The CD that accompanied this book has been replaced by
a web site that can be found at the following address:
http://www.awprofessional.com

Note that all references to the CD in the book now pertain
to the web site.

Praise for *XForms: XML Powered Web Forms*

"Reusable components such as E-Forms are at the heart of the U.S. Federal Enterprise Architecture and E-Government, and XML standards-based solutions are
starting to appear for use across the government. T. V. Raman's book meticulously
explains how XForms leverages the power of using XML for E-Forms and has been
designed to abstract much of XML's functionality into a set of components referred
to as MVC (Model, View, Controller), which separate the model from its final presentation. This XForms component architecture serves as an excellent roadmap for
the reader. T. V. eloquently shows how XForms makes the original promise of 'the
document is the interface' a reality so the collected data can be directly submitted
to a Web service—thus putting a human face on Web services!"

> —Brand Niemann, Ph.D.
> Chair, XML Web Services Working Group, U.S. CIO Council

"XForms is an exciting new technology for designing Web forms in an elegant
and accessible way. Raman's book provides strong motivations for flexibility in the
design of human-machine interactions, and explains how to use XForms to this end
in crystal-clear prose."

> —Eve Maler
> XML Standards Architect, Sun Microsystems

"Interactive forms technology is the logical evolution of Web user interface design.
XForms represents a significant leap forward in that evolution."

> —Sean McGrath
> CTO, Propylon

"The greatest strength of this book is the skill with which T. V. Raman links the XForms technology with the larger context of the Web. The limitations of HTML forms, the ways in which XForms provides a better foundation for Web and Web service user interfaces, and the opportunities for an XForms-powered Web that is accessible to all users and devices are outlined and brought together in a compelling way."

> —Michael Champion
> Advisory Research and Development Specialist, Software AG

"Raman's book gives the reader an excellent explanation of the emerging W3C XForms recommendation. It's a well-organized and well-written book that begins with a gentle introduction to the concepts that motivated the development of XForms and then provides a reasonable overview of the relevant XML technology related to XForms.

Most of the book covers XForms components: user interface controls, model properties, functions, actions, and events. It concludes with XForms as a Web service, offering multi-modal access and accessibility.

In light of the October 2003 deadline for U.S. federal agencies to comply with the mandate of the Government Paperwork Elimination Act (GPEA) to give citizens the opportunity to provide information online, this important technical work comes none too soon. As T. V. masterfully elucidates, XForms provides the 'last mile' in 'connecting users to their data.' Insightfully, he also observes 'the document is the [human] interface' to data—an understanding without which the challenge to make eGov services 'citizen-centered' simply cannot and will not be met."

> —Owen Ambur
> Cofounder and Cochair, XML Working Group, U.S. CIO Council

"I found the author's straightforward style quite comfortable and informative. I heartily recommend this book, especially for government XML developers interested in the broader area of E-Forms. Understanding XForms is key to developing robust and flexible E-Forms solutions that separate content, logic, validation, and presentation. You'll never look at (X)HTML forms the same way after reading Raman's book."

> —Kenneth Sall
> GSA eGov Technical Architect/XML Specialist, SiloSmashers

XFORMS

XFORMS
XML POWERED WEB FORMS

T. V. Raman

♦▼Addison-Wesley

Boston · San Francisco · New York · Toronto · Montreal
London · Munich · Paris · Madrid
Capetown · Sydney · Tokyo · Singapore · Mexico City

The publisher offers discounts on this book when ordered in quantity for bulk purchases and special sales. For more information, please contact:

U.S. Corporate and Government Sales
(800) 382-3419
corpsales@pearsontechgroup.com

For sales outside of the U.S., please contact:

International Sales
(317) 581-3793
international@pearsontechgroup.com

Visit Addison-Wesley on the Web: www.awprofessional.com

Library of Congress Cataloging-in-Publication Data

Raman, T. V., 1965-
    XForms : XML powered Web Forms / T. V. Raman.
        p. cm.
    Includes bibliographical references and index.
    ISBN 0-321-15499-1 (alk. paper)
    1. Web site development. 2. Application software–Development. 3. Internet
    Programming. 4. XML (Document markup language) I. Title.

TK5105.888.R35 2003
006.7'6—dc22

2003057742

ISBN: 0-321-15499-1

Text printed on recycled paper
1 2 3 4 5 6 7 8 9 10—CRS—0706050403
First printing, September 2003

To my guiding eyes, ASTER and Bubbles

ASTER Labrador

Bubbles Labrador

CONTENTS

LIST OF FIGURES

LIST OF TABLES

PREFACE

W3C XForms—XML powered Web forms—is an overhaul to HTML forms from 1993. On-line forms are critical to electronic commerce on the Internet, and the HTML forms design from 1993 is now beginning to show its age. The advent of XML on the Web and the subsequent move to Web Services as a means of connecting disparate information technologies to deliver end-to-end customer solutions have now made XML documents central to the fabric of the Web.

XForms leverages the power of using XML in modeling, collecting, and serializing user input. The XForms design enables simple browser-based interfaces for creating and editing XML documents with the client providing interactive support for ensuring that the XML document is valid. Thus, XForms enables the *last mile* of connecting the end user to Web Services.

XForms user agents provide an easy-to-use browser-based interface that enables the end-user to interact directly with information technologies that have been published as Web Services. As the Web moves from being a desktop-only phenomenon to a means of ubiquitous electronic access, Web transactions need to be available from a variety of end-user access devices ranging from desktop computers to smart phones. The XForms-authored interface is well suited for delivery to a variety of interaction modalities and end-user devices, thus assuring content developers the widest audience for their transaction-based applications.

From the user's perspective, XForms revolutionizes the way business-critical information is collected and published on the Web. A key consequence of this evolution is that information technologists can continue to model business data using abstract structures that are amenable to machine processing; XForms binds a user-friendly Web browser interface to such abstract XML models, thereby empowering the end user to edit and update these abstract structures. In this sense, XForms enables a standard Web browser to associate *editable views* to the underlying XML models. This ability to view and edit XML documents from within a standard Web browser is likely to prove a key empowering technology.

ACKNOWLEDGMENTS

This work was made possible by the help and support of my IBM colleagues and the stimulating intellectual environment provided by IBM Research. I would also like to thank my fellow members of the W3C XForms Working Group—and in particular the WG cochairs Steven Pemberton and Sebastian Schnitzenbaumer—who have worked hard over the last three years in successfully turning a collection of useful ideas into a practicable end-to-end solution.

My friend Professor M. S. Krishnamoorthy provided valuable comments throughout the writing of this book. XForms coeditors Leigh Klotz and Roland Merrick checked the text and examples for errors against the XForms 1.0 specification. In addition, Leigh Klotz created the screen images for the examples in the book using the various XForms implementations that are in progress.

I would also like to thank James C. King of Adobe Systems for his comments and feedback on early versions of this book. I also had a wonderful team of proofreaders made up of research colleagues at IBM who gave me valuable feedback throughout the writing of this book. Finally, I would like to acknowledge the help and support of the production team at Addison-Wesley, including the excellent team of proofreaders who helped me turn the final manuscript into a well-structured book. Eve Maler and Mike Champion provided especially insightful comments as the book was being developed.

HOW TO READ THIS BOOK

This book is targeted primarily at Web authors wishing to use XForms in their work. It is also meant to help IT specialists transition from using legacy HTML forms for their Web projects. The book has been written to complement the W3C XForms specification, not to replace it.

Each chapter of this book has a specific theme and concludes with a section that presents the material covered by that chapter *at a glance*. The book is organized in three parts:

Welcome   The first part gives a bird's-eye view of XForms and the various XML standards that it uses.

Components   The second part details the various components making up the XForms architecture.

Emerging Areas   The final part covers the relevance of XForms in the areas of Web services, multimodal interaction, and accessibility.

Welcome to XForms

The first chapter of this book presents a bird's-eye view of XForms after motivating the need for this new technology. This chapter should be sufficient to give decision makers a taste for the benefits of this exciting new standard. Web authors will find an introductory example that is first authored using the now familiar legacy HTML forms and then recast as an XForms application.

W3C XForms is built on a set of XML standards. The second chapter reviews these various standard building blocks and is meant as a quick tutorial. The material presented here is sufficient to get a taste for these standards and understand the examples in this book. However, it is not meant to be a complete review of these various standards. Readers familiar with XML Schema, XML namespaces, and XPath will find this chapter a useful review. Readers new to these specifications will find the chapter a useful starting point as they get acquainted with the space of XML standards.

XForms Components

The next six chapters present the components making up XForms. Each chapter consists of numerous examples that illustrate each concept as it is introduced; the examples have been designed to build on one another, and, as a consequence, examples in each chapter increase in complexity. XForms authors will find the index at the end of the book useful when looking up the usage pattern for the various XForms constructs. Implementors should find this useful in testing their implementations against the various XForms features.

XForms and the Next Generation Web

The final part of the book focuses on three key areas where XForms is likely to play a significant role:

Web Services	Creating user interfaces to Web Services.
Multimodal Interaction	Deploying multimodal interaction where users are able to interact using a variety of synchronized modalities such as spoken and visual interaction. This aspect is extremely relevant in deploying Web interaction to the plethora of emerging mobile devices.
Accessibility	Ensuring that Web content and applications are accessible to all. Implementing accessibility assures Web authors of the widest possible audience for their content; it also ensures that Web content meets U.S. Federal Access Guidelines.

These areas are at the center of intense activity within the standards community and are the focus of emerging customer solutions from the various major vendors. These chapters are designed to give IT specialists a leg up in coming up to speed on how the new XForms standard meshes with these three key areas of Web development.

Typographical Conventions

The book uses the following typographical conventions when presenting the various constructs introduced by XForms. All uses of these constructs are indexed.

element XML element names are typeset in a bold font within angle brackets, for example, ⟨**model**⟩.

attribute XML attribute names are typeset in a slanted font, for example, *ref*.

event Event names are typeset in a sans serif font, for example, DOMActivate.

function Function names are typeset in an italic font, for example, *max*.

In addition, references that have a Web site have been offset with the Web location specified in the footnote, for example, W3C[1]; in the HTML version found on the accompanying CD, these are hyperlinks that can be activated.

---

[1]http://www.w3.org

PART I

Welcome to XForms

CHAPTER I

XML Powered Web Forms

Since their inception in 1993, HTML forms have come to form the underpinnings of user interaction on the World Wide Web (WWW). The convenience afforded by the ability to deploy applications at all levels of complexity on the Web, and thereby provide consistent end-user access to information and application services via a universal Web client, created a platform-independent environment for electronic commerce across the Internet.

However, building on the essential simplicity of HTML forms has resulted in an extremely complex Web programming model; today, Web application developers are forced to work at different levels of abstraction—and, consequently, duplicate application and business logic in multiple programming languages—in order to deliver a satisfactory end-user experience. These problems become even more complex given the need to perform electronic transactions with a variety of different devices and user interface modalities. As we deploy Web access to software at all levels of complexity ranging from business back-ends to simple electronic transactions, these issues can be better addressed by revisiting the design of HTML forms that are the essential underpinnings of the transactional Web.

XForms—a revision to the existing HTML forms technology developed by the World Wide Web Consortium (W3C)[1]—builds on the advantages of XML to create a versatile forms module that can stand the Web in good stead for the next decade.

---

[1]http://www.w3.org

Section 1.1 traces the evolution of Web applications and describes the problems inherent in the present-day Web programming model that motivated the work on XForms. We design a simple questionnaire application using HTML forms in Section 1.2 and enumerate the software components needed to deploy the questionnaire on the Web. We then recast this application in XForms in Section 1.3 to give a bird's-eye view of the various components that constitute W3C XForms. We conclude this chapter with a summary of key XForms features and their benefits in Section 1.4. The remaining chapters of this book will cover these components in detail along with numerous examples that illustrate their use.

1.1 Background

HTML forms for creating interactive Web pages were introduced in 1993. The addition of a handful of simple markup constructs that allowed HTML authors to create input fields and other user interaction elements enabled Web sites to deploy Web pages that could *collect* user input as simple name-value pairs. The values input by the user were transmitted via HTTP and processed on the server via Common Gateway Interface (CGI) scripts. This new innovation spawned a multitude of interactive Web sites that experimented with these constructs to create interfaces ranging from simple user surveys to prototype shopping applications.

As electronic commerce on the Web gained momentum during the mid-90s, Web developers moved from experimenting with HTML forms to deploying real end-user applications to the Web. These forms-powered HTML pages provided a Web interface to standard transaction oriented applications. In this programming model, the Web developer authored a user interface in HTML and created corresponding server-side logic as CGI scripts that processed the submitted data before communicating it to the actual application. The combination of the HTML user interface and the server-side logic used to process the submitted data is called the *Web application*. The *Web application* in turn communicates user input to the application, receives results, and embeds these results in an HTML page to create a user interface to be delivered as a *server response* to the user's Web browser.

This method of deploying electronic transactions on the Web where end users could interact via a standard browser created a platform-independent environment for conducting electronic commerce across the Internet. Examples of such Web applications range from CNN's opinion polls to electronic storefronts like amazon.com. During this period, the server-side components making up Web applications gained in sophistication. The simple-minded CGI script came to be superseded by server-side technologies such as Java servlets, specialized Perl environments optimized to run in a server context such as Apache's modperl,[2] and a plethora of other server-side processing tools. These technologies were designed to aid in the processing of user data submitted via HTTP and the generation of dynamic content to be transmitted as the *server response*. The underlying HTML forms technology however remained unchanged—except for the addition of file upload and client-side Javascript to enable a more interactive end-user experience on the client.

As the *e*commerce Web matured, vendors rushed to deploy server-side middleware and developer tools to aid in the authoring and deployment of interactive Web applications. By this time, such tools were almost mandatory, since the essential simplicity of HTML forms resulted in scalability problems when developing complex Web applications.

Consider some of the steps that are carried out by a typical Web application. User data obtained via HTTP is validated at the server within servlets or other server-side software. Performing such validation at the server after the user has completed the form results in an unsatisfactory end-user experience when working with complex forms; the user finds out about invalid input long after the value is provided. This in turn is overcome by inserting validation scripts into the HTML page. Notice that such scripts essentially duplicate the validation logic implemented on the server side. This duplication often has to be repeated for each supported browser to handle differences in the Javascript environment.

Using this programming model, developing, deploying, and maintaining a simple shopping application on the Web require authoring content in a variety of languages at several different levels of abstraction. Once developed, such Web applications remain expensive to maintain and update. Notice that the move from experimenting with Web interaction technologies to deploying real-world applications to the Web brings with it a significant change; in most real-world scenarios, the application to be deployed to the Web *already* exists. Even in the case of new applications, only a portion of the application in question gets deployed to the Web. As an example, only the electronic storefront of a shopping site gets deployed to the Web; such shopping sites are backed by software that manages customer information, product catalogs, and other business objects making up an electronic store. Thus, deploying complex interactive sites involves creating the business logic and then exposing relevant portions of this application to a *Web application* that creates a user interface accessible via a Web browser.

---

[2]http://www.apache.org/modperl

One way of simplifying this development process is to make business applications themselves aware of the need to deliver a Web user interface. This approach is followed by many of today's popular middleware solutions, with some commercial database engines going so far as to incorporate a Web server into the database. However, making back-end business applications aware of the details of the user interface markup can make systems difficult to evolve and maintain. The resulting lack of separation of concerns ties Web applications to a particular back-end system.

As we deploy Web access to software at all levels of complexity ranging from business applications to electronic transactions, the problems outlined earlier can be better addressed by revisiting the essential underpinnings of the transactional Web. Today, Web applications need to be accessible from a variety of access devices and interaction modalities—Web applications may be accessed from a variety of clients ranging from desktop browsers to smart phones capable of delivering multimodal[3] interaction. Thus, a travel application that is being deployed to the Web needs to be usable from within a desktop browser, a Personal Digital Assistant (PDA), and a cell phone equipped with a small display. Thus, the interface needs to be usable when interacting via a graphical or speech interface.

Notice that the problems with HTML forms outlined earlier become even more serious when confronted with the need to perform electronic transactions with a variety of different end-user devices and user interaction modalities.[4] W3C XForms[5]—a revision to the existing HTML forms technology from 1993—builds on the advantages of XML to create a powerful forms module that can stand the Web in good stead for the next decade.

1.2 A Simple Web Application

This section introduces a simple Web application developed using today's HTML forms and illustrates the various software modules that would be authored on the client and server to deploy a complete end-to-end solution. This sample application will be recast using XForms in the remaining sections of this chapter to illustrate the advantages inherent in the various components making up the XForms architecture.

---

[3] The use of multiple means of interaction, for example, synchronized spoken and visual interaction, is called *multimodal* interaction.

[4] A user interaction modality denotes one of possibly many different means for providing input and perceiving output.

[5] http://www.w3.org/tr/xforms

1.2.1 Questionnaire Form

Consider a questionnaire application that collects the following items of user information:

name   User's first and last names as strings
age   User's age as a number
gender   User's gender: m for male and f for female
birthday   Fields making up the user's date of birth
address   Fields making up the user's mailing address
email   User's email address as a string
ssn   User's Social Security number, if available

Data collected by this questionnaire will be communicated to a survey application that imposes the following validity constraints on the data:

- All requested data items *must* be provided.
- Values *must* be legal for each field; for example, value of field age must be a number; fields making up the value of birthday need to be valid date components.
- Field ssn must contain a 9-digit Social Security number; if none is available, a default value of 000-000-000 must be used.

1.2.2 Developing the Web Application

The Web developer models the various items of data to be collected as simple name-value pairs; for example, age=21. Compound data items like address and name are made up of subfields, and in modeling these as simple string value pairs, the developer introduces additional field names such as name.first. Here is a list of the field names the developer might create for this application:

name.first	name.last	age
address.street	address.city	address.zip
birthday.day	birthday.month	birthday.year
email	ssn	gender

Next, the developer creates the server-side software component that will receive the submitted data as name-value pairs—this typically starts off as a stand-alone CGI script that evolves to encompass more and more functionality as the application gains in sophistication. Functions performed by this component include:

- Produce the HTML page that is displayed to the user; this generates the initial user interface and displays default values if any.
- Receive submitted data as name-value pairs via HTTP.
- Validate received data to ensure that all application constraints are satisfied.
- Generate a new HTML page that allows the user to update previously supplied values if one or more fields are found to be invalid.
- Make all fields *sticky*, that is, user does not lose previously supplied values during client-server round-trips.
- Marshal the data into a structure that is suitable for the survey application when all fields have valid values. This is necessary because intermediate fields created by the Web developer such as name.first may not match what the survey application expects.
- Transmit the collected data to the back-end, process the resulting response, and communicate the results to the user by generating an appropriate HTML page.

1.2.3 Developing the User Interface

The user interface is delivered to the connecting browser by producing appropriate HTML markup and transmitting this markup via HTTP to the user's browser. Interaction elements, for example, input fields, are contained in HTML element ⟨**form**⟩ that also specifies the URI where the data is to be submitted; the HTTP method to use, for example, GET or POST; and details on the encoding to use when transmitting the data. HTML markup for user interface controls, for example, ⟨**input**⟩, is used to create input fields in the resulting user interface. This markup refers to the field names defined earlier, for example, name.first, to specify the association between the field names defined by the Web developer and the values provided by the end user. The markup also encodes default values, if any, for the various fields. Notice the tight binding between the HTML markup and the server-side logic developed earlier with respect to the following:

- Field names used in the HTML markup need to match the names used in the server-side component.
- Making all fields *sticky*, that is, retaining user supplied values during multiple client-server round-trips requires that the previously received values be embedded in the generated HTML.

To achieve this, early Web applications produced the HTML markup from within the CGI script. Though this works in simple cases, this approach does not scale for creating more complex Web applications. This is because of the lack of separation of concerns that results from mixing user interface generation with server-side application logic. Maintaining and evolving the user interface markup require the developer to edit the server-side component. However, the skills required to edit server-side software components are different from those needed to design good user interfaces. This increases the cost of designing good Web user interfaces and makes it tedious to keep the result synchronized with the software components that implement the interaction.

1.2.4 A More Sophisticated Implementation

The lack of separation of concerns that arises when incorporating presentational markup within executable CGI scripts is typically overcome by developing Web applications using more sophisticated server-side technologies such as Hypertext Preprocessor (PHP),[6] Java Server Pages (JSP)[7] or Active Server Pages (ASP).[8] All of these technologies follow a Model, View, Controller (MVC) decomposition by factoring out the user interface markup from the program code that implements the server-side application logic. Thus, the user interface is created as an XML[9] document with special tags that invoke the appropriate software components when processed by the server. As a result, the user interface designer can work with intuitive authoring tools that generate XML markup while the software developer builds software objects using traditional programming tools.

Thus, the simple Web application developed earlier would be created as a set of software objects that implements the validation and navigation logic and a set of markup pages used to generate the user interface at each stage of the interaction—see Figure 1.1 for a high-level overview of the resulting components and their interdependencies.

Higher level Web application frameworks, such as struts[10] based on JSP and servlets, provide further abstractions that allow the Web developer to create the application by defining the *model* as Java beans, defining the user interaction *views* as JSP pages, and wiring up the resulting *model* and *views* via a standard *controller* component that manages the navigation among the various views.

---

[6]http://www.php.net
[7]http://java.sun.com/products/jsp
[8]http://www.asp.net/
[9]http://www.w3.org/tr/REC-xml.html
[10]http://jakarta.apache.org/struts

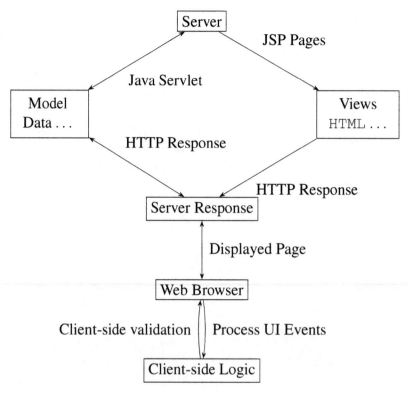

Figure 1.1. A simple Web application made up of software components that together
implement server-side validation and client-side user interaction.

Finally, an interface where the user learns about invalid input only after submitting the data to the server can prove unsatisfactory. To achieve a rich interactive end-user experience, simple tests such as checking for valid values for age or
birthday are better performed on the client during user interaction to provide
immediate feedback. This is achieved by embedding client-side validation scripts in
the HTML markup. Notice that such validation code duplicates the validation rules
already authored as part of the server-side validation component, but this time in a
client-specific scripting language. Variations in the scripting environment provided
by Web browsers on various platforms make such scripts hard to develop, test, and
maintain.

1.3 XForms Components

The previous section traced the development of a simple Web application using
present-day technologies predicated by the HTML forms architecture. The questionnaire application evolved from a simple stand-alone CGI script to a more

complex Web application consisting of software components dedicated to managing the application state within a servlet, markup pages designed to create the user interaction, and navigation components designed to connect the various views with the application state. In doing so, we saw that the Web developer needed to implement significant application-specific functionality in custom software to deliver the questionnaire to a Web browser.

XForms leverages the power of using XML in modeling, collecting, and serializing user input. XForms has been designed to abstract much of this functionality into a set of components that enable the Web developer to rely on a standard set of services and off-the-shelf XML tools when developing the final Web application. This allows the Web developer to focus on key aspects of the application and rely on the underlying XForms platform for the following services:

- Produce user interfaces appropriate for the connecting device.
- Provide interactive user feedback via automated client-side validation.
- Validate user input on the server automatically.
- Marshal user input on the server into a structure suitable for the back-end application.

Based on what has been observed in the design of today's Web applications and the need to deliver such applications to an ever-increasing array of end-user devices, the overall XForms architecture has been divided into the following components. A key feature of this MVC decomposition is a clear separation of the *model* from its final *presentation*.

Model All nonpresentational aspects of a Web application are encapsulated by the XForms data model. The data model incorporates an XML instance that holds user input, the constraints used to validate this input, and the necessary metadata about how this user input should be communicated to the Web server.

UI XForms defines a user interface vocabulary that consists of abstract controls and aggregation constructs used to create rich user interfaces. The user interface vocabulary is designed to capture the underlying intent of the user interaction, rather than its final presentation on any given device or in any specific modality. This makes it possible to deliver XForms-based Web applications to different devices and modalities.

Submit This allows the Web application author to specify where, how, and what pieces of data to submit to the Web server. It also permits the application developer to specify what actions to take upon receiving a response from the server.

1.3.1 XForms Overview

Next, we reexamine the questionnaire and recast it as an XForms application. The questionnaire will be created as an XHTML document that contains the XForms model and user interface components. The following subsections detail each of these components and show how they are used within an XHTML document. The XForms model (contained in ⟨**model**⟩) is placed within XHTML element ⟨**head**⟩. XForms user interface controls create the user interaction and appear within the body of the document, that is, within XHTML element ⟨**body**⟩, and are rendered as part of the document content. In this overview, we will describe a few of the XForms user interface controls to give the reader a feel for XForms markup; subsequent chapters will detail all the constructs defined in XForms 1.0.

1.3.2 XForms Model

As before, we start by enumerating the various items of user information collected by the Web application. Since we are now using XML, we no longer need restrict ourselves to a flat data model consisting of a set of untyped name-value pairs. Instead, we encapsulate the information collected from the user in a structured XML document. This is called the *XML instance*. Further, we pick the structure of this XML instance to suit the survey application—see Figure 1.2.

```
<model xmlns="http://www.w3.org/2002/xforms" id="p1">
  <instance>
    <person xmlns="">
      <name><first/><last/></name>
      <age/><email/>
      <address><street/><city/><zip/></address>
      <birthday><day/><month/><year/></birthday>
      <ssn>000-000-000</ssn>
      <gender>m</gender>
    </person>
  </instance>
</model>
```

Figure 1.2. Element ⟨**instance**⟩ declares the XML template that holds user input and default values.

```
<model xmlns="http://www.w3.org/2002/xforms"
  xmlns:xsd="http://www.w3.org/2001/XMLSchema"
  schema="person.xsd" id="p1">
<instance>
  <person xmlns="">...</person>
</instance>
</model>
```

Figure 1.3. Constraining instance data by specifying an XML Schema.

Notice that compound data items such as address are now modeled to reflect the structure of the data, unlike when using flat name-value pairs. This also obviates the need to introduce intermediate fields to hold portions of the user data and the subsequent need to marshal such intermediate fields into the structure required by the application.

Next, this XML instance can be annotated with the various constraints specified by the application, for example, age should be a number. When using XML, such constraints are typically encapsulated in an XML Schema[11] document that defines the structure of the XML instance—see Figure 1.3.

Alternatively, such type constraints can be specified as part of the instance using attribute *xsi:type*[12] as shown in Figure 1.4. Both techniques have their place in Web development; the former is especially relevant when creating Web applications that access existing business logic, and the latter is useful when creating a one-off Web application with relatively simple type constraints.

In the questionnaire application, the constraints shown in Figure 1.4 encapsulate type constraints—the default type is string. Complex schemas typically encapsulate more constraints, such as specifying the rules for validating a 9-digit Social Security Number or specifying the set of valid values for the various fields. Note that this example has been kept intentionally simple—later chapters will build real-world examples where we will use the full richness of the built-in type mechanisms provided by XML Schema.

The advantage of specifying such constraints using XML Schema is that the developer can then rely on off-the-shelf XML parsers to validate the data instance against the supplied constraints. With the increasing adoption of XML Schema by database vendors, complex business applications are likely already to have an XML

---

[11] http://www.w3.org/tr/xschema
[12] Attribute *xsi:type* is defined by XML Schema.

```
<model id="p1" xmlns:xsi=
  "http://www.w3.org/2001/XMLSchema-instance"
  xmlns="http://www.w3.org/2002/xforms"
  xmlns:xsd="http://www.w3.org/2001/XMLSchema">
  <instance>
    <person xmlns="">
      <name><first/><last/></name>
      <age xsi:type="xsd:number"/>
      <birthday>
        <day xsi:type="xsd:number"/>
        <month xsi:type="xsd:number"/>
        <year xsi:type="xsd:number"/>
      </birthday>
      <address>
        <street/><city/><zip/>
      </address>
      <email/><ssn>000-000-000</ssn>
    <gender>m</gender></person>
  </instance></model>
```

Figure 1.4. XML representation of the data collected by a questionnaire application, along with some simple type constraints.

Schema definition for the data model, and the developer can leverage such existing assets when creating a Web application. XML processor xerces[13] is available from the Apache project implements XML Schema and can be used to validate data collected on the server.

Finally, the constraints on the data instance are now encapsulated in declarative XML—as opposed to imperative program code—thus making it easier to maintain and revise these constraints using XML-aware tools without having to reprogram the application.

1.3.3 XForms User Interface

This section creates a sample XForms user interface for the questionnaire application and binds this user interface to the XForms data model defined in the previous section. XForms user interface markup appears within XHTML element ⟨**body**⟩

---

[13] http://xml.apache.org/xerces-j

along with other document markup. Notice that because of the separation of the model from the user interaction, XForms user interface markup can appear *anywhere* within the contents of XHTML element ⟨**body**⟩; in contrast, when using HTML forms, user interface controls can appear only within element ⟨**form**⟩.

In the questionnaire application, XForms user interface control ⟨**input**⟩ can be used to collect each item of data. User interface control ⟨**input**⟩ is intentionally designed to be generic. The type of information available about the underlying data item, for example, `birthday` is a *date*, can be used to advantage in generating a user interface representation that is appropriate to the connecting device, for example, rendering it as a calendar on a desktop browser. Notice that in addition to making the resulting user interface customizable for the connecting device, this design provides a rich level of accessibility for supporting users with different needs.

UI Control Input

Here, we review different aspects of UI control ⟨**input**⟩ in some detail; later chapters will review all of the XForms user interface controls. See Figure 1.5 for the markup that creates the input field for obtaining the user's age and Figure 1.6 for the resulting user interface. XForms controls encapsulate the following pieces of information

```
<input xmlns="http://www.w3.org/2002/xforms"
  xmlns:ev="http://www.w3.org/2001/xml-events"
  model="p1" ref="/person/age" class="edit"
  ev:event="DOMActivate" ev:handler="#speak"
  accesskey="a"><label>Age</label>
<help>Specify your age as a number e.g., 21</help>
<hint>How young are you?</hint>
<alert>The age you specified,
  <output ref="/person/age"/>is not a valid age.
</alert></input>
```

Figure 1.5. User interface control for obtaining the user's age.

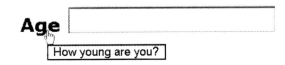

Figure 1.6. User interface for obtaining the user's age.

needed to render the interaction and connect the result to the appropriate portion of the XForms data model:

- Binding attributes that wire control to model
- Metadata for giving feedback to the user
- Wiring up of events and event handlers
- Presentation hints
- CSS style rules
- Keyboard shortcuts and navigation hints

Figure 1.5 illustrates the following XForms features:

Binding   Attributes *model* and *ref* on element ⟨**input**⟩ specify the portion of the instance to be populated by the value obtained via this control. Attribute *model* gives the id of the person model; Attribute *ref* addresses node /person/age of this instance. The syntax used to address portions of the instance is defined by XPath.[14]

Metadata   Elements ⟨**label**⟩, ⟨**help**⟩, ⟨**hint**⟩, and ⟨**alert**⟩ encapsulate metadata to be displayed to the user at various times. Notice that in XForms the label for the user interface control is *tightly bound* to the associated control; this is an extremely useful accessibility feature. Elements ⟨**hint**⟩ and ⟨**help**⟩ encapsulate tool tip text and detailed help to be displayed upon request. Finally, element ⟨**alert**⟩ holds the message to be displayed in the case of invalid input. Notice that the alert message uses element ⟨**output**⟩ to access the value supplied by the user. Element ⟨**output**⟩ uses XPath to address the relevant portion of the data model.

For simplicity, this example has shown elements ⟨**label**⟩, ⟨**hint**⟩, and ⟨**help**⟩ with inline content. For more complex applications, the contents of these elements can be specified indirectly via a URI by using attribute *src*. This feature can be used to advantage in localizing XForms-based Web applications by factoring all such messages into an XML file, referring to portions of that XML file using URIs within the XForms Web application, and loading these XML files to provide locale-specific messages.

---

[14]http://www.w3.org/tr/xpath

Eventing Attribute *ev:event* on element ⟨**input**⟩ sets up control ⟨**input**⟩ to respond to event **DOMActivate** by calling the handler located at #speak. This uses the syntax defined in XML Events[15] for authoring DOM2 Events and is described in Section 2.3.

Presentation Hints can be provided via attribute *appearance*.

Styling Attribute *class* specifies a Cascading Style Sheet (CSS[16]) style to use for styling this control. CSS is a style sheet language that allows authors and users to attach style (for example, fonts, spacing, and aural cues) to structured documents (for example, XHTML documents).

Navigation Attribute *accesskey* specifies an accelerator key for navigating to this control. This was an accessibility feature first introduced in HTML and has been incorporated into XForms.

UI Control select1

The field corresponding to the user's gender can have one of two legal values, m or f. The user *must* pick one of these values. Using traditional HTML forms, the corresponding user interface would be authored as a group of radio buttons. Notice that the HTML design hard-wires a particular presentation (radio buttons) to the underlying notion of allowing the user to select *one and only one* value. However, radio buttons may not always be the most appropriate (or even feasible) representation, given the device or modality in use; for instance, a radio button does not make sense when using a speech interface.

XForms separates *form* from *interaction* by capturing abstract notions such as *select from a set*. This enables the XForms author to create user interfaces that can be delivered to different target modalities and devices. XForms user interface control ⟨**select1**⟩ can be used instead of ⟨**input**⟩ to obtain the user's gender in the questionnaire example—see Figure 1.7 for the XML markup and Figure 1.8 for the resulting user interface.

As in the previous example, binding attributes *model* and *ref* specify the location where the value is to be stored. Attribute *appearance* is set to full to indicate that the client should create a full representation of this control; in the case of a visual presentation, this might be realized by using a group of radio buttons. Element ⟨**item**⟩ encodes each of the available choices. Subelement ⟨**label**⟩ contains the *display value*; subelement ⟨**value**⟩ encodes the value to be stored in the instance. The default value m is obtained from the model—see Figure 1.2. The author can style the interface further by using Cascading Style Sheets (CSS).

---

[15]http://www.w3.org/tr/xml-events
[16]http://www.w3.org/TR/CSS2/

```
<select1 xmlns="http://www.w3.org/2002/xforms"
  model="p1" ref="/person/gender" appearance="full">
  <label>Select gender</label>
  <help>...</help>
  <hint>...</hint>
  <item><label>Male</label>
  <value>m</value></item>
  <item><label>Female</label>
  <value>f</value></item>
</select1>
```

Figure 1.7. XForms user interface control for selecting a single value.

Select gender ⊙ Male ○ Female

Figure 1.8. XForms user interface for selecting a single value.

1.3.4 XForms Submit

The final stage of the questionnaire user interaction is to have the user submit the information. Using HTML forms, this is achieved by creating a *submit* button within HTML element ⟨**form**⟩. Activating the corresponding user interface control results in *all* values created as part of the containing ⟨**form**⟩ being submitted to the URI specified via attribute *action*.

As mentioned earlier, a key feature of XForms is to separate the model from the interaction. XForms preserves this separation in its design of data submission. Submission details covering

- What to submit,
- Where to submit,
- How to submit

that are independent of the presentation are encapsulated by element ⟨**submission**⟩ within element ⟨**model**⟩. XForms user interface control ⟨**submit**⟩ when activated dispatches an appropriate **xforms-submit** event to the relevant ⟨**submission**⟩ element. Upon receiving this event, the XForms processor serializes the values stored in the instance before transmitting the result as specified by element ⟨**submission**⟩.

For the questionnaire example, we first extend the model shown in Figure 1.2 with an appropriate ⟨**submission**⟩ element—see Figure 1.9.

```
<submission xmlns="http://www.w3.org/2002/xforms"
   id="s0" method="post"
action="http://example.com/survey"/>
```

Figure 1.9. Element ⟨**submission**⟩ models what, where, and how to submit.

User interface control ⟨**submit**⟩ in Figure 1.10 uses attribute *submission* to connect the user interface to the model. We show the resulting user interface in Figure 1.11.

```
<submit xmlns="http://www.w3.org/2002/xforms"
   submission="s0"><label>Submit</label>
</submit>
```

Figure 1.10. XForms user interface control for submitting the questionnaire.

Figure 1.11. Visual representation of XForms submit control.

1.3.5 The Complete XForms Questionnaire

This section combines the model and user interface developed so far to create the complete XForms questionnaire. The resulting XForms application is contained in an XHTML document. The complete example uses XML namespaces so that markup elements defined by different XML languages such as XForms and XHTML are clearly identified—see Figure 1.12.

1.3.6 Deploying the XForms Questionnaire

The XForms questionnaire can be deployed in a variety of ways depending on the XForms processor being used. This section details a variety of deployment scenarios.

The questionnaire can be deployed on an XForms-aware Web server that provides the following:

Serve content   The server produces a presentation that is appropriate for the connecting device.

Code generation   The XForms server can generate client-side validation code to be embedded in the markup being served to the connecting

```
<html xmlns="http://www.w3.org/1999/xhtml"
  xmlns:xf="http://www.w3.org/2002/xforms"
  xmlns:xsd="http://www.w3.org/2001/XMLSchema">
  <head><title>XForms Questionnaire</title>
    <xf:model schema="questionnaire.xsd">
      <xf:instance xmlns="">
        <person>...</person>
      </xf:instance>
      <xf:submission action="..."
      method="post" id="s0"/>
  </xf:model></head>
  <body>...
    <xf:input ref="/person/address/street">
    ...</xf:input>...
    <xf:submit submission="s0">
      <xf:label>Submit questionnaire</xf:label>
  </xf:submit></body>
</html>
```

Figure 1.12. The complete XForms questionnaire.

client. This provides client-side validation and immediate user feedback, but without the cost of requiring the Web developer to hand-craft such validation scripts.

Data Validation   Validate user data against the constraints given in the model.

State management   Maintain application state by implementing the XForms processing model. As a result, the developer of the questionnaire need write no special software for maintaining values submitted by the user between client-server round-trips.

The XHTML document hosting the XForms questionnaire could be served to conforming XForms clients. An XForms client would implement the following:

Consume   Consume the XForms-authored application to produce the client-side user interface.

Validate   Check user input against the validation rules to provide live feedback.

Submit   Submit a valid XML instance on completion.

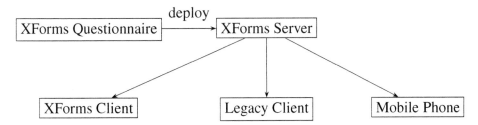

Figure 1.13. Deploying the XForms questionnaire.

Notice that in the deployment scenarios, the Web developer need only create the XForms questionnaire; contrast this with the application-specific components needed when deploying HTML forms—compare Figure 1.1 with the software components needed to deploy the XForms questionnaire shown in Figure 1.13.

1.4 Summary of XForms Benefits

We conclude this chapter with a summary of XForms features and highlight the consequent benefits over using traditional HTML forms for developing Web applications. A key differentiator when using XForms is the separation of purpose from presentation. The *purpose* of the questionnaire application is to collect information about the user. This is realized by creating a *presentation* that allows the user to provide the required information. Web applications typically render such a presentation as an *interactive document* that is continuously updated during user interaction. By separating the purpose from its presentation, XForms enables the *binding* of different interactions to a *single* model. In practice, this enables the application developer to deploy user interfaces that are appropriate to the target audience without having to create custom software components for processing the data collected via each distinct user interaction. Finally, by using structured XML to collect, validate, and communicate data, XForms processors can provide these functions to the Web developer as part of a standard XForms service.

1.4.1 XForms Features

Declarative	Declarative authoring makes XForms applications easier to maintain.
Strong typing	Submitted data is strongly typed and can be checked using off-the-shelf XML Schema tools. Strong typing also

	enables automatic client-side validation. As an example, a native XForms browser can use these types of constraints for validating user input; when serving the same XForms document to a legacy browser, these constraints can be used to generate client-side Javascript automatically.
Schema reuse	XForms enables the developer to reuse business rules encapsulated in XML Schemas. This obviates duplication and ensures that a change in the underlying business logic does not require reauthoring validation constraints at multiple layers of the Web application.
Schema augmentation	This enables the XForms author to go beyond the basic set of constraints available from the underlying business application. Providing such additional constraints as part of the XForms Model enhances the overall usability of the resulting Web application.
XML submission	This obviates the need for custom server-side logic to marshal the submitted data to the business application.
Internationalization	Using XML 1.0 for serializing data ensures that the submitted data is internationalization ready.
Accessibility	User interface controls encapsulate all relevant metadata such as labels, thereby enhancing accessibility of the application when using different modalities; as an example, a nonvisual client can speak relevant information when navigating through an XForms user interface.
Device independence	Abstract user interface controls lead to intent-based authoring of the user interface; this makes it possible to deliver the XForms application to different devices. Thus, Web pages authored using XForms can be deployed to a range of accessing devices including desktop browsers, PDAs, and cell phones with small displays.
Localization	Labels and help text can be referenced via URIs, thereby making it possible to localize XForms user interfaces.
Actions	XForms defines declarative XML event handlers such as ⟨**setfocus**⟩ and ⟨**setvalue**⟩ to obviate the most common use of scripting in Web applications. Consequently, most XForms applications can be statically analyzed; contrast this with the use of imperative scripts for event handlers.

1.5 XForms at a Glance

Table 1.1 shows the various XForms components at a glance; this also serves as a road map for the rest of this book. For each component, we enumerate its role in the XForms architecture, the underlying technology used by the component, and its concomitant benefits.

Table 1.1. XForms at a Glance

Component	Description
Model	• Encapsulates all data aspects of a form • Uses XML Schema to define constraints • Uses XPath to define model properties • Attaches model properties to instance nodes • Captures *what*, *how*, and *where* to submit
Properties	• Capture application constraints • Enable reactive user interfaces
UI Binding	• Connects user interface to the model using XPath
UI Controls	• Collect user input • *Bind* to underlying model • Encapsulate all relevant metadata • Access by design • Encourage device independence
UI	• Aggregates user interface controls • Encourages intent-based authoring • Creates dynamic user interaction
Events	• Bring user interface to life • Give access to eventing via XML Events • Attach dynamic behavior • Obviate common use of scripts via declarative actions

CHAPTER 2

Standard Building Blocks

2.1 Introduction

XForms models, collects, and transmits user input by building on several existing W3C standards. Reusing existing standards makes it possible to construct XForms processors from existing software that is designed to work with the standards being reused. On the other hand, the reliance on a set of complex standards can make the XForms specification hard to understand because the reader is often pointed to a never-ending chain of technical terms and complex specifications.

To alleviate this problem, we give a quick overview of these building blocks in a tutorial form with a focus on their use within XForms. The goal is not to explain each of these standards in detail; instead, the focus is on providing an introduction to the underlying technologies to enable the reader to work productively with XForms. We recommend skimming the content of this chapter and using it as a reference while working with the rest of the material in this book.

XPath XForms user interfaces are created by controls that *bind* to an underlying data model. In creating the necessary *binding* between model and instance, XForms uses XPath 1.0, described in Section 2.2, for addressing relevant portions of the XML instance. XPath 1.0 is also used for declaring model properties and expressing dependencies between related fields in a form.

XML Events User interfaces authored by binding form controls to an underlying data model come to life when combined with event handling facilities that process user interaction events. As a technology designed to be hosted primarily in Web application environments, XForms uses the DOM2 events model as exposed by XML Events, described in Section 2.3. DOM2 event listeners and handlers authored using XML Events enable the XForms author to attach application-specific behavior to user interface controls. The XForms 1.0 specification defines the XForms processing model via XML Events, thereby enabling the author to integrate application-specific behavior at all stages of XForms processing.

XML Namespaces and XML Schema   XForms applications collect user input using XML 1.0, described in Section 2.4. Such XML instances use XML namespaces, described in Section 2.4.2, to avoid name conflicts when encapsulating unrelated but similarly named data fields. XML instances for collecting user input are modeled using XML Schema 1.0, described in Section 2.5. XML Schema provides a declarative means of authoring data constraints and enables the automatic validation of XML instances against such constraints.

XForms Implementations   Emerging XForms implementations are detailed in Section 2.6. XForms is still a new W3C technology, and these implementations continue to evolve at the time of writing. Readers are encouraged to download one or more of these implementations while working through the material in this book.

2.2 XPath: XML Path Language

XPath is a language for addressing parts of an XML document and was originally designed to be used by both XSLT and XPointer. XPath gets its name from its use of a path notation, as in URLs, for navigating through the hierarchical structure of an XML document. XForms uses XPath 1.0[1] to *bind* user interface controls to the XForms model. This was illustrated in the questionnaire example in Figure 1.5 where we used XPath expression /person/age as the value of attribute *ref* on user interface control ⟨input⟩ to *bind* it to the data model.

The primary purpose of XPath is to address parts of an XML document. In support of this primary purpose, it also provides basic facilities for manipulation of strings, numbers, and booleans.[2] XPath uses a compact syntax to facilitate use of XPath within URIs and XML attribute values. This aspect of XPath makes it suitable to be a minimalistic expression language within XML documents.

---

[1]http://www.w3.org/tr/xpath

[2]XPath 2.0 has a richer set of data types and is a work in progress at the time of writing. Future versions of XForms are likely to use XPath 2.0.

XForms also uses XPath to express interdependency constraints among fields in an application. Such constraints are recalculated as the user interacts with the form; this can be used to advantage in creating dynamic Web interfaces. Unlike languages like ECMAScript, XPath is not a Turing-complete programming language; this ensures that the ability to encode interdependencies among fields is not abused by complex scripts to consume excessive resources on the client. In addition, it preserves the declarative nature of XForms applications. As a language designed for working on XML tree structures, nodes and node-sets are the most important object types when working with XPath expressions.

XPath expressions are evaluated with a given *context node* and in a given evaluation *environment*. Informally, the context node determines the portion of the tree relative to which the expression is evaluated. The *environment* determines the variable bindings that are in scope and the functions that are available, as well as the namespace declarations that are in effect.

XPath leaves it to the host language, for example, XSLT, to specify the rules used to determine the *context*; additionally, the host language is free to supply an appropriate library of functions. The rules used by XForms in determining the evaluation context are defined formally by the XForms 1.0 specification and will be explained in detail in later chapters of this book.

2.2.1 Location Paths

XPath expressions that address a node (or set of nodes) are called *location paths*. A location path selects a set of nodes relative to the context node. Location paths are evaluated from left to right, that is, given the expression /person/age, the first portion, /person, is evaluated to locate the node-set consisting of *all* person nodes occurring at the root. Next, the expression age is applied to this set to locate *all* age children of *all* /person nodes.

Formally,[3] location paths are either *relative* or *absolute*. A relative location path consists of a sequence of one or more *location steps* separated by /. The steps in a relative location path are composed together from left to right. Each step in turn selects a set of nodes relative to a context node. An initial sequence of steps is composed together with a following step as follows:

- The initial sequence of steps selects a set of nodes relative to a context node.
- Each node in that set is used as a context node for the following step.
- The *set union* of the sets of nodes identified by that step is the final result.

---

[3] This description is taken from the XPath 1.0 specification.

An absolute location path consists of an initial /, optionally followed by a relative location path. A / by itself selects the root node of the document containing the context node. If it is followed by a relative location path, then the location path selects the set of nodes that would be selected by the relative location path relative to the root node of the document containing the context node.

For the questionnaire example shown in Figure 1.12, the subtlety of this left-to-right evaluation rule does not matter because there is only one `person` child of the root element. However, it is important to remember that XPath location paths *always* work in terms of node-sets; this is important when understanding filters in location paths.

A *filter* is an XPath expression that is used to test the nodes in a node-set. Filters are typically used to select a subset of the nodes returned by a location path. Note that although sets in the traditional sense are *unordered*, members of XPath node-sets are treated in document order. For example, an XPath filter expression that selects nodes having a specific attribute might be used to filter a node-set. Other commonly used filters select the first or last element of a given node-set. As an example, if the `person` structure in our questionnaire example holds multiple `address` elements as direct children of `person`, we might use the expression

```
/person/address[1]
```

to select the first of these `address` elements.

Assuming that each `address` element contains an attribute *type* indicating the address type, we might use the expression

```
/person/address[@type='work']
```

to locate the work address.

2.2.2 Location Path Syntax

Location paths in XPath consist of three logical components:

- An axis, for example, all children of this node
- A node test, for example, the name of the node to select
- Optional sets of predicates, each enclosed in [ ] that specify expressions to filter the selected set of nodes

Table 2.1. XPath Abbreviated Syntax for Use in Location Paths

Syntax	Description	Example
.	*self*	`./age`
..	*parent*	`../address`
@	*attribute*	`address/@type`
*	*all* children	`address/*`
@*	*all* attributes	`address/@*`
//	*all descendants*	`person//address`

The XPath specification first describes the semantics of location paths in terms of an unabbreviated syntax and then describes the mapping to the abbreviated syntax used in this book. The XPath specification formally defines the various axes that can be used in constructing location paths; the abbreviated syntax covers all the axes that are commonly encountered when authoring XForms.

We summarize this abbreviated syntax in Table 2.1. Special note should be made of the syntax // used to select descendants of a given node; this selects *all* matching descendants starting from the context nodes. Thus, given an HTML document, the expression body//p would select all ⟨**p**⟩ elements that occur anywhere in the body of the document.

2.2.3 Variables, Functions, and Expression Evaluation

Variable[4] references use the syntax $v; function calls take the form f(a1,...). The definition of the function or the value of a variable is looked up in the current evaluation environment. The XPath specification defines a core set of functions that operate on the basic XPath types—node-set, string, boolean, and number. In addition, XForms 1.0 defines a set of functions for use in XForms.

XPath contains a core set of operators used in constructing expressions; these operations use the same syntax as found in most programming languages and will not be described here. A key difference to note is that since XPath uses / as the path separator character, the division operator is written 3 div 2. XPath also provides a mod operator that is the same as the % operator in ECMAScript. We conclude this section with examples of XPath expressions that one might encounter when creating common Web applications using XForms, as in Table 2.2.

---

[4]Note that XForms 1.0 does not use XPath variable references.

Table 2.2. Expressions Commonly Found in XForms Web Applications

Expression	Description
`count(person/children)`	Number of children
`price * tax-table[@state='NY']`	Compute tax
`camera[@price=min(../camera/@price)]`	Cheapest cameras
`sum(cart/item/@price)`	Price of items in cart
`avg(person/income)`	Average income

2.3 DOM2 Events

The purpose of Web applications created using XForms is to deliver dynamic user interfaces. User interfaces come to life when integrated with an eventing mechanism that enables application authors to listen for user and system events and to invoke handlers that trigger application-specific behavior. Today, Web programmers commonly achieve this by using ECMAScript event handlers that operate against the Document Object Model (DOM).

XForms uses this same DOM2 eventing model as specified in DOM2 Events[5] to specify how user and system events are processed in the context of XForms applications. However, instead of relying exclusively on ECMAScript, XForms provides a set of declarative event handlers that covers many common use cases, thereby obviating the need for custom scripts. In addition, rather than using the somewhat ad hoc events syntax used by HTML, XForms authors access the events model via markup specified by XML Events[6]—an XML module that provides XML languages with the ability to integrate event listeners and associated event handlers uniformly with Document Object Model (DOM) Level 2 event interfaces. The result is to provide an interoperable way of associating behaviors with document-level markup. This section gives a brief overview of the syntax defined by XML Events.

2.3.1 Introduction to DOM Events

An event is the representation of some asynchronous occurrence, for example, a user interface event such as a mouse click or the onset of speech, or a system-generated event, for example, an alert to warn the user about invalid input. In the DOM events model, an event is said to *target* the element in the XML document with which it

---

[5] http://www.w3.org/tr/DOM-Level-2-events/
[6] http://www.w3.org/tr/xml-events

is associated. The general behavior is that, when an event occurs, it is *dispatched* by passing it down the document tree in a phase called *capture* to the element where the event occurred (called its *target*). It may then be passed back up the tree again in the phase called *bubbling*. In general, an event can be responded to at any element in the path (by an *observer*) in either phase:

- By invoking an action
- By stopping the event
- By canceling the default action for the event at the place it is responded to

We illustrate this in Figure 2.1.

An *action* is some way of responding to an event; a *handler* is some specification for such an action, for instance, using scripting or some other method. A *listener* is a binding of such a handler to an event targeting some element in a document.

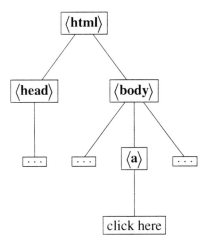

Event flow when *click here* is activated.

- **Capture**—Event travels from the root (⟨**html**⟩) to the target (click here).

- **Target**—Event arrives at the target (the text click here).

- **Bubble**—Event bubbles back to the root—element ⟨**html**⟩.

Figure 2.1. The DOM2 event propagation model.

2.3.2 XML Events

Understanding XML events depends on one key fact that is independent of the authoring syntax used. Creating an event listener at an element in the document tree requires three pieces of information: the element, the event to listen for, and a handler. Thus, we need to specify a triple (element, event, handler). Depending on the usage scenario, it may be convenient to do one of the following:

1. Author the triple by itself (see Figure 2.2)
2. Attach the *event* and *handler* to the *element* (see Figure 2.3)
3. Attach the *element* and *event* to the *handler* (see Figure 2.4)

The XML Events specification supports all three forms of authoring, thereby creating a generic eventing syntax for use in XML languages. We illustrate these three forms of event binding in the examples shown in Figure 2.2, Figure 2.3, and Figure 2.4.

```
<listener event="DOMActivate" observer="button1"
handler="#do-it"/>
```
- Call handler identified by #do-it, and
- Event DOMActivate occurs, and
- Element id=button1, and Or any of its children.

Figure 2.2. Authoring event binding via element ⟨**listener**⟩.

```
<p xmlns:ev="http://www.w3.org/2001/xml-events">
  <a ev:event="click" ev:handler="#popper"
    ev:defaultAction="cancel" href="link.html">
special link</a></p>
```
- Catch **click** targeted at element ⟨**a**⟩ or its children,
- Invoke action at #popper, and
- Stop further propagation of this event.

Figure 2.3. Attaching event listener on the *observer*.

```
<head xmlns:ev="http://www.w3.org/2001/xml-events">
  <script type="text/javascript"
    ev:event="xforms-submit" ev:observer="form1">
  return do_check(); </script>
</head>
```

- Declares script handler for event *submit*, and
- Arrives at element id="form1".

Figure 2.4. Attaching event listener to the *handler*.

2.4 XML: Extensible Markup Language

Extensible Markup Language—XML 1.0—was designed to bring the best features of Standard Generalized Markup Language (SGML) to the Web. XML can be used to encode structured documents; it can also be used to encode structured data.

As an example, a text book might be authored as a structured XML document; in this case, one is likely to find the hierarchical structure of the book encoded via appropriately named elements, for example, ⟨**chapter**⟩ and ⟨**section**⟩. Alternatively, XML can be used to encode structured data records; in this case, the XML document is likely to be made up of markup constructs that capture the various fields and values that appear in the data record—see the questionnaire example shown in Section 1.2.1.

As a vocabulary designed for integration into other XML-based languages, XForms uses XML to encode document structure. XForms also uses XML to model, collect, and transmit information as described in Section 1.4. In this chapter, we primarily focus on this latter use of XML to encapsulate structured data.

2.4.1 Encapsulating Structured Data Using XML

Software applications typically encapsulate structured data using primitives provided by the programming language in which the application is implemented. As an example, a C programmer might use C `structs`, whereas a Java or C++ programmer might use `classes`. In all such cases, data structures provide a means of bundling together related data items into appropriate aggregations and later checking data for conformance to a given structure, for example, checking that a *mailing address* is a valid `address`. This form of checking is commonly called *type checking*.

Elements and attributes form the basic building blocks of XML. HTML authors are already familiar with these concepts. As an example, HTML uses element ⟨**title**⟩ to encapsulate the title of a Web page, whereas it uses attribute *href* when specifying a URI to follow within a hyperlink. XML uses these same concepts but is stricter when it comes to ensuring that *all* tags are matched—this is commonly referred to as the need for documents to be *well formed*. As a reward for being strict about well-formed documents, XML allows the language designer to create elements and attributes that reflect the needs of a given usage scenario; thus, we were able to define element ⟨**person**⟩ for holding the data record in our questionnaire application.

When modeling structured data using XML, the hierarchical structure present in the data is captured via nested elements. Attributes are used to capture properties of specific elements.[7] Using XML for encoding structured data has the advantage of being independent of any given implementation language or machine representation. Although XML encodings can be verbose in comparison to native representations used by implementation languages like C or Java, they enhance interoperability among disparate computing systems.

Typically, software systems that consume the declarative XML representations are implemented using languages like Java or C++. In contrast, the declarative nature of XML permits the creation of authoring tools that hide the underlying plumbing involved in implementing the system.

2.4.2 Namespaces for Compartmentalizing XML Data

Large software systems often need to work with data created by different software modules. Programming languages typically enable different modules to coexist by providing a **namespace** facility, for example, `package` in Java; such mechanisms avoid name collisions among symbols defined in different modules. Using XML for interchanging structured data among disparate systems has requirements similar to those found when integrating different software modules into large software systems. The tree-structured nature of XML encodings modifies these requirements in subtle ways. XML namespaces[8] is designed to enable XML encodings from different vocabularies to coexist, while taking into account the special requirements imposed by XML.

Consider the `person` instance defined as part of the questionnaire application. We used element names `first` and `last` to capture the user's first and last names. When integrating the data generated by the questionnaire into a larger business application, we might need to distinguish element ⟨**first**⟩ defined by the questionnaire from element ⟨**first**⟩ defined by another component of the larger system, for

---

[7] Note that the decision as to when one uses an attribute in favor of an element is often hotly debated among XML designers.

[8] http://www.w3.org/TR/REC-xml-names

example, element ⟨**first**⟩ might be used by another part of the system in encoding an ordered list of persons based on some ranking.

XML distinguishes between element types having the same name but different underlying semantics by *compartmentalizing* the space of all element names into distinct *namespaces*. Thus, when using XML namespaces, each element (and attribute) name has a *global* and *local* part. The *local* (or unqualified) name is what we showed when outlining the XML representation used by the questionnaire. To distinguish element names defined by the questionnaire application, we would define a questionnaire namespace whose name gives the *global part* of each element name used in encapsulating `person`.

It remains to pick a representation for the *global part* of this namespace that can be guaranteed to be unique. The XML namespaces recommendation from the W3C uses Universal Resource Identifiers (URI) as the means for selecting the global part in a manner that is likely to guarantee uniqueness while remaining human-readable. Thus, the developer of the questionnaire application can choose `http://example.com/q` to identify the questionnaire namespace. Notice that the namespace URI is chosen to provide a reasonable guarantee of uniqueness and has no additional semantics, that is, there is no guarantee that accessing this URI will result in a resource that further documents the questionnaire application.

Finally, typing the complete URI that is the global part of the questionnaire namespace can become tedious very quickly; it would also violate XML syntax rules since URIs often contain characters that are not permissible in XML element names. To alleviate this, developers can associate a *local prefix* to the namespace URI and use this local prefix to qualify all elements belonging to a given namespace within the context in which that local namespace prefix is declared. We demonstrate this in Figure 2.5.

2.5 XML Schema

XML Schema is designed to enable object-oriented descriptions of XML. The rich type system introduced in XML Schema was specifically designed to allow the encoding of structured data in XML. In XForms, XML Schema's ability to create

```
<q:person xmlns:q="http://example.com/q">
  <q:name>...</q:name>...
</q:person>
```

Figure 2.5. Declaring a namespace and associating a local namespace prefix.

object-oriented descriptions of XML data is used to advantage in modeling the data to be collected by the application.

User input can be checked against these declarative constraints using XML processors. The rest of this section gives a brief tutorial on the features of XML Schema that prove useful in designing data models for XForms applications. The interested reader is referred to the wealth of XML Schema resources for additional details.

With the maturing of XML on the Web, the use of XML for structured data interchange is becoming increasingly popular. Data repositories, such as relational databases, also find XML representations of structured data a convenient means of exchanging data among different systems. These uses of XML for encapsulating and interchanging structured data create the need for static type checking of XML data. Type information can be captured using XML Schema, and such type constraints can be automatically checked using off-the-shelf XML processors such as xerces.[9] Such structured data can be *bound* to specific implementation languages such as Java using *data binding*. This proves a convenient means of interchanging data among systems distributed across the network and automatically marshaling such data between the XML interchange representation and the run-time representation used by a given environment.

We illustrate the XML Schema declaration for USAddress in Figure 2.10 and compare it to an equivalent Interface Definition Language (IDL) declaration of the same type in Figure 2.6. Notice that the IDL representation is biased toward implementation languages, whereas the XML representation is biased toward declaratively capturing the required information in an implementation-independent manner. These representations should not be viewed as competing approaches; rather, each reflects different design points in the overall spectrum of possible solutions.

```
<idl>
  interface USAddress {
  String name; String  street; String city;
  //Enumeration of  two letter codes
  USState  state;
  Integer zip; Float gpsLatitude; Float gpsLongitude;
  }
</idl>
```

Figure 2.6. IDL declaration of type USAddress

---

[9]http://xml.apache.org/xerces

2.5.1 Schema Built-in Types

The following built-in types from XML Schema are especially relevant for modeling structured data to be collected from the user. Note that XML Schema also has a few built-in types that are more relevant to defining document grammars, for example, `token` that will not be discussed in detail in this book. The complete list of built-in schema data types is described in XML Schema Part 2.[10]

These built-in types help constrain the lexical values of leaf nodes in an XML structure. These constraints can thus be applied to the text contents of an element or the value of an attribute. This set of basic types can be extended as described in the next section. XML Schema defines several additional data types derived from the above set of built-in types. We illustrate the use of the enumerated built-in types with an example in Figure 2.7. An XML instance document is shown with the type of each element declared using attribute `xsi:type`. Later, we extend this example to define a complete schema for invitations in Section 2.5.3.[11]

Table 2.3. Commonly Used XML Schema Data Types

Type	Description	Example
string	Text	`simple`
boolean	Logic	`false`
decimal	Numbers	`1.25`
integer	integers	`2002`
float	32-bit float	`67.433E12`
double	64-bit float	`7.33E32`
duration	Time period	`P1DT1H`
dateTime	ISO 8601 date-time	`2003-01-01T00:00:00`
time	Instant of time	`12:00:00`
date	Calendar date	`2003-01-01`
gYearMonth	Calendar month	`2003-01`
gYear	Calendar year	`2003`
gMonthDay	Monthly recurring date	`15`
gDay	Annually recurring day	`12-15`
gMonth	Annually recurring Month	`12`
base64Binary	Binary data	`...`
anyURI	URI	`http://example.com`

---

[10]http://www.w3.org/TR/xmlschema-2/

[11]Note that the types in this initial example are shown using *xsi:type* for clarity. In a real-world example, these would be provided by the XML Schema definition.

```
<invitation xmlns:xsi
  ="http://www.w3.org/2001/XMLSchema-instance"
  xmlns:xsd="http://www.w3.org/2001/XMLSchema">
  <title>BubbleDog's 5th Birthday</title>
  <age xsi:type="xsd:integer">5</age>
  <born xsi:type="xsd:Date">1997-12-21</born>
  <!-- party At a palindromic moment -->
  <party xsi:type="xsd:dateTime">
  2002-12-21T20:02:00-07:00</party>
  <!-- lasts 1 hour -->
  <duration xsi:type="xsd:duration">PT1H</duration>
  <!-- Recurs annually on December 21 -->
  <annual xsi:type="xsd:gMonthDay">12-21</annual>
  <!-- if celebrated monthly -->
  <monthly xsi:type="xsd:gDay">21</monthly>
  <location  xsi:type="USAddress">...</location>
  <replyTo  xsi:type="xsd:anyURI">...</replyTo>
  <picture xsi:type="xsd:anyURI">...</picture>
</invitation>
```

Figure 2.7. Illustrates the use of some of the built-in data types provided by XML Schema.

2.5.2 Extending Built-in Types

New data types can be defined starting from the set of XML Schema built-in types. Such *type derivations* are carried out by imposing appropriate restrictions on the set of allowable values for a given built-in type. Allowable values in XML Schema are governed by several *facets*; by restricting these facets, one can define subtypes of the built-in types described thus far. Table 2.4 lists facets that can be used in defining subtypes of the built-in types; type derivation by restricting values along one or more facets is called *restriction*. Note that not all of the facets listed in Table 2.4 are available on all built-in types; for details, see the XML Schema specification.

Simple types are defined in XML Schema using element ⟨**simpleType**⟩. We show examples of the use of element ⟨**simpleType**⟩ in defining two user-defined types, USState and ZIPCode. We show an example of using string enumeration to define a new type called USState in Figure 2.8.

We define type ZIPCode by restricting xsd:string in Figure 2.9; the set of allowable values is specified via facet *pattern*. XML Schema also allows the definition

Table 2.4. Facets Restrict Values of Built-in XML Schema Data Types

Facet	Description
pattern	Regular expression
enumeration	Enumerate values
minLength	Minimum length
maxLength	Maximum length
minExclusive	Lower Bound
minInclusive	Minimum allowed value
maxExclusive	Upper bound
maxInclusive	Maximum allowed value
length	Length
minLength	Minimum length
maxLength	Maximum length

```
<xsd:simpleType name="USState"
  xmlns:xsd="http://www.w3.org/2001/XMLSchema">
  <xsd:restriction base="xsd:string">
    <xsd:enumeration value="AK"/>
    <xsd:enumeration value="AL"/>
    <xsd:enumeration value="AR"/>
    <!-- and so on ...-->
  </xsd:restriction>
</xsd:simpleType>
```

Figure 2.8. Type USState is derived by restricting type xsd:string.

```
<xsd:simpleType name="ZIPCode"
  xmlns:xsd="http://www.w3.org/2001/XMLSchema">
  <xsd:restriction base="xsd:string">
    <xsd:pattern value="\d{5}"/>
  </xsd:restriction>
</xsd:simpleType>
```

Figure 2.9. Using facet *pattern* to define type ZIPCode that can hold five-digit U.S. ZIP codes.

of list and union types using element ⟨**simpleType**⟩. Complete details of the use of element ⟨**simpleType**⟩ are beyond the scope of this book, and the interested reader is referred to the references on XML Schema.

2.5.3 Defining Aggregations Using Complex Types

Higher level data aggregations are encoded in XML using elements and attributes. The previous section described simple types as defined by XML Schema. XML structures that are the result of attaching attributes or element children are called *complex types* in XML Schema.

Constructs for creating complex types are defined in XML Schema Part 1,[12] and XML Schema Primer[13] gives a good tutorial introduction to this topic. This section gives a high-level overview of how these constructs can be used to define data aggregations.

In XML Schema, complex types allow elements in their content and may carry attributes; simple types cannot have element content and cannot carry attributes. XML Schema *definitions* create new types, and XML Schema *declarations* enable elements and attributes with specific names and types to appear in XML instances. In this section, we focus on defining complex types and declaring the elements and attributes that appear within them.

We illustrate these concepts by first defining complex type USAddress and then using this to define a more complete schema for the party invitation introduced in Figure 2.7. The schema in Figure 2.10 defines a new type called USAddress. It declares that data conforming to type USAddress *must* have 5 element children and 2 attributes. It further constrains the values of these elements and attributes using XML Schema built-in types.

New complex types are defined using element ⟨**complexType**⟩, and such definitions contain a set of element declarations, element references, and attribute declarations. The declarations are not themselves types, but rather an association between a name and the constraints that govern the appearance of that name in conforming XML instances. Thus, these are similar to statements in programming languages used to declare identifiers of a given type.

Elements are declared using element ⟨**element**⟩; attributes are declared using element ⟨**attribute**⟩. For example, we define InvitationType as a complex type, and within that definition, we see element and attribute declarations as shown in Figure 2.11.

---

[12]http://www.w3.org/TR/xmlschema-1/
[13]http://www.w3.org/TR/xmlschema-0/

```
<x:complexType name="USAddress"
  xmlns:x="http://www.w3.org/2001/XMLSchema">
  <x:sequence>
    <x:element name="name"   type="x:string"/>
    <x:element name="street" type="x:string"/>
    <x:element name="city"   type="x:string"/>
    <x:element name="state"  type="x:string"/>
    <x:element name="zip"    type="x:integer"/>
  </x:sequence>
  <x:attribute name="gpsLatitude" type="x:decimal"/>
  <x:attribute name="gpsLongitude" type="x:decimal"/>
</x:complexType>
```

Figure 2.10. Type Definition for complex type USAddress.

```
<s:schema xmlns:s="http://www.w3.org/2001/XMLSchema">
  <!-- insert USAddress definition here -->
  <s:complexType name="InvitationType">
    <s:sequence>
      <s:element name="title" type="s:string"/>
      <s:element name="age" type="s:integer"/>
      <s:element name="born" type="s:date"/>
      <s:element name="party" type="s:dateTime"/>
      <s:element name="duration" type="s:duration"/>
      <s:element name="annual" type="s:gMonthDay"/>
      <s:element name="monthly" type="s:gDay"/>
      <s:element name="location" type="USAddress"/>
      <s:element name="replyTo" type="USAddress"/>
      <s:element name="picture" type="s:anyURI"/>
    </s:sequence></s:complexType></s:schema>
```

Figure 2.11. Definition of type InvitationType.

The consequence of the definition shown in Figure 2.11 is that any element whose type is declared to be InvitationType must consist of the requisite number of elements and attributes. These elements must be named as specified by the values of the name attributes appearing in the definition, and each element *must* appear in the same order as declared. The USAddress definition contains only declarations involving the simple types xsd:string and decimal. More advanced type definitions, like the one for InvitationType shown in Figure 2.11, can use complex types defined earlier by using the same mechanism shown here.

In defining InvitationType, two of the element declarations, replyTo and location, associate different element names with the same complex type USAddress. The consequence of this definition is that any element appearing in an instance document whose type is declared to be InvitationType *must* consist of elements named replyTo and location, each containing the five subelements (name, street, city, state, and zip) that were declared as part of type USAddress. These elements may also carry the GPS attributes that were declared as part of USAddress.

Finally, notice that the declaration of child elements is enclosed in element ⟨**sequence**⟩. Attributes *minOccurs* and *maxOccurs* on element ⟨**sequence**⟩ may be used to specify cardinality constraints on the number of child elements. If omitted, these default to 1 as in the examples shown in Figure 2.11.

2.6 XForms Implementations

A complete list of XForms implementations is maintained by the XForms WG.[14] This section covers some of the major implementations at the time of writing to get readers started on XForms. Readers are encouraged to download one or more of these implementations as they work through the material in this book.

2.6.1 X-Smiles: An Open Source XML Browser

X-Smiles is an open source XML browser with support for numerous emerging W3C standards. It has full support for XForms 1.0 and provides an excellent example of how modular specifications lead to modular implementations. X-Smiles integrates existing implementations of XML Schema, XPath, and other W3C standards to create a powerful and versatile browser that supports an increasing list of W3C specifications, including:

- CSS for creating Web sites in style
- XHTML 2.0 for creating clean, easy to maintain Web pages
- XForms for creating interactive user experiences

---

[14]http://www.w3.org/MarkUp/Forms/overview.html#implementations

- for Exposing XForms' multidevice capabilities
- SMIL for creating synchronized multimedia experiences
- XFrames for creating frame-based Web sites that really work
- SVG support for creating high-quality vector graphics
- XSL Flow Objects[15] for creating high-quality print representations

By supporting all of these technologies within a well-integrated XML browser, X-Smiles helps Web developers experiment with different combinations of these standards. As an example, X-Smiles permits the use of XForms, SVG, and SMIL within a single Web page for creating rich end-user interaction.

2.6.2 Novell XForms Preview

This is a stand-alone Java client for interacting with XForms applications. It enables Web developers to experiment with XForms in a stand-alone environment. This technology preview comes with numerous examples, including a demonstration of how XForms can be connected to Web Services.

2.6.3 FormsPlayer—XForms for Internet Explorer

FormsPlayer is a plug-in for Internet Explorer that extends this widely deployed yet legacy Web browser with XForms functionality. It includes numerous examples of how XForms can be integrated within a Web browser to create a rich end-user experience. The FormsPlayer site provides tutorials and other learning materials in addition to the XForms plug-in.

2.6.4 IBM XForms Preview

The IBM XForms technology preview consists of several components designed to encourage experimentation with XForms. It includes the following:

- XForms client for Mozilla
- XForms client for Internet Explorer
- XForms processor for use in conjunction with JSP

---

[15]http://www.w3.org/tr/xsl/

2.7 XML Standards at a Glance

The various standard building blocks covered in this chapter are summarized in Table 2.5. For each of these standard building blocks, we give a brief summary of their role in the overall XForms architecture.

We conclude this chapter with a brief summary of existing implementations of the various standard building blocks described in this chapter in Table 2.6. This serves to illustrate the advantages resulting from designing XForms based on existing standards. XForms implementations can be put together using the implementations of these building blocks in much the same manner as the XForms specification itself.

Table 2.5. XML Standards at a Glance

Standard	Role in XForms
XML	• Encapsulates structured instance data. • XML DOM provides underlying model. • Serialized instance data is I18N ready.
Namespaces	• Partition space of element and attribute names. • Enable different XML vocabularies to coexist. • Create modular XForms applications. • Key to integrating XForms into XML host languages.
Schema	• Enables object-oriented descriptions of XML. • Provides rich set of data types. • Enables off-the-shelf validation. • Captures static constraints in the model.
XPath	• Locators address portions of an XML instance. • Locators used to bind controls to the model. • Locators used to bind model properties. • A side-effect free expression language. • Expresses dynamic properties within XForms.
DOM2	• Cross-platform API for eventing. • Used to attach *behavior*. • Enables hosting XForms processors in a browser.
XML Events	• XML access to DOM2 Events. • Defines common XML markup for eventing. • Attaches event handlers in XForms documents. • Enables declarative authoring in place of scripts.

Table 2.6. Implementations of Relevant W3C Standards

Standard	Implementation
XML Schema	• Apache xerces on all platforms • MSXML.dll on Windows
XPath	• Apache Xalan on all platforms • Mozilla on all platforms • MSXML.dll on Windows
DOM2 events	• Mozilla on all platforms • Internet Explorer
XML Events	• Apache xerces on all platforms • All XForms implementations
XForms	• X-Smiles—an open source XML browser • FormsPlayer—an XForms plug-in for IE • Novell XForms technology preview • IBM XForms technology preview for Mozilla and IE

PART II

XForms Components

CHAPTER 3

XForms User Interface Controls

User interface *widgets* collect user input and are responsible for providing a pleasant end-user experience when interacting with an application. The presentation and interaction exhibited by such widgets determines the *look and feel* of the user interface. With markup languages such as XForms, such user interface widgets are created by special markup constructs called, in this book, *user interface controls*. We begin our technical overview of XForms with a tour of the available user interface controls. Each such control adds a specific type of functionality and will be introduced alongside examples that motivate its use.

XForms user interface controls have been designed to be familiar to HTML authors and provide a smooth transition from today's HTML forms. In contrast to HTML form controls, XForms user interface controls are designed to match the structure of XHTML documents. User interface controls are designed to be *accessible*, *localizable*, and *internationalizable*. Presentational hints, such as visual styling, are clearly separated to better enable the delivery of XForms user interfaces to a variety of end-user devices and modalities. We summarize the design philosophy underlying the XForms user interface in Section 3.1.

We begin our overview of the various user interface controls by describing the overall structure of XForms user interface controls in Section 3.2.

XForms user interface controls share a number of common markup features. Markup features such as attributes and child elements common to all XForms user interface controls are described here. User interface controls designed to allow free-form textual input are described in Section 3.3. By leveraging the type information from the XForms data model, such input controls can be rendered using platform-specific widgets to enable rich data entry.

Traditional user interfaces provide a variety of widgets that enable *controlled* user input, for example, pull-down lists that allow the user to pick from a given set of choices. XForms provides this functionality via controls ⟨**select**⟩ and ⟨**select1**⟩, described in Section 3.4. These controls are useful when the set of values that the user can provide is constrained in some manner, for example, picking a state from a list of states. XForms select controls provide a flexible yet device-independent means of creating such user interfaces.

The notion of selecting from a set of available values can be further refined when the underlying set of values is *ordered*. This manifests itself in traditional user interfaces in the form of widgets, such as *sliders* and *spin dials*, that make the structure of the space of available values apparent to the user. XForms includes control ⟨**range**⟩, described in Section 3.5, that can be used for this purpose.

Control ⟨**upload**⟩, described in Section 3.6, provides the familiar *file upload* feature of HTML forms; at the same time, it is designed to be usable on devices that do not contain a file system but need to upload data to a Web server, for example, digital cameras.

Finally, we describe XForms controls that enable the user to invoke specific commands. Traditional visual interfaces provide a generic *button* widget that is used to invoke a given command; control ⟨**trigger**⟩, described in Section 3.7, generalizes this idea by enabling the XForms author to specify one or more *action handlers* to be invoked when the *trigger* is activated. The familiar *submit* control used to submit data from a Web form is enabled via XForms action ⟨**send**⟩. Control ⟨**submit**⟩, described in Section 3.8, is thus a special case of control ⟨**trigger**⟩ that invokes action ⟨**send**⟩. We conclude the chapter with a summary of the various user interface controls in Section 3.9.

3.1 XForms User Interface Design

We begin this chapter with an overview of the design philosophy that motivated the creation of the XForms user interface vocabulary. The primary goal as we overhauled HTML forms from 1993 was to make the next generation Web forms technology robust with respect to accessibility, internationalization, and the ability to deliver user interaction to a variety of modalities and end-user devices. Looking forward to a ubiquitous Web that would be accessible using devices and modalities best suited to a user's needs and abilities at a given time meant that we had to step back from commonly held notions of visual interaction and create an abstract user interface vocabulary capable of withstanding the test of time.[1]

Addressing the need to create an abstract user interface vocabulary had the advantage of contributing directly to our primary goals of accessibility. Once we freed the user interface vocabulary from fixed ideas driven purely by visual interaction, we were able to leverage the separation of the XForms model from the user interface to the fullest degree in creating a set of controls that could be easily retargeted to different user interaction environments. Cascading Style Sheets (CSS) is now a mature Web technology, and this has made it significantly easier for the XForms working group to defer stylistic and presentational issues to the CSS layer. Having separated out presentation by using CSS, we used the XML binding to DOM Events provided by XML Events to factor out interaction behavior of the various controls. Thus, the XForms user interface design separates content, presentation, and interaction to create an XML vocabulary that lends itself to *intent-based* authoring of user interaction:

Content   Separating the *model* from the user interaction allows user interface controls to *bind* to display-independent content.

Presentation Factoring out presentation and style via CSS makes XForms user interface controls presentation independent.

Interaction   Using XML Events to connect events and the actions they invoke enable XForms user interface controls to remain independent of specific user interaction environments. Thus, none of the XForms user interface controls as defined depend on specific UI peripherals such as mouse, keyboard, or monitor.

Once we had achieved the above three-way separation, it became possible to define a user interface vocabulary that encourages *intent-based* authoring. This style of authoring encourages authors to specify fully the underlying intent behind a given user interaction—rather than the mere physical representation of a particular user interface. Thus, authors specify that the user should be allowed to pick from a set of choices via XForms element ⟨**select**⟩—rather than by hard-wiring a specific representation of such a control, for example, a list box.

The abstract nature of the XForms user interface vocabulary, combined with each XForms control encapsulating all the metadata needed to represent the user interaction effectively, makes it well suited for delivering applications to different modalities and devices. Notice that encapsulating such metadata as part of the user

---

[1]Or at least survive as long as HTML forms from 1993 have survived!

Table 3.1. Mapping HTML Forms Vocabulary to XForms

HTML Forms	XForms
⟨**input** *type*="text"⟩	⟨**input**⟩
⟨**input** *type*="password"⟩	⟨**secret**⟩
⟨**input** *type*="textarea"⟩	⟨**textarea**⟩
⟨**input** *type*="hidden"⟩	Default—values shown only when controls are bound
⟨**input** *type*="checkbox"⟩	⟨**input**⟩ bound to *type* xsd:boolean
⟨**input** *type*="radio"⟩	⟨**select1**⟩
⟨**select**⟩	⟨**select**⟩
⟨**input** *type*="submit"⟩	⟨**submit**⟩
⟨**input** *type*="reset"⟩	⟨**trigger**⟩ with handler ⟨**reset**⟩
⟨**input** *type*="file"⟩	⟨**upload**⟩
⟨**input** *type*="image"⟩	⟨**trigger**⟩ with image label
⟨**input** *type*="button"⟩	⟨**trigger**⟩

interface controls makes the resulting vocabulary accessible by design. This is a major step forward from the past where accessibility was typically bolted in after the rest of the system had been designed.

The effect of building accessibility as a first-class citizen into the XForms design is most noticeable when reading the XForms 1.0 specification, which makes very few explicit references to accessibility. This is not an oversight in the specification— on the contrary, having designed XForms to be accessible and usable from the very beginning, the working group needed to say very little in terms of explicit accessibility guidelines when authoring XForms applications.

Finally, the XForms vocabulary was designed to be familiar to HTML authors in order to smooth the transition to XForms. HTML authors will recognize the equivalences shown in Table 3.1 between familiar HTML Forms constructs and their XForms counterparts.

3.2 Common Aspects of XForms Controls

XForms user interface controls are used to collect user input. The various XForms user interface controls provide a consistent markup interface to ease authoring. The XML markup is designed to be familiar to today's HTML authors, while overcoming some of the idiosyncrasies found in HTML forms. This section presents a high-level design overview before presenting the syntactic details of the various user interface controls. In doing so, we will cover all aspects of common markup found in XForms user interface controls.

3.2.1 Anatomy of a User Interface Control

XForms defines a set of abstract user interface controls that collect and display user input. The XForms design separates these user interface controls from the data that is collected from the user. Abstract user interface controls are designed to capture the underlying intent of the user interaction, rather than its final presentation on any given device or in any specific modality. This makes it possible to deliver XForms applications to different devices and modalities. More generally, this design enables the creation of editing interfaces that allow the user to view and modify XML data and documents. The separation of the user interface from the underlying model and the design of this user interface as a set of abstract user interface controls result in all XForms controls having the following structure:

Bind   Binding attributes that wire control to model
Metadata   Metadata for giving feedback to the user, for example, labels
Presentation   Hints used to affect the rendering of the control
Style   CSS-based styling
Shortcuts   Keyboard shortcuts and accelerator keys
Navigation   Where this control appears in the navigation sequence
Behavior   Action handlers for custom behaviors

These aspects are authored via a set of attributes and child elements common to all XForms user interface controls. These characteristics of a user interface control can be grouped according to their functionality as pertaining to the model, presentation, and interaction behavior, respectively—see Figure 3.1. We summarize these for easy reference in Table 3.2.

3.2.2 Binding Controls to the Model

XForms user interface controls are connected to the underlying data model using *binding attributes*. Attribute pair (*model*, *ref*) specifies the portion of the instance to be populated by a given control. We use a pair of attributes here since XForms permits the creation of Web applications that use multiple models, for example, when creating a complex application that needs to submit data to multiple locations on the Web. Binding attribute *model* identifies the model that contains the instance being populated; Attribute *ref* holds an XPath locator that identifies the location in the instance that is being populated. Binding user interface controls to the model was illustrated in Figure 1.5 and Figure 1.7.

Table 3.2. Common Aspects of XForms User Interface Markup

Markup	Purpose
	Binding Attributes (Section 3.2.2)
model	Identifies the model containing the bound instance
ref	Identifies single node from the instance that is bound
nodeset	Identifies set of nodes from the instance
bind	Identifies bound instance data via a binding site
	Common Presentation Attributes (Section 3.2.3)
appearance	Presentation hint—one of *full*, *compact*, or *minimal*
class	CSS selector to specify rendering style
	Common Presentation Child Elements (Section 3.2.3)
⟨**label**⟩	Label for the user interface control
⟨**help**⟩	Help text for the user interface control
⟨**hint**⟩	Tooltip for the user interface control
⟨**alert**⟩	Message to display in case of invalid input
	Common Interaction Attributes (Section 3.2.4)
accesskey	Specifies keyboard shortcut for navigating to this control
navindex	Specifies position of the control in the navigation sequence
inputmode	Facilitates text input on small devices
eventing	XML Events attributes for wiring up events
incremental	Specifies if text input generates continuous stream of events
	Common Interaction Child Elements (Section 3.2.4)
⟨**action**⟩	Declarative action handlers defined by XForms

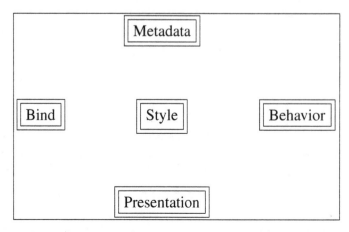

Figure 3.1. Anatomy of an XForms user interface control.

Thus, binding attributes *wire* user interface controls to the appropriate portion of the underlying XForms model. In addition to attribute pair (*model*, *ref*) described earlier, XForms provides a syntactic shortcut for creating binding expressions that involve complex XPath expressions. When defining the XForms model, the author can identify certain locations with a designated id declared via element ⟨**bind**⟩. Such *binding sites* can be later used when binding user interface controls by specifying the id of the binding site as the value of attribute *bind*.

This mechanism is useful when binding multiple controls to the same location in multipage forms. For instance, consider a tax form that collects multiple items of information and displays the most important items on a summary page—see Figure 3.2.

The author can identify those information items that appear on multiple pages as *binding sites* when defining the model. Later, when authoring the user interface, attribute *bind* can be used when binding user interface controls to these binding sites.

```
<html xmlns="http://www.w3.org/1999/xhtml">
  <head>
    <model xmlns="http://www.w3.org/2002/xforms">
      <instance>
        <data xmlns="">...<wages/>...</data>
      </instance>
      <!-- identify binding site -->
      <bind ref="/data/wages" id="wages"/>
    </model></head>
  <body>
    <h1>Page 1</h1>
    <group xmlns="http://www.w3.org/2002/xforms">
      ...<input bind="wages">...</input>...
    </group>...
    <h1>Summary Page</h1>
    <group xmlns="http://www.w3.org/2002/xforms">
      <output bind="wages">
        <label>Total Wages Reported</label>
    </output></group>
  </body></html>
```

Figure 3.2. Using binding sites for connecting user interface controls to the model.

This has the advantage if the structure of the instance needs to be changed at a later date. When such changes are made, the XPath locators need be edited only in one place, namely the model where the binding site is declared. If the attribute pair (*model*, *ref*) were used in this scenario, this would require the editing of the binding attributes on the different user interface controls. This said, using attributes (*model*, *ref*) is more convenient, except in such complex examples, since the extra level of indirection introduced by the use of binding sites makes the resulting markup less obvious.

3.2.3 Rendering User Interface Controls

End-user experience is controlled via a set of attributes and child elements common to all XForms user interface controls. These common markup constructs hold metadata associated with the user interface control, for example, the label to be displayed to the user; they also encapsulate presentation hints that can be used in delivering the desired presentation.

Common Presentation Attributes

appearance   Attribute *appearance* can be used by the author to specify *presentational* hints. XForms specifies three predefined values for this attribute:

1. `full`
2. `compact`
3. `minimal`

The meaning of these predefined values is a function of the user interface control. As an example, `appearance="full"` might be used to request that a (**select**) selection control be presented as a list of checkboxes with all the available choices being visible to the user. In contrast, `appearance="minimal"` might be used to request that the same control be rendered to take up a minimal amount of display real estate and, as a result, appear as a pop-up menu in a visual interface.

In addition to the predefined values, attribute *appearance* encourages innovation by accepting application-specific values as long as these values are properly namespace qualified. Thus, an author creating an (**input**) control that binds to a value of type `xsd:date` can request that the control be presented using a custom date picker with

```
<input model="invite" ref="/invitation/date"
  appearance="my:date-picker">
<label>Invitation Date</label>...</input>
```

Figure 3.3. Requesting a custom date picker via attribute *appearance*.

markup (shown in Figure 3.3). The advantage of this design is that user agents not capable of using the custom date picker control can still effectively represent the user interface by using a regular text input field.

class   When using XForms controls in HTML, attribute *class* can specify a CSS style to be used.

Common Presentation Child Elements

label   Holds the label for the containing user interface control

help   Holds help text to be displayed on request

hint   Holds tooltip information for the containing control

alert   Holds a message to be displayed if the form control is an invalid state, for example, when an illegal value is entered by the user

Note that elements ⟨**label**⟩, ⟨**help**⟩, ⟨**hint**⟩, and ⟨**alert**⟩ when used *must* appear in this specific order.

Element ⟨**label**⟩ is *required* on all XForms user interface controls. In addition to providing a label for the user interface control, the content of this element can be useful to accessibility aids; for example, an accessibility aid might speak the contents of this element when the user navigates to a control.

Element ⟨**label**⟩ was designed to be a child element of the user interface control in order to improve accessibility of electronic forms. Traditional HTML form controls did not capture the label as part of the markup for the user interface control; this resulted in authors visually aligning labels for user interface controls using HTML tables. Though this delivers a visual presentation that clearly displays the association between labels and user interface controls, it presents a serious accessibility problem. Accessibility aids were forced to guess the association between labels and controls by examining the visual layout. By making element ⟨**label**⟩ a *required* child of all user interface controls, XForms takes a major step forward with respect to enhancing the accessibility of Web applications.

Elements ⟨**label**⟩, ⟨**help**⟩, ⟨**hint**⟩, and ⟨**alert**⟩ can directly encapsulate the information to be shown to the user. Alternatively, this metadata can be specified indirectly by specifying a URI as the value of attribute *src*. Specifying such metadata indirectly can be helpful when creating user interfaces that need to be localized. In such cases, one can create locale-specific sets of messages and use attribute *src* to refer to the messages.

3.2.4 Interaction Behavior of Form Controls

End-user experience—the look and feel delivered by a user interface—is a function of the end-user presentation as well as the behavior exhibited by the user interface in response to user actions such as key presses and mouse clicks. Interaction behavior of XForms user interface controls can be customized via the common attributes and child elements described in this section.

Common Interaction Attributes

accesskey	Specifies the shortcut key to navigate to the containing control.
navindex	Specifies the position in the navigation sequence.
inputmode	Attribute *inputmode* was added to user interface controls that collect textual input to facilitate text entry on different devices. This feature is especially useful on small devices that need to provide the necessary aids to enable efficient user input when using various international character sets.
eventing	XML Events attribute pair (*event*, *handler*) is used to turn user interface controls into *listeners*. Attribute *event* specifies the event to listen for; attribute *handler* specifies the handler to be invoked upon receiving the specified event.
incremental	Optional boolean attribute *incremental* (`false` by default) specifies if the containing user interface control fires events as the value is being entered. This is an advanced feature that might be used by user agents to update different parts of a form as the user is entering a value; leveraging the XForms processing model for implementing sophisticated user interfaces will be described in a later chapter.

Attributes *accesskey* and *navindex* are important accessibility features first introduced in HTML4. Specifying keyboard shortcuts via attribute *accesskey* can enhance the usability of an online form by enabling the user to navigate directly to a control via the keyboard. Specifying the position of a user interface control in the navigation sequence via attribute *navindex* gives the author the ability to influence the order in which the user navigates through a sequence of controls.

Common Interaction Child Element

action   Holds one or more action handlers. XForms defines a set of declarative
             event handlers that provides functionality commonly found in online forms.
             All of these handlers can appear within XForms user interface controls.
             Such handlers are executed when the user interface control is activated by
             the user.

3.3 Collecting Text Input

Inputting free-form textual input is perhaps one of the most common tasks when
working with electronic forms. In fact electronic forms can be viewed as a means
of collecting semistructured information from the user and automatically tagging
such information for later processing. Thus, a travel report might be modeled as
an electronic form where most if not all of the fields collect free-form textual input
from the user. Yet, when the travel report is filled in using a well-designed form
that populates an underlying data model like the one provided by XForms, the
information that is collected is immediately ready for further machine processing.
In contrast, if the same travel report were directly authored as a word processor
document, the data collected by the travel report would need to be reentered into
the relevant systems in order to be processed further.

As an example, consider a more detailed version of the questionnaire form
introduced in Section 1.2.1 and shown in Figure 3.4. Once the information collected
by the questionnaire is modeled using XML Schema, binding a set of user interface

```
<questionnaire xmlns:q="http://example.com/q">
  <name><first/><initial/><last/></name>
  <email xsi:type="q:email"/>
  <home-phone xsi:type="q:phone"/>
  <work-phone xsi:type="q:phone"/>
  <address>
    <name/><street/><city/><state/>
    <zip xsi:type="q:zip"/>
  </address>
  <age xsi:type="xsd:integer"/>
  <date-of-birth xsi:type="xsd:date"/>
</questionnaire>
```

Figure 3.4. Data collected by the questionnaire.

controls that facilitate entering this information creates an efficient user interface for editing and maintaining XML documents that conform to the questionnaire schema.

XForms provides three variants of the generic *enter some text* user interface control, all of which have the same markup structure:

⟨**input**⟩   Edit field for entering values

⟨**secret**⟩   For entering a value that should not be echoed as it is entered

⟨**textarea**⟩ For entering multiple lines of text, for example, the body of an e-mail message

We demonstrate the use of these controls to author a simple e-mail application in Figure 3.5.

Controls ⟨**input**⟩, ⟨**secret**⟩, and ⟨**textarea**⟩ use all of the common markup attributes and child elements described in Section 3.2.

3.3.1 Customizing Input Controls

Controls ⟨**input**⟩, ⟨**secret**⟩, and ⟨**textarea**⟩ are commonly rendered as edit boxes in a visual interface. Notice, however, that the XForms design leaves considerable flexibility for a client to implement these controls in a manner most suitable for the facilities available on the accessing device.

This section gives examples of how different clients and interaction modalities might leverage the information encapsulated in the XForms markup to deliver an appropriate end-user experience. We illustrate these scenarios using the e-mail application introduced in Figure 3.5; see Figure 3.6 for the visual rendering of this interface.

End-user experience is a function of the look and feel delivered by a user interface. As the phrase *look and feel* implies, this is made up of two halves: the presentation that is delivered to the user and the interaction behavior exhibited by the user interface, that is, the way the interface reacts to different user interface events.

In XForms, the *look* is authored via CSS; the *feel* is specified using XML Events. Notice that in Figure 3.5, we used

```
class="address"
```

on the input controls used to collect the from and to e-mail addresses. An accompanying email.css can define appropriate presentational properties that help visually distinguish input fields that collect e-mail addresses; the same CSS style sheet might also define presentation rules for other output modalities, for example,

```
<html xmlns="http://www.w3.org/1999/xhtml">
  <head><link rel="stylesheet" href="email.css"/>
    <model xmlns="http://www.w3.org/2002/xforms"
      id="m1" schema="email.xsd">
      <instance>
        <email xmlns="">
          <from type="email"/><to type="email"/>
          <pin/><message/>
        </email></instance>
    </model></head>
  <body>
    <group xmlns="http://www.w3.org/2002/xforms">
      <input class="address" appearance="my:email"
        model="m1" ref="/email/from">
        <label class="address">From</label>
      <help>Enter your email address</help></input>
      <input class="address" appearance="my:email"
        model="m1" ref="/email/to">
        <label class="address">To</label>
      <help>Recipient's address</help></input>
      <secret class="pin" ref="/email/pin">
        <label>Pin</label>
      <help>Secret phrase</help></secret>
      <textarea class="message"
        model="m1" ref="/email/message">
        <label>Message</label>
        <help>...</help><hint>...</hint>
    </textarea>...</group>
</body></html>
```

Figure 3.5. Sending e-mail using XForms.

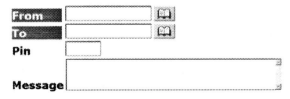

Figure 3.6. Visual presentation of the XForms e-mail composer.

```
<style type="text/css">
  @namespace xf url(http://www.w3.org/2002/xforms);
  xf|label {
  font-weight: bold; font-size: 20px;   width:100px;}
  xf|input::value.address {
  font-weight:bold; width:500px;}
  xf|secret::value.pin {
  font-weight:bold; width:100px;}
  xf|label.address {
  color:white; background-color:blue;}
  xf|textarea::value {
  width:800px;}
  @media speech {
  xf|input.address {pitch: 1; pitch-range: 9;
  }
  xf|label.address {pitch: 1; pitch-range: 9;
  } }
</style>
```

Figure 3.7. CSS style that defines how fields for collecting e-mail addresses should be rendered in various presentation modes.

aural output, by defining aural presentational rules for class="address"—see Figure 3.7.[2]

Further media specific sections in the CSS file might fine-tune the presentation for different device types.[3] Factoring out presentational aspects from the user interface markup and delegating this responsibility to CSS enable the XForms author to design applications that can be delivered to a variety of different devices and presentation modalities.

The interaction behavior of user interface controls is primarily determined by the *type* of the bound instance data. As an example, input controls that bind to instance nodes of type date might be rendered as a *date picker* control. This can be further customized via attribute *appearance*.[4] XForms 1.0 defines three standard values for this attribute as described in Section 3.2. In addition, it allows for custom

---

[2]Note that CSS uses | as the namespace separator character unlike XML which uses :.

[3]The CSS WG is working on a mechanism called CSS Media Query to facilitate such fine tuning.

[4]As a working group, we struggled long and hard to come up with a suitable name for this attribute and eventually settled on *appearance*, even though it does not do full justice.

controls by allowing additional values for attribute *appearance* as long as such values are namespace qualified.

The example shown in Figure 3.5 takes advantage of this feature by setting attribute *appearance* to `my:email` on the input controls used to collect e-mail addresses.[5]

Notice further that when defining the model in Figure 3.5, we declared the type of the `/email/from` and `/email/to` fields to be `my:email`. An XForms client that includes an e-mail picker—a widget that can access the user's e-mail address book—can use that widget rather than a plain edit field. Notice that this mechanism enables clients to deliver an end-user experience that best leverages the facilities available on a client. At the same time, the XForms e-mail application can be used on a device that does not provide an e-mail picker control.

We declared field `date-of-birth` in Figure 2.11 to be of type `xsd:date`. This information could be used to pick a custom date picker control when rendering an input control that binds to the `date-of-birth` field. By setting an appropriate value for attribute *inputmode*, entering the date or e-mail address can be made easier when using devices such as cell phones. More ambitious use cases would include invoking an appropriate speech interface that is capable of collecting a valid date; advanced user interaction including speech and multimodal interfaces will be discussed in Chapter 10.

3.4 Selecting from a Set of Values

Next to free-form input, user selection based on a set of constraints is perhaps one of the most common facilities provided by user interfaces today. Such *selection* often manifests itself in a visual interface in the form of pull-down lists or radio buttons. When using smaller sized devices, for example, digital cameras or cell phones, such selections show up as nested menus that progressively guide the user to a specific selection.

XForms defines selection controls based on the functionality provided, rather than their appearance in a given environment. This design has the advantage of capturing the underlying intent in a given user interaction rather than its mere visual appearance. Thus, consider a selection control that allows one to specify one's gender by picking from a pair of mutually exclusive values. Rendering such a control as a group of radio buttons may be appropriate for a visual interface; however, designing the user interface markup based on this choice of presentation

---

[5]We have used `my:` as the namespace prefix for the e-mail application.

```
<fieldset>
  <input id="g1" type="radio" checked="checked"
  value="m" name="gender"/>
  <label for="g1">Male</label>
  <input id="g2" type="radio"
  value="f" name="gender"/>
<label for="g2">Female</label></fieldset>
```

Figure 3.8. HTML radio buttons fail to capture the intent underlying the user interface.

leads to content that fails to capture sufficient information. For instance, the HTML markup shown in Figure 3.8 does not explicitly capture the underlying intent of the user interaction being authored. An ideal auditory representation of the user interface created by Figure 3.8 might be to produce a spoken prompt of the form

Please specify your *gender*; default is male.

As a consequence of the HTML markup in Figure 3.8 failing to capture explicitly the relationship among the radio buttons, providing the desired nonvisual presentation of this control becomes difficult. Capturing the appearance of a user interface, rather than its underlying intent, can make it significantly harder to retarget an application to different modalities and devices.

Notice further that the markup in Figure 3.8 uses HTML construct ⟨**label**⟩ to associate each control with its label. This association is made by creating a unique id for each control and specifying this id as the value of attribute *for* on the label elements. This construct was added in HTML4 for enabling the design of accessible Web interfaces; however, the level of indirection present in this design has caused it to be rarely if ever used on today's mainstream Web.

Contrast this with the XForms version of the same user interface shown in Figure 3.9; here, the interface is accessible by design since the user interface labels are a mandatory part of the markup making up the control. Notice further that when working with the HTML markup shown in Figure 3.8, the relationship among the radio buttons needs to be inferred from the fact that both controls have an identical value of gender for attribute *name*. The XForms markup makes this fact explicit by encapsulating the available choices as child elements of control ⟨**select1**⟩.

Finally, notice that there is no means of explicitly associating a label for the group of radio buttons in the HTML markup. The XForms version of the same control can encapsulate label Gender as an immediate child of element ⟨**select1**⟩.

```
<select1 xmlns="http://www.w3.org/2002/xforms"
  ref="/person/gender"><label>Gender</label>
  <item><label>Male</label>
  <value>m</value></item>
  <item><label>Female</label>
  <value>f</value></item>
</select1>
```

Figure 3.9. XForms user interface markup for picking from a pair of mutually exclusive values.

In addition, common elements ⟨**help**⟩ and ⟨**hint**⟩, described in Section 3.2.3, can be used to attach tooltips and help to each of the choices; similar functionality would require using browser-specific scripting in the case of traditional HTML forms.

3.4.1 Types of Selection Controls

Presentation and interaction behavior aside, selection controls can be characterized by the *atomic* or *list* nature of the data they collect. XForms defines selection control ⟨**select1**⟩ for creating selection controls that return an *atomic* value; control ⟨**select**⟩ creates selection controls that return a *list* of values.[6] Notice that this design creates separate selection controls based on the underlying functionality, rather than the appearance of these controls in any given interface, for example, pull-down lists or radio buttons.

Consider the selection control used in a questionnaire that allows the respondent to specify one of two gender values, M or F. These values are mutually exclusive, that is, the user can pick *one and only one* of the available values. A typical visual interface might render this control as a group of two radio buttons, and the result of user interaction with such a user interface control is an atomic value.

Contrast this with a U.S. tax form that lets users specify the states in which they worked during a given calendar year. Users can pick one or more values from the 50 states; here the selections are not mutually exclusive. This control might be rendered by a typical visual interface as a pull-down list, and the result of user interaction with this control is a *list* of one or more states.

Controls ⟨**select**⟩ and ⟨**select1**⟩ share a common set of attributes and child elements in addition to the ones described in Section 3.2. These selection-related

---

[6]Note that the working group agonized long and hard over these names, and we went through a sequence of name choices. The final choice was agreed on because it was both succinct and did not require the use of mixed case in the element names.

```
<select xmlns="http://www.w3.org/2002/xforms"
  ref="/pizza/topping" selection="open">
  <label>Toppings</label>
  <item><label>Mushrooms</label>
  <value>mushrooms</value></item>
...</select>
```

Figure 3.10. Open selections permit selecting from a set as well as free-form input.

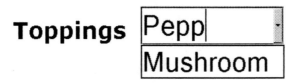

Figure 3.11. Open selections permit selecting from a set as well as free-form input.

attributes and child elements will be described in the rest of this section along with examples that illustrate their use.

3.4.2 Open and Closed Selections

Selections such as picking a state from a list of available states *require* the user to pick from the set of choices; such controls are called *closed* selections. Contrast this with a user interface where the user can pick from a set of predetermined choices, or alternatively specify a conceptual *other* value, that is, a value that does not appear in the set of predefined values. Such controls are called *open* selections. XForms selections controls ⟨**select**⟩ and ⟨**select1**⟩ are *closed* by default; a selection control can be declared *open* by setting attribute *selection* to open. See Figure 3.10 for an example. Visual user agents might render such an open selection by juxtaposing a text entry field next to the selection control (see Figure 3.11).

3.4.3 Default Selection

Selection controls often come with one or more default choices already selected when appropriate. In the HTML example shown in Figure 3.8, this is achieved by setting attribute *checked* to the value checked. Notice that the equivalent XForms example shown in Figure 3.9 does not have any of the choices *checked*. The question therefore arises as to how one specifies default choices when using XForms.

The *missing checked* attribute in the XForms version of the selection controls is a consequence of the separation of the *model* from the *interaction* present in the

```
<model xmlns="http://www.w3.org/2002/xforms" id="p1">
  <instance>
    <person xmlns="">...
      <gender>m</gender>...
  </person></instance>
</model>
```

Figure 3.12. XForms model fragment for gender picker.

XForms design. The values selected via the selection controls ⟨**select**⟩ and ⟨**select1**⟩ are stored in the XForms model and not within the user interface control. Consequently, it is more natural to set default values in the model. Notice that doing so treats default values in the same way as values picked by the user. Figure 3.12 shows the corresponding model for the gender picker shown in Figure 3.9 with a preassigned value of m. When the user interface control shown in Figure 3.9 *binds* to this model, the choice corresponding to m becomes selected.

The design shown earlier has numerous advantages over the traditional HTML design of specifying default values within the user interface markup.

Auto Fill   It is now significantly easier to fill a form automatically with a set of values. Doing this in the case of HTML requires locating *every* user interface control that collects a particular value and then setting the default values of that control by manipulating its markup. Contrast this with the XForms design that permits one to *load* data from an XML document into the form.

Defaults   Storing default values in the model ensures that such defaults are valid for a given application. In contrast, specifying default values within the user interface controls would mean that an incorrectly authored form might potentially contain incorrect defaults. This can lead to a bad end-user experience when a user does not change an erroneous default and later gets an error for something the user was not responsible for.

3.4.4 Selections Using Static Choices

The previous section described how the XForms model is used to provide default values for user interface controls, including the various selection controls. Viewed from the viewpoint of separating the model from the interaction, the selection controls as shown so far do not go all the way with respect to this separation. Notice also that in the examples shown so far, the available choices, including the values that get stored in the model, appear in the user interface markup.

This design pattern was adopted intentionally to smooth the transition from traditional HTML forms to XForms. One consequence of authoring the available choices within the user interface controls is that the choices become *static*, that is, the available choices need to be determined at the time the XML markup is authored. However, this design works well only in cases where the available choices are known at authoring time. The next section describes XForms constructs that allow the author to move the available choices from the user interface markup to the XForms model. This introduces a level of indirection that enables the creation of dynamic selections. Lacking this facility, today's HTML authors resort to browser-specific scripting in order to update dynamically the list of available choices as the user interacts with an application.

3.4.5 Dynamic Selections

Dynamic selections in XForms are enabled by having selection controls refer to a portion of the XForms model that contains the choices rather than enumerating these choices directly within the user interface markup. Element ⟨**itemset**⟩ can be used as a child element of selection controls ⟨**select**⟩ and ⟨**select1**⟩ to specify the location that holds the choices. The location is specified using the standard XForms binding mechanism based on XPath described so far. As the name implies, element ⟨**itemset**⟩ points at the set of available choices.

Referring to such sets comes naturally to XPath, which has been designed to work with sets of nodes. In fact, XPath locators *always* evaluate to node-sets. In the examples shown so far in this book, we have used XForms binding expressions that needed to select a single node; we consequently specified such expressions using attribute *ref*. When attribute *ref* is used, XForms processors use the *first* element of the resulting node-set. Binding expressions that wish to operate on an entire node-set use binding attribute *nodeset* instead of attribute *ref*. To summarize,

Single Node   Use attribute pair (*model*, *ref*) to specify the location when bind-
                     ing to a single node. The result is to operate on the first node in
                     the node-set addressed by the XPath expression specified as the
                     value of attribute *ref* from model *model*.

Multiple Nodes   Use the attribute pair (*model*, *nodeset*) to specify the location
                     when binding to set of nodes. The result is to operate on all of
                     the nodes in the node-set addressed by the XPath expression
                     specified as the value of attribute *nodeset* from model *model*.

To return to the topic of dynamic selections, element ⟨**itemset**⟩ is used to specify the location in the model that holds the available alternatives. Child elements ⟨**value**⟩

```
<head xmlns:xf="http://www.w3.org/2002/xforms">
  <xf:model id="bookshelf">
    <xf:instance xmlns="">
      <shelf><books-picked/></shelf>
    </xf:instance>
  </xf:model>
  <xf:model id="catalog">
    <xf:instance xmlns="">
      <catalog>
        <book isbn="0-2014-8541-9">
          <title>Art of Computer Programming</title>
          <author>Donald E. Knuth</author>
        </book>
        <book isbn="0-7923-9984-6">
          <title>Auditory User Interfaces</title>
          <author>T. V. Raman</author>
        </book>...
      </catalog></xf:instance>
  </xf:model></head>
```

Figure 3.13. Book catalog used to provide available choices.

and ⟨**label**⟩ of element ⟨**itemset**⟩ refer to a prototype member of this set. The XForms processor expands element ⟨**itemset**⟩ at run-time to produce the list of choices by instantiating child elements ⟨**label**⟩ and ⟨**value**⟩ once for each element in the node-set just selected. Child elements ⟨**label**⟩ and ⟨**value**⟩ in turn can refer to portions of an individual element in the set by using XPath locators. Thus, in the case of an electronic book store, the available alternatives may be extracted from an online catalog. Such an online catalog might hold each book as an XML structure, with appropriate attributes and child elements. When creating a dynamic selection that operates over such a catalog, how the constructs described so far would be used are shown in the following figures: Figure 3.13 and Figure 3.14 for the XML markup and Figure 3.15 the corresponding visual interface.

Model　　Create a model that holds an appropriately filtered instance of the book catalog. The contained instance might appear inline or be addressed via a URI.

UI Select　　Create a selection control that stores selected values in the bookshelf instance. For this example, we assume that the ISBN of each selected book is stored in the bookshelf.

```
<select xmlns="http://www.w3.org/2002/xforms"
  model="bookshelf" ref="/shelf/books-picked">
  <label>Select books</label>
  <itemset model="catalog" nodeset="/catalog/book">
    <label ref="title"/><value ref="@isbn"/>
</itemset></select>
```

Figure 3.14. Available choices can be updated dynamically.

Select books | Auditory User Interfaces |
| The Art of Computer Programming |

Figure 3.15. Visual presentation of the bookstore user interface.

Alternatives   Create an ⟨**itemset**⟩ child element of the selection control that locates the set of available alternatives via an appropriate binding expression.

Label   Within element ⟨**itemset**⟩, create element ⟨**label**⟩ that specifies the label to display for a given choice. For this example, we will display the title of the book. The title is retrieved by addressing subelement ⟨**title**⟩ of element ⟨**book**⟩.

Value   Create child element ⟨**value**⟩ of element ⟨**itemset**⟩ to specify the value to be stored as the result of selecting a given book. We have decided to store the ISBN in the bookshelf, and it is found as the value of attribute *isbn* in each book element. We therefore create the appropriate binding attributes for element ⟨**value**⟩ that extracts attribute *isbn* from ⟨**book**⟩.

In the case of this example, an XForms processor can dynamically update the available books during user interaction. This is because the choices are not statically authored within the user interface control; instead, like the XForms user interface controls, the choices too are *bound* to the model. Thus, dynamically updating the available choices in the model results in the user interface being refreshed to display the newly available choices.

3.4.6 Selecting XML Structures

In the examples shown so far, selection controls have been used to pick atomic data types from a set of choices. When viewing XForms as the means to edit and manipulate XML structures interactively from within a Web browser, it is often

```
<head xmlns:xf="http://www.w3.org/2002/xforms">
  <xf:model id="bookshelf1">
    <xf:instance xmlns="">
      <shelf>
        <books-picked/>
        <book>...</book>
      </shelf>
    </xf:instance>
  </xf:model>
  <xf:model id="catalog">
    <xf:instance xmlns="">
      <catalog>
        <book isbn="0-7923-9984-6">
          <title>Auditory User Interfaces</title>
          <author>T. V. Raman</author>
        </book>...
      </catalog>
    </xf:instance>
  </xf:model></head>
```

Figure 3.16. Bookshelf stores complete book structure.

useful to select entire XML subtrees as opposed to just selecting atomic data types such as strings and numbers.

As an example, we stored the isbn of the book being selected in the example shown in Figure 3.14. Consider an example where the entire book structure is to be stored in the bookshelf model. In this case, the storage value is not a string value as was the case when storing the isbn; instead, here we are *copying* the entire book structure to the bookshelf model. XForms enables this via element ⟨**copy**⟩, which can be used in place of element ⟨**value**⟩.

Element ⟨**copy**⟩ encodes the information about what nodes are to be copied via standard XForms binding expression—see Figure 3.16 and Figure 3.17.

The shelf model has been updated to hold one or more book elements and is given an id of bookshelf1. The user interface has been modified to use element ⟨**copy**⟩ instead of element ⟨**value**⟩. The binding expression on element ⟨**copy**⟩

```
ref="."
```

specifies that selecting a given item results in the *current node* being copied to the storage location specified by the containing ⟨**select**⟩ control.

```
<select xmlns="http://www.w3.org/2002/xforms"
  model="bookshelf1" ref="/shelf/books-picked">
  <label>Select books</label>
  <itemset model="catalog" nodeset="/catalog/book">
    <label ref="title"/><copy ref="."/>
</itemset></select>
```

Figure 3.17. Element ⟨**copy**⟩ used to select XML structures.

The *current node* is determined by the current evaluation context; in this case, this context is set by the containing ⟨**itemset**⟩. As before, element ⟨**itemset**⟩ iterates over the books in the catalog. When processed, this example produces the same user interface as when using element ⟨**value**⟩ to store the isbn into the bookshelf; however, the XML instance that is produced by these two user interfaces is different.

The example shown in Figure 3.14 results in a bookshelf structure that contains a set of string values; in contrast, the example in Figure 3.17 produces a bookshelf structure that contains one or more ⟨**book**⟩ children.

Thus, when providing dynamic selections via element ⟨**itemset**⟩, the XForms author has two options:

⟨**value**⟩   Use element ⟨**value**⟩ if the value to be stored is an atomic data type, for example, a string or number.

⟨**copy**⟩   Use element ⟨**copy**⟩ if the value to be stored is an XML structure, for example, the subtree corresponding to a given book.

3.4.7 Grouping Available Choices

Navigating through large lists of choices can become cumbersome when using small-sized displays or nonvisual modalities such as speech. Imposing additional structure on the available choices can help in presenting a more usable interface in such cases. Element ⟨**choices**⟩ provides functionality similar to that provided by HTML ⟨**optgroup**⟩; however it has better support for attaching labels to each group of choices. We demonstrate this with an example in Figure 3.18 along with the corresponding visual presentation in Figure 3.19.

3.4.8 Rendering Selection Controls

Attribute *appearance* can be used to influence the concrete representation used for a selection control. XForms 1.0 recommends the interpretation that follows for the predefined values of attribute *appearance* when used with selection controls.

```
<select xmlns="http://www.w3.org/2002/xforms"
  ref="/pizza/topping" selection="open">
  <label>Toppings</label>
  <choices><label>Vegetarian</label>
    <item><label>Mushrooms</label>
    <value>mushrooms</value></item>
    <item><label>Tomatoes</label>
    <value>tomatoes</value></item>
  </choices>
  <choices><label>Meat</label>
    <item><label>Pepperoni</label>
    <value>pepperoni</value></item>
    <item><label>Salami</label>
    <value>salami</value></item>
  </choices>
</select>
```

Figure 3.18. Grouping available choices.

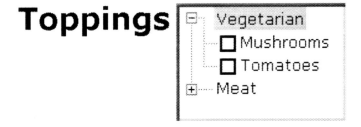

Figure 3.19. Visual presentation of a hierarchical selection control.

minimal   Requests a presentation that takes a minimal amount of display real estate. A visual browser might choose to render selection controls having `appearance=minimal` as a pop-up list.

compact   Requests a presentation that displays some of the available choices with facilities for navigating through the remaining choices. Visual browsers render such controls as scrolling lists.

full   Requests that all of the available choices be displayed if possible. Visual interfaces use radio buttons in the case of ⟨**select1**⟩ and checkboxes for ⟨**select**⟩.

```
<html xmlns="http://www.w3.org/1999/xhtml">
  <head><title>Volume Control</title>
    <model xmlns="http://www.w3.org/2002/xforms"
      id="sound" schema="units.xsd">
      <instance>
        <settings xmlns="http://example.com/volume">
          <volume xsi:type="percentage"/>...
        </settings></instance>
    </model></head>
  <body>
    <group xmlns="http://www.w3.org/2002/xforms">
      <range model="sound" ref="/settings/volume"
        appearance="full" step="5">
        <label>Volume</label>
        <help>...</help><hint>...</hint>
      </range></group>
  </body></html>
```

Figure 3.20. Volume control authored using element ⟨**range**⟩.

3.5 Selecting from a Range of Values

Modern user interfaces provide widgets such as sliders and rotary dials, for example, volume controls. Such user interface controls can be viewed as a special case of selection control where the underlying set of choices has additional structure in that the available values are well ordered. XForms defines a generic *range control* that can be used to pick a value from a set of well-ordered values.

Element ⟨**range**⟩ returns a single value from the set of available values. As with other XForms controls, the set of available values is declared in the XForms model. Thus, it is meaningless to bind control ⟨**range**⟩ to types whose value space is not well ordered. Element ⟨**range**⟩ accepts all the common attributes and child elements described in Section 3.2; in addition, special attributes on element ⟨**range**⟩ are used to tune the presentation and interaction behavior of the resulting control—see Figure 3.20 for an example of a volume control authored using element ⟨**range**⟩.

start   Optional attribute *start* specifies the start value to be made available by the control. By default, the start value is the minimum permissible value as defined in the model.

end   Optional attribute *end* specifies the maximum value to be made available by this control. By default, the end value is the maximum permissible value as defined in the model.

step   Attribute *step* determines the offset used when moving through the set of available values. If specified, it should be appropriate for expressing the difference between two valid values from the underlying set of values. As an example, when picking from an ordered set of numbers, for example, when setting the volume, specifying `step=5` would change the volume in steps of 5.

Notice that the volume control shown in Figure 3.20 uses the minimum and maximum permissible values defined in the model rather than further constraining these via attributes *start* and *end*. Attribute *step* specifies that the volume should be changed in steps of 5. Attribute *appearance* is set to `full` to request that the control be presented with the full range of available values; as a result, a visual interface might present this control as a slider that shows both the minimum and maximum acceptable values—see Figure 3.21.

In contrast, specifying a value of `minimal` for attribute *appearance* might result in a presentation that takes up less display real estate.

Specialized widgets such as rotary controls or spin dials might be requested by specifying a namespace qualified value such as

```
appearance="my:dial".
```

This is similar to requesting a custom date picker as illustrated in Section 3.3. Notice that this design permits the author to create user interfaces that degrade gracefully, that is, the control can be presented as a spin dial on a device that makes such a widget available; however, the interface is still usable on a device that does not contain a spin dial widget. Alternatively, devices that contain a spin dial might choose to use that representation for presenting all range controls; this enables the XForms author to create user interfaces that eventually get delivered in a manner that is optimal for the target device.

Figure 3.21. Visual rendering of a volume control created using ⟨**range**⟩.

3.6 Uploading Data

Uploading data using online forms was first introduced into HTML via the now familiar *file upload* feature. In HTML forms, this feature was added to the input control by adding an extra attribute that caused the input control to be represented using a *file picker* dialog. Today, Web sites commonly use this feature to allow for the creation of attachments when sending e-mail using Web-mediated e-mail services.

XForms defines element ⟨**upload**⟩ to enable equivalent functionality. Control ⟨**upload**⟩ goes further in the functionality provided. At the time HTML forms were designed, Web browsers ran primarily on desktop machines, and this made file upload the primary use case for this functionality. Today, Web access is available on a variety of devices ranging from desktop clients to PDAs and mobile phones. As a result, the ability to upload data has far wider applicability than merely *uploading* a file. For instance, a cell phone that is equipped with a digital camera might use control ⟨**upload**⟩ to create user interfaces that allow the user to transmit pictures taken with the on-board camera.

XForms user interface control ⟨**upload**⟩ has been designed to cover all of these use cases. This flexibility comes from designing the control as an abstract *upload data* control, rather than as a *file browser*. Notice that this allows the control to be used effectively on devices that may not contain a file system but have the ability to capture data, for example, scanners and digital cameras.

Like the rest of the XForms user interface controls, control ⟨**upload**⟩ can use all of the common attributes and child elements defined in Section 3.2. XForms binding attributes are used to specify the location in the data model that is to hold the data to upload. Control ⟨**upload**⟩ collects binary data and should bind to instance data having type `anyURI`, `xsd:base64Binary`, or `xsd:hexBinary`. The following special attributes and child elements can be used to tune further the behavior of control ⟨**upload**⟩:

mediatype   Attribute *mediatype* can be used to constrain the choices made available to the user.

⟨**filename**⟩   Child element ⟨**filename**⟩ specifies the location in the instance where control ⟨**upload**⟩ should store the filename.

⟨**mediatype**⟩   Element ⟨**mediatype**⟩ specifies the location in the instance where control ⟨**upload**⟩ should store the media type of the data being uploaded.

Figure 3.22 shows the use of control ⟨**upload**⟩ to create a user interface that allows the user to transmit an image. A visual interface might render this control as a file browser (see Figure 3.23).

```
<html xmlns="http://www.w3.org/1999/xhtml">
  <head><title>Image Upload</title>
    <model xmlns="http://www.w3.org/2002/xforms"
      id="message">
      <instance>
        <mail xmlns="">
          <picture filename="" content-type="">
            <attach1 xsi:type="xsd:base64Binary"/>
          </picture>
        </mail></instance>
    </model></head>
  <body>
    <group xmlns="http://www.w3.org/2002/xforms">
      <upload ref="/mail/picture/attach1"
        mediatype="image/jpg">
        <label>Select image:</label>
        <filename ref="../@filename"/>
        <mediatype ref="../@content-type"/>
      </upload></group>
  </body></html>
```

Figure 3.22. Element ⟨**upload**⟩ enables uploading data from a variety of devices.

Figure 3.23. Visual interface that enables uploading data.

When used in an environment having a file system, control ⟨**upload**⟩, shown in Figure 3.22, might be rendered as a file dialog that allows the user to pick from a collection of images. Attribute *mediatype* requests that the user be presented with images of type image/jpg.

If the user selects file bubbles.jpg, the binary data contained in that file will be encoded as base64Binary and stored in the instance as specified by the binding attributes on control ⟨**upload**⟩. Elements ⟨**filename**⟩ and ⟨**mediatype**⟩ specify the locations that will hold the filename and content type of the selected image. Thus, the instance data after selecting file bubbles.jpg might look like the XML tree shown in Figure 3.24.

```
<mail>
  <picture filename="bubbles.jpg"
    content-type="image/jpg">
    <attach1>
      /9j/4AAQSkZJRgABAQAAAQABAAD/2wBDAA0JCgsK
      ...
      RobjMxr2gfdCFHiU8dRVmSIktsBqLIVxnfX/2Q==
    </attach1></picture>
</mail>
```

Figure 3.24. Instance data corresponding to image upload.

Notice that this user interaction can be deployed meaningfully to a desktop client that contains a file system, as well as to devices that do not necessarily contain a traditional file system.

3.7 Triggering Actions

The previous sections have described the various XForms user interface controls for collecting data from the user. Data collection apart, user interface controls are used to trigger specific actions. In traditional visual interfaces, such controls manifest themselves as buttons. Buttons in a visual interface are wired to an underlying action to be executed upon *activation* of the button. The visual rendering of the button is styled to indicate whether the underlying action is currently available to the user. A specific user action, for example, pressing the button, causes the underlying action to be triggered.

XForms defines abstract control ⟨**trigger**⟩ that provides a generic framework for connecting user events and actions. Notice that this is in line with the rest of the abstract user interface markup provided by XForms. The design of user interface control ⟨**trigger**⟩ is not specific to a given representation, for example, buttons in a visual interface; nor does it restrict the interaction behavior to specific user events, for example, pressing a button.

Element ⟨**trigger**⟩ holds all the metadata needed to produce appropriate renderings of the control on a given target modality or device. The event that *activates* the trigger, as well as the action to be invoked upon activation of the trigger, is authored using XML Events described in Section 2.3. XForms defines a number of declarative action handlers that can be used within ⟨**trigger**⟩ to create specialized interactions. This section first describes the design of element ⟨**trigger**⟩ and then

```
<body xmlns:ev="http://www.w3.org/2001/xml-events">
  <trigger xmlns="http://www.w3.org/2002/xforms"
    id="getPersonal">
    <label>Collect Personal Information</label>
    <setfocus   control="personalInfo"
  ev:event="DOMActivate"/></trigger>...
  <group id="personalInfo">
  <label>Personal Information</label> ...</group>
</body>
```

Figure 3.25. Using ⟨**trigger**⟩ to wire up events and actions.

describes XForms action handlers that can be used with element ⟨**trigger**⟩. A complete catalog of XForms event types and declarative actions is given in Chapter 7 and Chapter 8.

3.7.1 Anatomy of Element ⟨trigger⟩

Element ⟨**trigger**⟩ uses all of the common attributes and child elements described in Section 3.2. In addition, it uses markup defined by module XML Events, described in Section 2.3, to wire up events and actions. Unlike other XForms control, ⟨**trigger**⟩ does not operate directly on instance data stored in the XForms data model. As a result, binding attributes are not mandatory on control ⟨**trigger**⟩.

Binding attributes may, however, be used to enable or disable the ⟨**trigger**⟩ conditionally. The XForms data model can hold dynamic properties that determine if a piece of instance data is *relevant* at run-time (see Section 5.3). Binding control ⟨**trigger**⟩ to such instance data results in the control becoming *enabled* if and only if the bound instance data is *relevant*. Figure 3.25 shows an example use of ⟨**trigger**⟩.

ev:event   Attribute *ev:event* specifies the event type that triggers the encapsulated action.[7] The specified event type may be any one of the standard DOM2 event types; it may also be any of the special event types defined by the XForms specification, for example, **xforms-reset**.

ev:handler   Attribute *ev:handler* specifies the action to be triggered upon receiving the desired event.

Binding   Optional binding attributes can be used to enable or disable the trigger conditionally.

---

[7]Here, namespace prefix ev is used to denote the XML Events namespace.

⟨**action**⟩   Child element ⟨**action**⟩ is used to hold one or more actions to be triggered. In most cases, the action to invoke is authored as a child element of ⟨**trigger**⟩ (as shown in Figure 3.25) rather than specified indirectly via attribute *ev:handler*. In the general case, any of the design patterns illustrated in Figure 2.2, Figure 2.3, or Figure 2.4 may be used when wiring up events and actions.

Figure 3.25 shows a fragment of a user interface consisting of multiple conceptual *pages*. Each group of controls is authored within a separate ⟨**group**⟩ construct described in detail in the next chapter. Depending on the characteristics of the target device, each *group* might be displayed on a separate screen. The ⟨**trigger**⟩ shown here is used to move to the section in the user interface that collects personal information by invoking XForms action handler ⟨**setfocus**⟩.

It achieves this by listening for event **DOMActivate**—a generic event that might be raised when the user activates the control, for example, by clicking a mouse when using a visual interface. Action ⟨**setfocus**⟩ specifies the control to move focus to the attribute *control* as shown in this example. Notice that action ⟨**setfocus**⟩ appears as a direct child of element ⟨**trigger**⟩ in this example. If there were multiple actions to be executed in response to the **DOMActivate** event, we would have used element ⟨**action**⟩ to group the various actions.

Notice further that attribute *ev:event* has been placed on element ⟨**setfocus**⟩, as opposed to placing it directly on element ⟨**trigger**⟩. This usage is consistent with XML Events and affords the ability to create triggers that invoke different actions based on the received event as illustrated in Figure 3.26. The ⟨**trigger**⟩ shown in

```
<body xmlns:ev="http://www.w3.org/2001/xml-events">
  <trigger xmlns="http://www.w3.org/2002/xforms"
    id="getPersonal">
    <label>Collect Personal Information</label>
    <action ev:event="DOMActivate">
      <setfocus  control="personal"/>
      <refresh ev:event="xforms-focus"/>
    </action></trigger>...
  <group xmlns="http://www.w3.org/2002/xforms"
    id="personal">
  <label>Personal Information</label>...</group>
  </body>
```

Figure 3.26. Element ⟨**trigger**⟩ can invoke different actions based on the received event.

that example responds to two separate events, **DOMActivate** and **xforms-focus**. It invokes action ⟨**setfocus**⟩ upon receiving event **DOMActivate**, as in the earlier example. In addition, it has been set up to *refresh* the XForms user interface when this control receives focus. This is achieved by attaching a ⟨**refresh**⟩ action that responds to event **xforms-focus**.

3.8 Submitting Data

The user interface controls described so far can collect user data and enable the triggering of actions in response to user interaction events and are sufficient to implement a large number of online interaction. When designing XForms, we felt that enabling the user to trigger the specific action of submitting the collected data to the Web server was sufficiently important to deserve its own user interface control. HTML4 had achieved such submit buttons by overloading the input control with a value of submit for attribute *type*. We decided to define element ⟨**submit**⟩ as a separate submit control because submit processing is significantly different from the role played by controls that allow the user to input data.

User interface control ⟨**submit**⟩ can be implemented using a ⟨**trigger**⟩ control that invokes action ⟨**send**⟩. In this sense, element ⟨**submit**⟩ is syntactic sugar that is present to ease authoring.

This section describes control ⟨**submit**⟩ and then details submit processing as defined by XForms. As with the rest of the XForms design, submit processing relies on the XForms model for encapsulating all of the display-independent aspects of submit processing. Submission-related information is encapsulated in XForms model element ⟨**submission**⟩, which will be described in Section 3.8.2.

3.8.1 Anatomy of Control ⟨submit⟩

Control ⟨**submit**⟩ can use all of the common attributes and elements described in Section 3.2. Control ⟨**submit**⟩, like ⟨**trigger**⟩, does not directly affect the underlying instance data, and XForms binding attributes are therefore not required. However, as in the case of element ⟨**trigger**⟩, XForms binding attributes may be used on element ⟨**submit**⟩ to enable or disable the submit control conditionally. In addition to these common markup components, required attribute *submission* on element ⟨**submit**⟩ is used to connect the submit control with the portion of the XForms model that specifies the details of the data to be submitted. Value of attribute *submission* specifies the id of the corresponding ⟨**submission**⟩ element. Details of

- *what* to submit,

- *where* to submit, and

- *how* to submit

are encapsulated in element ⟨**submission**⟩.

Figure 3.27 shows an example of control ⟨**submit**⟩. When the user activates control ⟨**submit**⟩, an **xforms-submit** event is dispatched to element ⟨**submission**⟩, identified by attribute *submission.*

In this example, the event is dispatch to element ⟨**submission**⟩, identified by buy. Notice that this design enables an XForms document to contain multiple submission elements, an advanced feature that makes authoring applications containing multiple forms significantly easier than when using HTML forms.

Notice further that the markup for element ⟨**submit**⟩ is completely independent of the final form representation used to render the control in a given modality. Further, the markup does not force the author to specify the user interaction event that should trigger the submit action. Leaving both the presentation and interaction behavior of submit controls to be determined by the target user interaction environment makes the XForms submit control suitable for deployment across a wide variety of end-user devices and interaction modalities.

3.8.2 Modeling What, How, and Where to Submit

Element ⟨**submission**⟩ within XForms element ⟨**model**⟩ holds the necessary details about what, where, and how to submit. Notice that in the older HTML forms design, this information is encapsulated within element ⟨**form**⟩ that appears as part of the user interface markup. When designing XForms, the working group made a

```
<html xmlns="http://www.w3.org/1999/xhtml">
  <head>
    <model xmlns="http://www.w3.org/2002/xforms">
      <submission id="buy">...</submission>
  </model></head>
  <body>
    <group xmlns="http://www.w3.org/2002/xforms">
      <submit submission="buy">
        <label>Submit Purchase Order</label>...
    </submit></group>
  </body></html>
```

Figure 3.27. Control ⟨**submit**⟩ encapsulates all presentational metadata associated with the submit control.

conscious decision to factor out all nonpresentational aspects of submit processing from the user interaction markup. This information is kept inside the XForms model element since it does not change when binding different interaction modalities to a given XForms model.

Thus, the data to be collected from the user, the location to which this data is transmitted, and the manner in which it is serialized during transmission are all *independent* of the user interaction that was used to collect the data. By encapsulating this information within the XForms model, this design makes it possible to bind either the XForms user interface controls described in this chapter or a different user interface vocabulary to the same underlying XForms model.

In addition, separating submission details from the user interface controls used to invoke the submission has the advantage of enabling a single XForms document to offer multiple submit controls within the same document, with each submit control possibly submitting different subsets of the data collected to a different network location. At the same time, the common use case of submitting all data collected from the user to a given location remains extremely simple.

3.8.3 Anatomy of Element ⟨submission⟩

XForms element ⟨**model**⟩ can contain one or more ⟨**submission**⟩ elements. Here, we describe the attributes and elements that are allowed in element ⟨**submission**⟩. Submission related metadata is carried within attributes on element ⟨**submission**⟩. Additionally, declarative XForms event handlers may appear as child elements within element ⟨**submission**⟩. Such event handlers are invoked before the data is submitted and enable authors to attach custom behaviors to form submission.

As described earlier in Section 1.3.4, element ⟨**submission**⟩ specifies the *what*, *how*, and *where* of the submission process. Attributes of element ⟨**submission**⟩ are described with respect to the following three categories:

What to Submit

Binding   Optional XForms binding attributes, that is, attribute pair (*model*, *ref*) or attribute *bind*, is used to specify the data that is to be submitted. These binding attributes are used to address a specific portion of the instance if only a part of the data collected is to be submitted. By default, the first data instance is submitted in its entirety.

Where to Submit

action   Attribute *action* specifies the protocol and location for data submission. The name was chosen to retain consistency with HTML forms that use an *action* attribute on element ⟨**form**⟩ for the same purpose.

How to Submit

method   Specifies the *method* used to submit the data. The value of this attribute may be one of a predefined set of values designed to cover commonly used methods on the Web today. It is also designed to be extensible to allow future methods. The predefined values include

Method	Description
post	Send XML using HTTP POST
put	Send XML using HTTP PUT
get	HTTP GET
multipart-post	Send XML using HTTP POST
form-data-post	Send data using multipart/form-data
urlencoded-post	Send url-encoded data

Method names not appearing in this list may be used as long as they are qualified with the appropriate namespace. This provides an extensibility mechanism for easily incorporating emerging XML protocols.

separator   Optional attribute *separator* (default is ;) specifies the separator character used when encoding multiple fields in conjunction with method get. This is present to enable authors to choose explicitly between using & and ; to separate encoded fields within a URL when using method get. The older HTML choice of & is not XML-friendly, and as a result Web forms are now beginning to use ; as the separator. This attribute is present to give the author explicit control if necessary.

encoding   Attribute *encoding* specifies the encoding to use when serializing the data.

replace   Attribute *replace* enables XForms-aware user agents and servers to process intelligently partial submission and data refresh. When using today's HTML forms, submitting data to a server results in the response being delivered as a new HTML page. As a consequence, transactions consisting of multiple stages require retransmission of the entire Web page from server to client at each stage of the transaction.

This was necessitated by the lack of separation between model and user interaction inherent in the HTML forms design. Given its model vs. interaction separation, XForms provides more design flexibility with respect to how the response to a form submission is processed on the client. Since we have separated the model from the user interface, the XForms author can specify whether a submission response is to update one of either the XForms model, the user interface, or both via submission attribute *replace*. XForms 1.0 specifies three predefined values for attribute *replace*:

Value	Description
all	Server response replaces current view
instance	Server response replaces *only* instance data
none	Server response treated as an acknowledgment

In addition to the values shown here, namespace qualified values may be used for attribute *replace* when experimenting with new interaction behaviors. The default behavior is to replace both the model and user interface to match the behavior of today's HTML forms. Replacing the instance provides a powerful means of refreshing the user interface without retransmitting all of the original markup. Note that an XForms model can contain more than one instance; this is an advanced concept that is introduced in a later chapter. When using multiple instances in a model, XForms always defaults to the first instance, and this is true in the case of attribute *replace* as well.

The metadata encapsulated by element ⟨**submission**⟩ about *how* to serialize instance data was modeled after XSLT element ⟨**output**⟩. XForms allows the following attributes taken from XSLT element ⟨**output**⟩ on element ⟨**submission**⟩. These are listed separately since they are used less often than the ⟨**submission**⟩ attributes described earlier:

indent   Boolean that specifies if the instance data should be indented when it is serialized as XML

version   Specifies the version of XForms in use

omit-xml-declaration   Specifies if the serialized instance data should include the following XML Processing Instruction:

```
<?xml version="1.0"?>
```

standalone   Specifies if the serialized instance data is a stand-alone XML document

```
<model xmlns="http://www.w3.org/2002/xforms">...
  <submission id="buy" ref="/e-store/cart"
    action="http://example.com/e-store" method="post"
    replace="instance">
    <action>
      <message> Ordering...</message>
  </action></submission>
</model>
```

Figure 3.28. Element ⟨**submission**⟩ that initiates a buy operation.

cdata-section-elements   Names elements in the instance whose contents should be escaped as XML CDATA sections when serializing as XML

3.8.4 Using Element ⟨submission⟩

Next, we create element ⟨**submission**⟩ (see Figure 3.28 for the markup) needed to complete the shopping cart example. Submitting the purchase order by activating control ⟨**submit**⟩ causes the data stored in /e-store/cart to be serialized and transmitted to the location specified by attribute *action*.

The server responds with an XML instance that holds updated information about the user's currently open orders in subtree /e-store/open-orders. When this response is received by the XForms client, the data model is updated, and any user interface controls that bind to updated portions of the data model are refreshed. Thus, activating the *buy* submit control results in the user interface being updated with information about the newly opened order.

Assume that the items bought by the user have been collected into the XML subtree rooted at ⟨**cart**⟩. Notice that in this example not all the nodes in the XForms model instance are to be submitted to the server. This situation often arises when an XForms application uses a portion of the data model to store intermediate computed values. Such partial submission is also useful if the XForms author has chosen to use a single model/instance pair to store all of the data for an application. For instance, the example shown in Figure 3.29 contains four XML subtrees under the ⟨**e-store**⟩ root element:

⟨**specials**⟩   Subtree rooted at ⟨**specials**⟩ holds special offers.
⟨**scratch**⟩   Subtree rooted at element ⟨**scratch**⟩ functions as a scratch pad for holding intermediate values needed by the shopping application.

```
<model xmlns="http://www.w3.org/2002/xforms">
  <instance>
    <e-store xmlns="">
      <specials>...</specials>
      <scratch>...</scratch>
      <cart>
        <item><sku/><quantity/><price/></item>
      ...</cart>
      <open-orders><order/>...</open-orders>
    </e-store></instance>
  </model>
```

Figure 3.29. Skeleton data model used by a shopping application.

⟨**cart**⟩   Subtree rooted at element ⟨**cart**⟩ holds one or more ⟨**item**⟩ elements.

⟨**open-orders**⟩   Subtree that holds information about the user's open orders. This subtree will be used by the XForms server hosting the e-store application to hold information about the user's currently open orders.

In this case, we use an appropriate binding attribute

```
ref="/e-store/cart"
```

on element ⟨**submission**⟩ to locate the data that is submitted to the server.

Attribute *action* specifies where the data is to be submitted. Attribute *method* specifies the method to use for serializing and transmitting the data. Attribute *replace* is used to specify how the server response is to be interpreted. In this application, the author has specified that the server response be treated as an update to the XForms data model.

Finally, the author has set up an event handler inside element ⟨**submission**⟩ (by using action ⟨**message**⟩) that displays a message to the user that the purchase order is being submitted. Event handlers inside element ⟨**submission**⟩ are invoked before the data is transmitted to the specified location. This gives authors the ability to add custom interaction behavior when data is being submitted. Note that today's HTML authors depend on scripting for achieving similar functionality by attaching an event handler to the **onsubmit** event.

3.8.5 Submit Round-up

We conclude this section with a round-up that summarizes submit processing from the time the user activates control ⟨**submit**⟩ to the final step of updating the user interface based on the server response. We describe this process using events and the actions they invoke. The XForms processing model is defined declaratively in the XForms specification to ensure that implementations achieve the same results irrespective of variations in the underlying implementation. Following are the steps that occur in sequence during submit processing in the example covered in this section:

Trigger   User triggers control ⟨**submit**⟩. As described earlier, control ⟨**submit**⟩ is syntactic sugar for a ⟨**trigger**⟩ that generates a **xforms-submit** event.

Target   Event **xforms-submit** is dispatched to the ⟨**submission**⟩ specified by attribute *submission*.

Handler   Upon receiving this event, element ⟨**submission**⟩ first invokes any event handlers that have been declared as child elements. In this example, invocation of action handler ⟨**message**⟩ displays a message indicating that the purchase order is being submitted.

Locate   Next, the binding attribute specified on element ⟨**submission**⟩ is evaluated to locate the portion of the instance data to be submitted. If no binding attributes are present, the entire instance is prepared for transmission.

Serialize   The located portion of the instance data is serialized in accordance with the values specified for attributes *method*, *mediatype*, and *encoding*.

Transmit   The resulting serialization is transmitted to the location specified via attribute *action* using the method specified by attribute *method*.

Response   The server response is processed as specified by attribute *replace*. The value of *instance* for this attribute causes the XForms client to treat the response as an update to the data model.

Refresh   Once the data model has been updated as specified by the server response, the user interface is refreshed. Here, the server response has updated sub tree /e-store/open-orders. User interface controls that *binds* to /e-store/open-orders are refreshed to display the newly available information.

Table 3.3. XForms Controls at a Glance

Control	Description
⟨**input**⟩	Generic input control
⟨**secret**⟩	Password entry
⟨**textarea**⟩	Multiline text entry
⟨**select**⟩	Select from a set
⟨**select1**⟩	Exclusive select from set
⟨**range**⟩	Pick from range of values
⟨**upload**⟩	Upload data
⟨**trigger**⟩	Activate command
⟨**submit**⟩	Trigger submission

3.9 XForms Controls at a Glance

Finally, Table 3.3 summarizes the various XForms controls covered in this chapter.

CHAPTER 4

Creating Complex User Interfaces

Complex user interfaces can be created by aggregating user interface controls described in Chapter 3. We begin this chapter with an overview of the XForms aggregation constructs. Like the user interface controls, aggregation constructs are designed to encourage intent-based authoring of the user interaction. The goal is to capture sufficient information about the underlying man-machine conversation and thereby deliver a satisfactory end-user experience on a variety of modalities and devices.

The need to *refactor* a user interface is the first requirement that arises when one attempts to deliver a given user interaction to a variety of end-user devices. As an example, a user interface authored for a large display often needs to be split into several screens (or a logical *deck of cards*) when rendered on a cell phone. Effective refactoring of user interfaces is best achieved if the information needed for refactoring is captured at authoring time. Aggregation construct ⟨**group**⟩ described in Section 4.1 was specifically introduced into XForms to play this role.

Efficient navigation among the parts of a complex user interface can be a major factor in determining overall usability. This is especially true when a complex user interface may be refactored into a number of logical transactional units. As the man-machine conversation gets more complex, the ability to introduce dynamic constructs that enable the conditional activation of relevant portions of the user interface lead to efficient navigation and task completion. Aggregation construct ⟨**switch**⟩ described in Section 4.2 can be used to author dynamic user interfaces that respond to user interaction events by appropriately revealing specific portions of a user interface.

Electronic forms (in contrast to paper forms) are characterized by their ability to adapt to the user's actions and grow as necessary. Thus, a shopping application might start off by displaying a *shopping cart* with space for a small number of entries. However, as the user proceeds to add items to the shopping cart, the interface adapts itself by creating additional *rows* in the shopping cart interface. This form of dynamism in XForms is enabled by aggregation construct ⟨**repeat**⟩ described in Section 4.3.

Construct ⟨**repeat**⟩ can be nested, and this ability can be used to advantage in creating user interfaces for manipulating complex hierarchical structures. Associated event handlers ⟨**insert**⟩ and ⟨**delete**⟩ can be used in conjunction with repeating constructs created via element ⟨**repeat**⟩ to edit and update complex hierarchical structures interactively.

We conclude this chapter in Section 4.4 with a step-by-step description of a complex user interface that uses the various user interface controls and aggregation constructs.

4.1 Aggregation Using ⟨group⟩

XForms aggregation construct ⟨**group**⟩ can be used to group logically related user interface controls. When introducing the notion of hierarchical data models, we saw how related variables were grouped into higher-level aggregations. Thus, the house number, street name, city name, and ZIP code are typically grouped into an `address` structure. Construct ⟨**group**⟩ enables similar functionality on the user interface side.

When modeling data, grouping related variables into appropriate hierarchical structures leads to data encapsulation. When creating user interfaces, grouping logically related controls results in related parts of a user interface being encapsulated in logical containers. When rendering the final presentation, this logical grouping can be used to advantage in refactoring the user interface in a manner appropriate for the target device. Such grouping can also help in navigating through a complex user interface. We show an example of the use of element ⟨**group**⟩ in grouping together the various user interface controls making up a conceptual `address` control in Figure 4.1. The result of rendering this example using X-Smiles is shown in Figure 4.2.

4.1.1 Labeling Groups

Element ⟨**label**⟩ can be used to attach a meaningful label to a group. As in the case of user interface controls, the contents of the label can be specified directly

```
<html xmlns="http://www.w3.org/1999/xhtml">
  <head><title>Address Form</title>
    <model xmlns="http://www.w3.org/2002/xforms">
      <instance>
        <address xmlns="">
          <name/><street/><city/><state/><zip/>
        </address></instance>
  </model></head>
  <body>
    <group xmlns="http://www.w3.org/2002/xforms"
    ref="/address" accesskey="a">
    <label>Mailing Address</label>
    <input ref="name"><label>Name</label></input>
    <input ref="street"><label>...</label></input>
    <input ref="city"><label>City</label></input>
    <input ref="state"><label>...</label></input>
    <input ref="zip"><label>ZIP</label></input>
</group></body></html>
```

Figure 4.1. Grouping related controls using construct ⟨**group**⟩.

Mailing Address

Name	
Street	
City	
State	
ZIP	

Figure 4.2. X-Smiles rendering of related controls using construct ⟨**group**⟩.

within element ⟨**label**⟩ or indirectly via a URI. Placing meaningful labels on element ⟨**group**⟩ has several advantages:

Accessibility   When the user navigates to a group, an accessibility aid can render the label for the group to give the user a high-level overview of the contents of the group. Thus, label Mailing Address in Figure 4.1 alerts the user about what to expect when moving through the controls in that group.

Refactoring   Consider a complex invoice that contains the address user interface shown in Figure 4.1. When rendered to a large display, the user is

presented sufficient context to interpret meaningfully the relationship of the address being input to the rest of the invoice. Consider
refactoring such a complex user interface for presentation on a small
display. The user interface will need to be split into a number of logical units and presented as a deck of cards. Alternatively, it might
be presented as a tab dialog with each *tab* containing a portion of
the interface. In either case, the group label can be used as the title
for each logical component of the interface to construct a naviga-
ble table of contents that lets the user move efficiently between the
various portions of the application.

4.1.2 Navigating among Groups

Logically grouped controls enable the user to navigate through complex user interfaces. As in the case of user interface controls, attribute *accesskey* on element
⟨**group**⟩ can be used to specify an accelerator key that moves focus to the group.
As an example, Figure 4.1 specifies a value of a for attribute *accesskey*. In this case,
pressing a with the appropriate platform-specific modifier key would move to the
address group. This moves focus to the user interface control within that group
that appears first in navigation order. Attribute *navindex* on element ⟨**group**⟩ can
be used to refine this process further if needed.

4.1.3 Groups and Binding Expressions

Attribute pair (*model*, *ref*) can be used on element ⟨**group**⟩, as in Figure 4.1. The
binding expression on element ⟨**group**⟩ sets up the *context* for resolving relevant
XPath expressions within element ⟨**group**⟩. The binding expression factors out
those parts of the XPath binding expression that are common to all user interface
controls in the group and therefore serves to ease authoring.

In addition, using element ⟨**group**⟩ to set up the XPath context for user
interface controls within a group and using relative binding expressions on the
various controls make the resulting XForms document easier to maintain. For
example, consider the example shown in Figure 4.1 where element ⟨**address**⟩ is
assumed to occur at the root of the instance tree. To change this example to be
more realistic where the mailing address appears lower down within the instance
tree, for example, /invoice/address, we need only edit the binding expression on element ⟨**group**⟩. Contrast this with using absolute XPath expressions on
the user interface controls making up the address user interface.

Using binding expressions on element ⟨**group**⟩ has one final subtle advantage.
One of the main reasons for HTML's early success was the ability of users to cut

and paste portions of the HTML source they saw on the Web to create their own Web pages. The XForms working group considered this a key enabler for rapid adoption of a new markup language. Using binding expressions on element ⟨**group**⟩ as described here enables such cut and paste authoring.

4.2 Dynamic User Interaction with ⟨switch⟩

A key feature of electronic forms is their ability to react to user input and use such dynamic updates to aid in rapid task completion. Thus, whereas paper forms are static, electronic forms typically aid the user in navigating through the various stages of a complex interaction by appropriately revealing or hiding sections of the form. This form of dynamic interaction is also commonly used to create task-oriented wizards that guide users through a given interaction. We described construct ⟨**group**⟩ in Section 4.1 for logically grouping user interface controls. Here, we describe construct ⟨**switch**⟩, which can be used to hide or reveal selectively such logical groups of controls.

4.2.1 Anatomy of Construct ⟨switch⟩

User interface construct ⟨**switch**⟩ holds sets of logically grouped controls and enables any one of these logical groups to be displayed to the user selectively. Element ⟨**switch**⟩ takes all common user interface attributes described in Section 3.2, and these can be used to advantage in styling the user interface.

In addition, XForms binding attributes can be used on element ⟨**switch**⟩ to establish an XPath context and thus aid in authoring relative XPath locators within binding expressions that appear within the body of construct ⟨**switch**⟩. Each logical group of controls is encapsulated within child element ⟨**case**⟩. Boolean attribute *selected* of element ⟨**case**⟩ determines the ⟨**case**⟩ that is currently *active*, that is, the group of controls currently displayed to the user. Setting this attribute to true results in the controls within that ⟨**case**⟩ becoming active. If none of the ⟨**case**⟩ children of a ⟨**switch**⟩ has *selected* set to true, the first ⟨**case**⟩ in document order is made active.

Each ⟨**case**⟩ is given a unique identifier via attribute *id* that is used later in activating a given ⟨**case**⟩. Element ⟨**case**⟩ can hold all of the XForms user interface controls, as well as the various aggregation constructs described in this chapter, including construct ⟨**switch**⟩ itself.

Construct ⟨**switch**⟩ derives its power from the use of XML Events. XForms defines a declarative event handler, ⟨**toggle**⟩, that is specifically designed for use with ⟨**switch**⟩. As an event handler designed for use with XML Events, element

⟨**toggle**⟩ uses the attributes defined by module XML Events in binding to the desired event. Attribute *case* on handler ⟨**toggle**⟩ identifies a particular ⟨**case**⟩ in a ⟨**switch**⟩ to activate. Invoking handler ⟨**toggle**⟩ results in the specified ⟨**case**⟩ becoming selected; as a side effect, the ⟨**case**⟩ that was previously selected becomes inactive. Thus, the effect of invoking handler ⟨**toggle**⟩ with a specific value for attribute *case* is

- The containing ⟨**switch**⟩ is located.
- The currently active ⟨**case**⟩ in that ⟨**switch**⟩ is made inactive by setting its *selected* attribute to `false`.
- The ⟨**case**⟩ identified by attribute *case* of element ⟨**toggle**⟩ is set to `true`.
- The presentation is updated to reflect the newly active ⟨**case**⟩.

4.2.2 A Simple Example of ⟨switch⟩

We illustrate the use of construct ⟨**switch**⟩ with a simple example in Figure 4.3. The ⟨**switch**⟩ construct shown here contains two ⟨**case**⟩ elements. The first of these is initially active and contains an input control that collects the user's first and last names; we show the visual rendering produced by X-Smiles in Figure 4.4.

```
<switch xmlns="http://www.w3.org/2002/xforms"
  xmlns:ev="http://www.w3.org/2001/xml-events"
  ref="/person/name">
  <case id="edit"><label>Editor</label>
    <input ref="first">
    <label>First name</label></input>
    <input ref="last"><label>Last name</label>
      <toggle ev:event="DOMActivate" case="view"/>
  </input></case>
  <case id="view">
    <label>
      <output ref="first"/><output ref="last"/>
    </label>
    <trigger><label>Edit</label>
      <toggle case="edit" ev:event="DOMActivate"/>
    </trigger></case>
</switch>
```

Figure 4.3. ⟨**switch**⟩ can selectively reveal or hide portions of an interface.

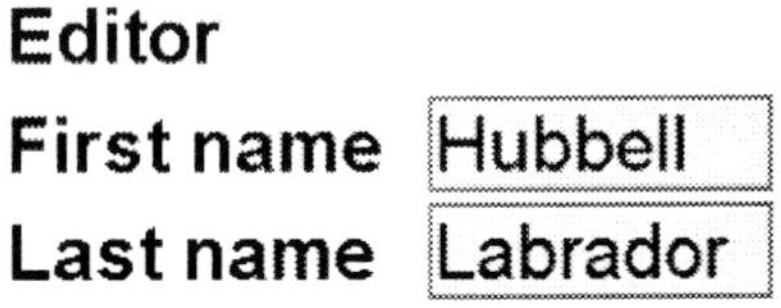

Editor

First name Hubbell

Last name Labrador

Figure 4.4. Initial state of the edit/view interface.

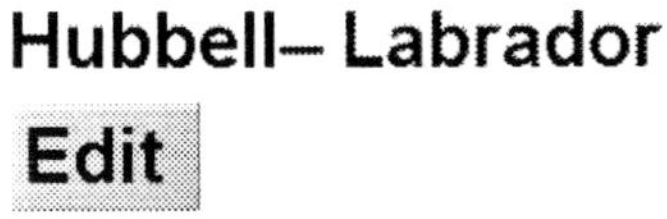

Hubbell– Labrador
Edit

Figure 4.5. ⟨**switch**⟩ can alternate between different portions of an interface.

Notice that we have used XForms binding attributes on element ⟨**switch**⟩ to set up the XPath context for the rest of this example. As a consequence, all the user interface controls appearing within this ⟨**switch**⟩ can use relative XPath expressions when binding to the underlying data model.

The input control that collects the user's last name contains an event binding that attaches handler ⟨**toggle**⟩ to event **DOMActivate**. This handler is invoked when the input control receives a **DOMActivate** event, that is, the user completes entry in the input field. Attribute *case* of this ⟨**toggle**⟩ handler is set to refer to the second ⟨**case**⟩ element in the containing ⟨**switch**⟩; thus, finishing entry into the input control results in the second ⟨**case**⟩ becoming active. The user interface now *switches* to displaying the rendering shown in Figure 4.5.

This second ⟨**case**⟩ element contains a label that displays a greeting using the values just entered. This ⟨**case**⟩ contains a trigger that functions as a conceptual *edit* button by invoking a ⟨**toggle**⟩ handler that activates the first ⟨**case**⟩ element.

Notice that as a consequence, the ⟨**switch**⟩ shown in Figure 4.3 functions as a read-only display of the user's name that when activated turns itself into an input control that allows the user to update the value.

4.2.3 Model and Interaction-Based Switching

Construct ⟨**switch**⟩ is used to enable dynamic navigation through complex interfaces. It's also useful when delivering a user interface to devices with small displays where it is advantageous to *reveal progressively* a user interface. Notice that activation and deactivation of ⟨**case**⟩ elements within construct ⟨**switch**⟩ is driven through the user interface, that is, cases are made active or inactive based on user interaction events.

Contrast this with the rest of the XForms user interface, where all updates to the presentation happen as a result of changes to the underlying model. This interaction-based switching introduced by construct ⟨**switch**⟩ is by design and is not an oversight on the part of the XForms working group. We feel that interaction-based switching is a sufficiently useful feature to be treated as a first-class citizen, given our interest in being able to deliver complex user interfaces to small devices.

XForms supports an alternative form of dynamism that is completely model driven; this is achieved via model property *relevant* detailed in Section 5.3. Model property *relevant* is a boolean value that is computed dynamically at run-time and can affect the availability of portions of the interface that bind to *relevant* portions of the model. Model-based switching is a powerful XForms feature and can often lead to more flexible interfaces than the pure interaction-based switching afforded by construct ⟨**switch**⟩. As an example, notice that ⟨**switch**⟩ can activate *one and only one* of the contained logical groupings encapsulated within the various ⟨**case**⟩ children. In contrast, model-based switching can hide or reveal more than one section of a user interface.

4.2.4 Creating Multipage Tab Dialogs Using ⟨switch⟩

Construct ⟨**switch**⟩ can be used to advantage in authoring *multipage* wizards that allow the user to complete a complex task. When such a task consists of several conceptual *pages*, construct ⟨**switch**⟩ enables the delivery of a rich end-user experience by avoiding client-server round-trips when switching between the various *pages* making up the task.

Notice that the Web metaphor of serving a Web page for each *dialog turn* in a complex task works well for large displays where the user interface can encompass multiple entry fields in a given page. As a consequence, matching each dialog turn with a client-server round-trip can still deliver a satisfactory end-user experience.

But when deploying to small devices, the quantity of information that can be displayed at a given time, and consequently the amount of data that can be collected on any given *page*, is relatively small. In the case of a purely nonvisual interface, this may be as small as a single item of information. Introducing client-server round-trips for each turn in such a man-machine conversation can lead to rapid degradation of the end-user experience.

Construct ⟨**switch**⟩ can be used to alleviate this problem. A complex task consisting of multiple conceptual pages can be organized within construct ⟨**switch**⟩ with each ⟨**case**⟩ containing a portion of the user interface that has been tailored to the small display. Control ⟨**trigger**⟩ within each ⟨**case**⟩ element can be used to create navigation controls that allow the user to move through the various stages

```
<switch xmlns="http://www.w3.org/2002/xforms"
  ref="/insurance/policy-form">
  <case id="general">
    <label>General Information</label>
    <group ref="general">...</group>
  </case>
  <case id="coverage">
    <label>Coverage</label>
    <group ref="coverage">...</group>
  </case>
  <case id="fees">
    <label>Annual Fees</label>
    <group ref="fees">...</group>
  </case>
  <case id="summary">
    <label>Summary</label>...</case>
</switch>
```

Figure 4.6. Using construct ⟨**switch**⟩ to navigate through a complex task.

of the task. Notice that in this case, there is no client-server round-trip as the user transitions between various stages of the task. Using construct ⟨**switch**⟩ in these situations improves the end-user experience. It also eliminates the need to write on the server a device-specific *controller* component that manages the user's navigation through the various *pages* making up the task.

Consider the multipage insurance form shown in Figure 4.6. The form is divided into logically separate pages, with each page contained within an individual ⟨**case**⟩ element.

Notice that all (except the last) ⟨**case**⟩ elements use a ⟨**group**⟩ to establish the XPath evaluation context for relative XPath locators appearing within that group. The final ⟨**case**⟩ shows a summary of the information collected—typically, such a summary displays key values collected by all of the earlier pages in the form. This summary uses the context set up by the containing ⟨**switch**⟩ for evaluating relative XPath locators.

As described earlier, navigation among the cases can be enabled by creating ⟨**trigger**⟩ controls that invoke handler ⟨**toggle**⟩. Handler ⟨**toggle**⟩ achieves its effect by dispatching the appropriate events to the ⟨**switch**⟩ to change the ⟨**case**⟩ that is active.

Notice that this design enables XForms clients to enhance the end-user experience by binding platform-specific keys that navigate through the different ⟨**case**⟩ elements in a ⟨**switch**⟩ construct. For example, consider an XForms browser designed for use on a cell phone with *forward* and *back* navigation keys. Pressing these keys typically raises a platform-specific event; the XForms client for this platform can map these device-specific events to the corresponding XForms events to allow navigation through a multipage user interface created via construct ⟨**switch**⟩.

4.2.5 Creating Wizards Using ⟨switch⟩

User interface wizards aids in rapid task completion. The combination of interaction-based switching provided by construct ⟨**switch**⟩ can be combined with model-based switching via model property *relevant* in creating task-based wizards. Application-specific knowledge can be codified in the XForms model; thus, in an insurance form, the portion of the user interface pertaining to questions about an applicant's children can be selectively revealed based on the user's response to an earlier question.

Binding attributes on the navigation controls used to move among the different ⟨**case**⟩ groupings in a ⟨**switch**⟩ construct can be used to ensure that the user does not leave a portion of the interface without providing critical items of information. As an example, consider a user interface that collects the necessary information before configuring the wireless network on a mobile device. This information might include authorization information such as a user id and password. Assume further that this task has been factored into a set of logically grouped *pages* to create a multipage dialog using construct ⟨**switch**⟩ (see Figure 4.7). The corresponding visual interface produced by X-Smiles is shown in Figure 4.8.

The application author can ensure that the user provides the requisite information before moving off the authentication page by attaching an appropriate binding expression to the ⟨**trigger**⟩ that navigates from this page. In this example, the model contains a second ⟨**instance**⟩ that holds a state variable `pin-check` used for this purpose. This field itself does not collect a value; instead, it is used to enable or disable the navigation control that allows the user to move from the authorization page to the `services` page. Within the model, an XForms binding expression created via ⟨**bind**⟩ is used to bind model property *relevant* to `instance('s')/pin-check`. The value of this property, an XPath expression, is evaluated at runtime to return a boolean value. In this example, we have

```
relevant="length(instance('m')/pin)>0
  and length(instance('m')/id)>0"
```

```
<html xmlns="http://www.w3.org/1999/xhtml"
  xmlns:ev="http://www.w3.org/2001/xml-events">
  <head><title>XForms Wizard</title>
    <model xmlns="http://www.w3.org/2002/xforms"
      xmlns:xsd="http://www.w3.org/2001/XMLSchema"
      schema="mobile.xsd">
      <instance id="m">
        <auth xmlns=""><id/><pin/></auth>
      </instance>
      <instance id="s">
        <data xmlns=""><pin-check/></data>
      </instance>
      <!-- Used by wizard -->
      <bind nodeset="instance('s')/pin-check"
        relevant=
        "string-length(instance('m')/id)&gt;0
        and string-length(instance('m')/pin)&gt;0"/>
  </model></head>
  <body>
    <switch xmlns="http://www.w3.org/2002/xforms"
      ref="/auth">
      <case id="auth"><label>Authorization</label>
        <input ref="id">...</input>
        <secret ref="pin">...</secret>
        <trigger ref="instance('s')/pin-check"
          ev:event="DOMActivate">
          <label>service details</label>
        <toggle case="service"/></trigger></case>
      <case id="service">
      <label>Service</label>...</case>
    </switch>
  </body></html>
```

Figure 4.7. Task wizard authored using ⟨**switch**⟩.

Figure 4.8. Visual representation of task wizard authored using ⟨**switch**⟩.

to specify that `pin-check` gets model property `relevant=true` if and only if the length of the value collected for `instance('s')/pin` is greater than 0. Within the user interface, control ⟨**toggle**⟩ in the ⟨**case**⟩ that collects authorization information binds to `instance('m')/pin-check`. As a consequence, this control becomes available to the user only if the `/auth/id` and `/auth/pin` values have been provided.

The functionality described here enhances end-user experience. The XForms model enables the application author to declare specific portions of the instance to be *required*, that is, the user may not submit the form until these *required* values have been provided. However, in the case of the multipage user interface rendered on a small device, ensuring that each *page* of the multipage task is correctly completed can often lead to more rapid task completion.

Finally, notice that this is the first example in this book to use the advanced XForms feature of having multiple ⟨**instance**⟩ elements in the model. Multiple instances are useful when an application needs to store temporary interaction state information that should not be submitted to the server. In this example, we have used element ⟨**instance**⟩ having `id="m"` to store the data to be transmitted to the server and element ⟨**instance**⟩ with attribute `id="s"` to hold interaction state. Access to multiple instances in the model is achieved via function *instance* described in Section 6.6. Model property *relevant* used in this example is described in Section 5.3.

4.3 Repeating Structures with ⟨repeat⟩

The ability to adapt dynamically to user interaction is one of the most important usability features of electronic forms. We saw examples of such dynamic behavior when reviewing construct ⟨**switch**⟩ in Section 4.2 and when creating dynamic selections via element ⟨**itemset**⟩ in Section 3.4.5. XForms construct ⟨**repeat**⟩, described in this section, completes this picture by enabling the creation of template-based user interfaces that grow or shrink during user interaction.

Such *repeating* constructs are most commonly found when interacting with electronic stores on the Web today where the metaphor of a dynamic shopping cart is implemented using appropriate looping constructs in either client-side or server-side scripts. XForms construct ⟨**repeat**⟩ defines a declarative construct that can be used to iterate over collections of *like* nodes in the XForms model, for example, the items in a shopping cart.

4.3.1 Designing Construct ⟨repeat⟩

The purpose of construct ⟨**repeat**⟩ is to create a user interface that *repeats* over a collection of nodes. To this end, ⟨**repeat**⟩ can be thought of as an *iterator*; contents of ⟨**repeat**⟩ can be thought of as a *template* of the user interface to be created for each node in the collection being iterated. The user interface created by construct ⟨**repeat**⟩ displays a portion of the collection being iterated with user interaction facilities that permit the user to scroll through the collection, and to add or delete nodes to the collection. Notice that all of these operations depend on the notion of a well-defined *current* node in the collection; XForms calls this the ⟨**repeat**⟩ *index*. Thus, construct ⟨**repeat**⟩ encapsulates the following information:

Id A unique `id` used to identify the ⟨**repeat**⟩ construct.

Collection The collection of nodes being iterated. This is a *node-set* identified using an XForms binding expression. The binding expression appearing on construct ⟨**repeat**⟩ also establishes the context for evaluating relative XPath locators within the body of ⟨**repeat**⟩.

Index An *index* that points at the *current* node in the collection. To maintain consistency with XPath, XForms uses a 1-based index to identify the *current* node in the collection, which is made available to authors via XPath extension function *index*.

UI Template The body of construct ⟨**repeat**⟩ contains a user interface template to be instantiated for each member of the collection. User interface controls appearing in this template use relative XPath locators in their binding expressions. These XPath locators use the binding expression of the containing ⟨**repeat**⟩ to establish the evaluation context; the *current* node, that is, . using XPath notation, is determined by the repeat index.

Controls Controls that enable the user to add to, delete, or scroll the nodes in the collection. These *add*, *delete*, and *scroll* controls are created by including the appropriate event handler within XForms control

⟨**trigger**⟩. All of these handlers use the repeat index, which they access by passing the id of the ⟨**repeat**⟩ to *index* function. Add, delete, and scroll controls may appear as part of the template user interface within element ⟨**repeat**⟩; alternatively, they may appear outside the body of construct ⟨**repeat**⟩. The former design might be used to create these controls once per element of the underlying collection; the latter can be used to create a *toolbar* that is presented along with the ⟨**repeat**⟩.

Presentation   Presentation hints that indicate the portion of the collection to display. This is achieved by specifying the index of the first node to display and the suggested number of members from the collection to display. These are only hints; the presentation *must* display the current node at all times.

4.3.2 Anatomy of Construct ⟨repeat⟩

Next, we define the XML markup that allows XForms authors to create *repeating* user interfaces. The information items enumerated in Section 4.3.1 are encoded via appropriately designed attributes and child elements. In addition to these, construct ⟨**repeat**⟩ can use all the common XForms user interface markup described in this chapter.

Attributes of Construct ⟨repeat⟩

startindex   Optional attribute *startindex* specifies the first member of the collection that is presented to the user. It defaults to 1 if not specified, that is, the presentation starts with the first member of the collection.

number   Optional attribute *number* specifies the number of members to display at any given time. This is a presentation hint, and the client can display fewer or more members of the collection as appropriate for the connecting device.

Binding   Attribute pair (*model, nodeset*) locates the collection of nodes to be iterated. Alternatively, this binding can be specified using attribute *bind* to address a predefined *binding site*.

Child Elements of ⟨repeat⟩

The body of construct ⟨**repeat**⟩ is the template user interface to be used when presenting each member of the collection. This can use all of the XForms user

Shopping Cart

Select Product   Quantity Price + Shipping
Item: Shoes Price: 1.50 ▾   1   2.62
Select Product   Quantity Price + Shipping
Item: Boots Price: 3.00 ▾   2   7.48

Shopping Cart Toolbar

Create Item   Remove Item   Scroll Forward   Scroll Back

Figure 4.9. X-Smiles rendering of the XForms shopping cart.

interface vocabulary[1] in addition to markup defined by the host language. Thus, when using XForms within XHTML, body of construct ⟨**repeat**⟩ might use XHTML markup in addition to markup defined by XForms. Conceptually, the contents of construct ⟨**repeat**⟩ can be thought of as being enclosed in an anonymous ⟨**group**⟩ construct. This is useful in answering common styling questions that arise with respect to the presentation of ⟨**repeat**⟩ user interfaces.

4.3.3 Shopping Cart Using Construct ⟨repeat⟩

Using the markup described so far, we define a shopping cart example that allows the user to add and remove products from a conceptual shopping cart interactively. The visual interface for the complete shopping cart example is shown in Figure 4.9.

The shopping cart display grows or shrinks appropriately and displays a portion of the cart that includes the *current item* at any given time. This example consists of two parts, the model and the user interface, each of which is described following. This shopping cart will be extended with *add*, *delete*, and *scroll* controls in Section 4.3.4.

Shopping Cart Model

For this example, we first define an XForms model that declares the structure of our shopping cart in Figure 4.10.

This model uses the schema defined in Figure 4.11 to define the type and structure of the instance data used by the shopping cart. The shopping cart holds one or more ⟨**line-item**⟩ elements, with each ⟨**line-item**⟩ containing details about a given item being purchased.

---

[1] An exception to this is construct ⟨**switch**⟩.

```
<model xmlns="http://www.w3.org/2002/xforms"
 xmlns:xsd="http://www.w3.org/2001/XMLSchema"
 id="cart" schema="cs.xsd">
 <instance id="c1">
   <cart xmlns="">
     <line-item><item><product>...</product></item>
       <quantity>1</quantity>
       <!-- cost includes: price, tax and shipping
       and will be computed -->
   <cost/></line-item></cart>
 </instance>
 <instance id="cat">
   <catalog xmlns="">
     <product sku="a1">
     <description/><price/></product>
 </catalog></instance>
 <bind nodeset="/cart/line-item/cost"
   calculate="../item/product/price *../quantity
   +../item/product/price *../quantity * 0.08
 +../item/product/shipping"/>
</model>
```

Figure 4.10. Shopping cart model defines the structure of element ⟨**cart**⟩.

Notice that this model includes two instances, the first to hold the items on the shopping cart, and the second to hold a product catalog; contrast this with the similar example on dynamic selections in Section 3.4.5 where we used separate models for the bookshelf and catalog. When using multiple instances, XForms binding expressions use XPath extension function *instance* to identify the instance being addressed; by default, XForms binding expressions address the *first* instance in the model.

Observe the following facts with respect to the model shown in Figure 4.10:

Structure   Element ⟨**product**⟩ in the catalog instance has the same type and structure as ⟨**product**⟩ in the shopping cart. This correspondence will be used to advantage during user interaction, where selection controls will be used to *copy* the selected product from the catalog into the shopping cart.

```
<x:schema id="cart-schema"
  xmlns:x="http://www.w3.org/2001/XMLSchema">
  <x:element name="cart">
    <x:complexType><x:sequence>
        <x:element ref="line-item"
        maxOccurs="unbounded"/>
    </x:sequence></x:complexType>
  </x:element>
  <x:element name="line-item">
    <x:complexType><x:sequence>
        <x:element ref="item"/>
        <x:element name="quantity" type="x:integer"/>
        <x:element name="cost" type="x:decimal"/>
    </x:sequence></x:complexType>
  </x:element>
  <x:element name="item">
    <x:complexType><x:sequence>
        <x:element ref="product"/>
    </x:sequence></x:complexType>
  </x:element>
  <x:element name="product">
    <x:complexType><x:sequence>
        <x:element name="description"
        type="x:string"/>
        <x:element name="price" type="x:decimal"/>
        <x:element name="shipping" type="x:decimal"/>
      </x:sequence>
      <x:attribute name="sku" type="x:string"/>
    </x:complexType>
  </x:element>
</x:schema>
```

Figure 4.11. Schema for the shopping cart.

Constraints   Later chapters will add additional dynamic constraints to the shopping cart via XForms element ⟨**bind**⟩.

Calculate   Some fields appearing in the shopping cart are computed as a function of other values. Thus, the total cost of an item might be computed from its price, tax, and cost of shipping. Such calculations are defined

```
<group xmlns="http://www.w3.org/2002/xforms">
  <label>Shopping Cart</label>
  <repeat id="cartUI" model="cart"
    nodeset="/cart/line-item"
    startindex="1" number="3">
    <select1 ref="item" appearance="minimal">
      <label>Select Product</label>
      <!-- Namespace qualify bindings.-->
      <itemset nodeset="instance('cat')/product">
        <label>
           Item: <output ref="description"/>
           Price: <output ref="price"/>
        </label>
        <copy ref="."/>
      </itemset></select1>
    <input ref="quantity">
    <label>Quantity</label></input>
    Price +  Shipping: <output ref="cost"/>
  </repeat></group>
```

Figure 4.12. Shopping cart user interface using construct ⟨**repeat**⟩.

via model property *calculate* using XForms element ⟨**bind**⟩ described in a later chapter.

Catalog   In this example, we have shown the catalog as an inline instance. In a real-world shopping application, element ⟨**instance**⟩ would instead refer to the catalog via a URI. This form of indirection leads to easier maintenance of the XForms application.

Shopping Cart User Interface

The markup shown in Figure 4.12 *binds* an XForms user interface to the shopping cart model. We use construct *repeat* to iterate the ⟨**line-item**⟩ elements in the shopping cart. Attribute *startindex* is set to 1 to cause the user interface to display a portion of the cart starting with the first ⟨**line-item**⟩ element; attribute *number* is set to 3 to serve as a presentation hint. The markup appearing within body of element ⟨**repeat**⟩ contains XForms user interface controls for populating an individual ⟨**line-item**⟩ in the cart.

Control ⟨**select1**⟩ is used within the body of ⟨**repeat**⟩ to enable the user to select a product from the catalog. We have used *appearance* to request a minimal presentation, that is, one that takes up minimal display real estate. A visual user agent might choose to render this control as a pull-down list. This is appropriate, since the user will be presented with this control once for each ⟨**line-item**⟩ appearing in the shopping cart.

Binding attributes on control ⟨**select1**⟩ specify that the value selected will be placed in the shopping cart at location

```
/cart/line-item/item
```

The available products are rendered via element ⟨**itemset**⟩ whose binding expression refers to the catalog instance to determine the available products at runtime. Note that this binding expression uses function *instance* as in

```
nodeset="instance('cat')/product"
```

to address the set of products listed in the catalog. Child elements ⟨**label**⟩ and ⟨**copy**⟩ also use this binding expression to set up the XPath context for evaluating relative XPath locators.

Element ⟨**itemset**⟩ creates the list of alternatives as described in Section 3.4.5. Notice that in this example, we have used element ⟨**output**⟩ within ⟨**label**⟩ to build up a label for each alternative that extracts the description and price fields from the product to be selected. Finally, element ⟨**copy**⟩ uses binding expression

```
ref="."
```

to declare that picking one of the alternatives should result in the *current node* operated on by the containing ⟨**itemset**⟩ being copied to the location specified by the ⟨**select1**⟩. The ⟨**select1**⟩ has been set up to populate the ⟨**item**⟩ child of the *current* ⟨**line-item**⟩. The result of this copy operation is therefore the addition of the selected ⟨**product**⟩ element as a child of element ⟨**item**⟩ in the current ⟨**line-item**⟩.

By definition, the ⟨**product**⟩ contained in line-item/item in the shopping cart has the same type and structure as the ⟨**product**⟩ appearing in the catalog; thus, the *copy* operation populates the shopping cart with structurally valid content.

The remainder of the template user interface in ⟨**repeat**⟩ is fairly simple; user interface control ⟨**input**⟩ allows the user to specify the quantity to be ordered. Element ⟨**output**⟩ is used to display the cost of this line-item. This is a computed value and is automatically recalculated when the user selects a product and specifies the quantity being ordered.

The markup shown in Figure 4.12 does not contain presentational or stylistic information. In a real-world shopping cart, this markup would be *hosted* in an appropriate host language, for example, XHTML; this would provide the necessary constructs for aligning the controls appearing within the body of 〈**repeat**〉 or styling them via CSS.

We will extend this example in a later chapter by extending the model to define cardinality constraints on the number of items that can be placed in the shopping cart. These constraints can then be used in enabling or disabling the *add* and *delete* controls shown in Figure 4.13. The shopping cart is contained within construct

```
<group xmlns="http://www.w3.org/2002/xforms"
  xmlns:ev="http://www.w3.org/2001/xml-events">
  <label>Shopping Cart</label>
  <repeat id="cartUI">...</repeat>
  <group model="cart" ref="/cart">
    <label>Shopping Cart Toolbar</label>
    <trigger id="addItem">
      <label>Create Item</label>
      <insert nodeset="line-item"
        at="index('cartUI')" position="after"
  ev:event="DOMActivate"/></trigger>
    <trigger id="del">
      <label>Remove Item</label>
      <delete nodeset="line-item"
        at="index('cartUI')"
  ev:event="DOMActivate"/></trigger>
    <trigger id="forward">
      <label>Scroll Forward</label>
      <setindex repeat="cartUI"
  index="index('cartUI')+1"/></trigger>
    <trigger id="back">
      <label>Scroll Back</label>
      <setindex repeat="cartUI"
  index="index('cartUI')-1"/></trigger>
  </group></group>
```

Figure 4.13. Adding *add*, *delete*, and *scroll* controls to shopping cart.

⟨**group**⟩ that has an appropriate label. This ⟨**group**⟩ will be used next in aggregating the ⟨**repeat**⟩ with the add, delete, and scroll controls.

4.3.4 Adding Controls to the Shopping Cart

Next, we add *add*, *delete*, and *scroll* controls to the shopping cart. These controls will use XForms declarative event handlers ⟨**insert**⟩, ⟨**delete**⟩, and ⟨**setindex**⟩, respectively. We first describe these event handlers before using them within control ⟨**trigger**⟩ to create the desired controls.

Event Handlers for Use with ⟨repeat⟩
Event handlers ⟨**insert**⟩ and ⟨**delete**⟩ enable the addition and deletion of nodes to a collection of nodes. In this sense, they are not specific to construct ⟨**repeat**⟩; however, in XForms 1.0 they are mostly used in conjunction with user interfaces created via ⟨**repeat**⟩. Handler ⟨**setindex**⟩ is specific to ⟨**repeat**⟩ since it manipulates the *index* that determines the *current node* for a construct ⟨**repeat**⟩. Invoking any of these handlers causes the user interface created via construct ⟨**repeat**⟩ to be updated appropriately to reflect the new state of the underlying collection.

⟨**insert**⟩ **and** ⟨**delete**⟩   Handlers ⟨**insert**⟩ and ⟨**delete**⟩ are symmetric with respect to their underlying design as well as the XML markup they expose. These handlers need to specify the following items of information:

Collection   Identify the collection of nodes that will be affected by the insert or delete operation. This is encoded used XForms binding attributes, either via attribute pair (*model*, *nodeset*) or via a predefined binding site.

Location   The location in the collection that is to be affected by the insert or delete operation. This is specified via an XPath expression in attribute *at*. This expression is evaluated to give a 1-based offset into the collection. This XPath expression can use extension function *index* to compute an offset that is relative to the *current* node in the collection.

Position   When inserting nodes into a collection, we need to know whether the new node is to be inserted *before* or *after* the specified location. Handler ⟨**insert**⟩ uses attribute required *position* to encapsulate this item of information. Attribute *position* can be set to one of either `before` or `after`.

Eventing   Attributes defined by module XML Events used to wire up these handlers to the appropriate user interface events.

⟨**setindex**⟩   Handler ⟨**setindex**⟩ can be viewed as a specialized assignment statement for modifying the value of the *index* for a given ⟨**repeat**⟩ construct. It takes the following items of information:

repeat   Required attribute *repeat* holds the id of the ⟨**repeat**⟩ construct to be affected.

index   Required attribute *index* holds an XPath expression that is evaluated to produce the new value for the repeat index. This expression can use extension function *index* to compute the new index value relative to the *current* node in the collection.

Add, Delete, and Scroll Controls

Here, we use actions ⟨**insert**⟩, ⟨**delete**⟩, and ⟨**setindex**⟩ within control ⟨**trigger**⟩ to create *add*, *delete*, and *scroll* controls for the shopping cart. For this example, we will place these controls outside the body of construct ⟨**repeat**⟩ to create a conceptual *toolbar* for the shopping cart. This toolbar will be placed inside a ⟨**group**⟩ that carries the relevant metadata for these controls. The toolbar and the user interface created via ⟨**repeat**⟩ are in turn placed inside a ⟨**group**⟩ to capture the fact that the toolbar and shopping cart are logically related.

Observe the following in the example shown in Figure 4.13:

Grouping   The controls are grouped using construct ⟨**group**⟩. XForms binding is used to specify the XPath context to be used in resolving relative XPath locators appearing within this ⟨**group**⟩.

Events   The ⟨**trigger**⟩ controls respond to event **DOMActivate**.

Location   The ⟨**insert**⟩ and ⟨**delete**⟩ handlers within the *add* and *delete* controls are set up to operate on the *current* line-item. This is achieved by calling extension function *index* with the id of the ⟨**repeat**⟩ construct in the value of attribute *at*.

```
at="index('cartUI')"
```

As a result, the *add* control creates a new line-item at the current position in the cart; the *delete* control removes the current line-item from the cart.

Position   The ⟨**insert**⟩ handler in the *add* control specifies that the new line-item should be inserted *after* the current line-item.

Scroll   Handler ⟨**setindex**⟩ is invoked by both the *scroll forward* and *scroll back* controls. Each of the contained ⟨**setindex**⟩ handlers has attribute *repeat* set to `cartUI` to identify the ⟨**repeat**⟩ construct that created the shopping cart user interface. Both scroll controls are set up to move through the shopping cart one line-item at a time by specifying a new value for *index* that is offset by 1 from the current index value.

```
index="index(cartUI)+1"
```

```
index="index(cartUI)-1"
```

4.3.5 User Interaction with Construct ⟨repeat⟩

We now review the various stages of user interaction with the shopping cart as created so far. The shopping cart starts off with one empty `line-item` when the user first accesses the application. This is because of the initial instance declared in the model shown in Figure 4.10. The `line-item` is empty; that is, no product is selected. The presentational hints on construct ⟨**repeat**⟩ in Figure 4.12 request that three line-items be displayed starting with the first line-item. Since there is only one line-item to display, the presentation starts off displaying only one line-item. The *index* of construct ⟨**repeat**⟩ is set to 1. The toolbar consisting of the *add*, *delete*, and *scroll* controls is rendered along with the shopping cart.

In rendering the template user interface specified within the body of construct ⟨**repeat**⟩ for the line-item in the cart, the XForms client creates a ⟨**select1**⟩ control with no product selected and fields that bind to the `quantity` and `cost` fields. Field `quantity` has an initial value of 1 as specified in the model. Next, the user activates control ⟨**select1**⟩ to pick a specific product using the pull-down list. Selecting a product causes the corresponding ⟨**product**⟩ node from the catalog to be *copied* to the shopping cart.

The current ⟨**line-item**⟩ is no longer empty. The ⟨**select1**⟩ control now displays the description of the selected product. When the shopping cart model is updated with this selected product, that update in turn triggers the computation of field `cost`. The shopping cart model has defined the value of `cost` as follows:

```
calculate="../item/product/price *../quantity
```

```
+../item/product/price * ../quantity * 0.08
```

```
+../item/product/shipping"/>
```

This expression is evaluated to produce the value to be stored in cost. The user interface is updated to reflect the updated value of field cost. Next, the user changes the value of quantity from 1 to 5. This again causes field cost to be recomputed and the user interface to be refreshed appropriately.

Next, the user adds a new line-item to the shopping cart by activating the *add* control. This invokes handler ⟨**insert**⟩ which clones the initial ⟨**line-item**⟩ node as declared in the ⟨**instance**⟩ element and inserts this copy into the shopping cart. Notice that each time handler ⟨**insert**⟩ is invoked, it will use the ⟨**line-item**⟩ from the initial instance when creating the new ⟨**line-item**⟩ to be inserted. As a result, each newly created ⟨**line-item**⟩ starts off as described in the initial step.

The user proceeds to add new ⟨**line-item**⟩ entries to the shopping cart. As the number of ⟨**line-item**⟩ entries grows beyond 3, the presentational hint provided via attribute *number* takes effect, and the user interface *scrolls* to display a portion of the cart that includes the *current* ⟨**line-item**⟩. Activating the *scroll forward* or *scroll back* controls results in the *index* being assigned a new value; this in turn results in the user interface being updated to display the current ⟨**line-item**⟩.

4.3.6 Using Construct ⟨repeat⟩ within XHTML Tables

When presenting the shopping cart user interface within an XHTML page, each line-item might be presented as a *row* of a table. The obvious solution would be to place element ⟨**repeat**⟩ within an XHTML ⟨**table**⟩ element and have the ⟨**repeat**⟩ produce the rows of the table; see Figure 4.14.

However, doing so would produce an invalid XHTML document; this is because as defined, the content model of XHTML element ⟨**table**⟩ cannot be extended. To cover this common use case while preserving the ability to create valid XHTML documents, XForms defines an alternative means of creating ⟨**repeat**⟩ structures via a set of attributes. We refer to this set of attributes as *repeat attributes*.

The *repeat attributes* encode the same set of information as encapsulated by element ⟨**repeat**⟩, and repeating structures created via *repeat attributes* have the same functionality as repeating structures created via element ⟨**repeat**⟩. Thus, the difference is one of concrete syntax, and there is no change to the underlying processing model.

To understand this alternative syntax for creating repeating structures, think of ⟨**repeat**⟩ as encapsulating its contents in an *anonymous* group—anonymous because in the case of element ⟨**repeat**⟩, this ⟨**group**⟩ element does not appear in the markup as seen in Figure 4.12.

Viewed this way, element ⟨**repeat**⟩ is present in the markup to carry the various information items needed to create the repeating structure; it achieves this by

```
<table xmlns="http://www.w3.org/1999/xhtml"
  xmlns:xf="http://www.w3.org/2002/xforms">
<!-- XHTML does not permit this -->
<xf:repeat id="cartUI" model="cart"
  nodeset="/cart/line-item"
  startindex="1" number="3">
<tr>
  <td>
    <xf:select1 ref="item" appearance="minimal">
      <xf:label>Select Product</xf:label>
      <xf:itemset
        nodeset="instance('cat')/product">
        <xf:label>
          Item: <xf:output ref="description"/>
          Price: <xf:output ref="price"/>
        </xf:label>
        <xf:copy ref="."/>
      </xf:itemset></xf:select1>
  </td>
  <td>
    <xf:input ref="quantity">
    <xf:label>Quantity</xf:label></xf:input>
  </td>
  <td>
    Price + Shipping: <xf:output ref="cost"/>
  </td></tr>
</xf:repeat></table>
```

Figure 4.14. Placing element ⟨**repeat**⟩ within element ⟨**table**⟩ produces invalid XHTML.

encoding the needed information via attributes appearing on element ⟨**repeat**⟩. Next, we make the *anonymous* group explicit as shown in Figure 4.15. The repeating structures thus created are identical by our definition.

Finally, we can move the attributes appearing on element ⟨**repeat**⟩ to element ⟨**group**⟩ before dropping the containing ⟨**repeat**⟩ element as shown in Figure 4.16.

There is one final twist; we prefix each attribute name in the *repeat attributes* with *repeat-* for clarity. See Table 4.1 for the correspondence between attributes of element ⟨**repeat**⟩ and the *repeat attributes*.

Table 4.1. Correspondence between *Repeat Attributes* and Attributes of Element ⟨**repeat**⟩

Attribute	Repeat Attribute
id	repeat-id
model	repeat-model
nodeset	repeat-nodeset
bind	repeat-bind
startindex	repeat-startindex
number	repeat-number

```
<repeat xmlns="http://www.w3.org/2002/xforms"
  id="cartUI" model="cart" nodeset="/cart/line-item"
  startindex="1" number="3">
  <!--Anonymous group made explicit -->
  <group>
    <select1 ref="item" appearance="minimal">
      <label>Select Product</label>
      <itemset nodeset="instance('cat')/product">
        <label>
          Description: <output ref="description"/>
          Price: <output ref="price"/>
        </label>
        <copy ref="."/>
    </itemset></select1>
    <input ref="quantity"><label>...</label></input>
    Price +  Shipping: <output ref="cost"/>
</group></repeat>
```

Figure 4.15. Element ⟨**repeat**⟩ contains an anonymous ⟨**group**⟩ element.

```
<group xmlns="http://www.w3.org/2002/xforms"
  repeat-id="cartUI" repeat-model="cart"
  repeat-nodeset="/cart/line-item"
  repeat-startindex="1" repeat-number="3">
  <!-- cart UI as before -->
</group>
```

Figure 4.16. Moving repeat attributes to the containing anonymous group.

The XForms working group defined repeating structures via an element (rather than via attributes) to ensure future extensibility. This is why the element version of repeating structures is still the preferred solution over the alternative of placing *repeat attributes* on element ⟨**group**⟩. However, XForms is also designed to be hosted in a variety of markup languages such as XHTML and SVG. As illustrated in the case of XHTML tables, these container languages may often define content models that are not extensible, thereby making it impossible to use element ⟨**repeat**⟩ at the appropriate point in the markup.

XHTML modularization enables host languages to *import* attributes and apply such foreign attributes to the various elements defined in the language. Thus, the *repeat attributes* from the XForms namespace can be imported into XHTML and applied to element ⟨**tr**⟩ when creating repeating rows inside a table; see Figure 4.17.

```
<table xmlns="http://www.w3.org/1999/xhtml"
  xmlns:xf="http://www.w3.org/2002/xforms">
  <!--Repeat via  attributes on element tr-->
  <tr repeat-id="cartUI" repeat-model="cart"
    repeat-nodeset="/cart/line-item"
    repeat-startindex="1" repeat-number="3">
    <td>
      <xf:select1 ref="item" appearance="minimal">
        <xf:label>Select Product</xf:label>
        <xf:itemset
          nodeset="instance('cat')/product">
          <xf:label>
            Item: <xf:output ref="description"/>
            Price: <xf:output ref="price"/>
          </xf:label>
          <xf:copy ref="."/>
      </xf:itemset></xf:select1></td>
    <td>
      <xf:input ref="quantity">
    <xf:label>Quantity</xf:label></xf:input></td>
    <td>
      Price + Shipping: <xf:output ref="cost"/>
</td></tr></table>
```

Figure 4.17. XHTML tables that grow and shrink dynamically.

To summarize, repeating structures can now be encoded by placing *repeat attributes* as defined earlier on any markup element and consequently on element ⟨**tr**⟩ appearing inside XHTML tables. This allows the creation of XHTML tables that grow or shrink dynamically while preserving the structural validity of XHTML documents.

4.3.7 Summary of Construct ⟨repeat⟩

We conclude this section with a summary of construct ⟨**repeat**⟩. Element ⟨**repeat**⟩ is similar in functionality to *iterator* constructs found in modern object-oriented languages like Java. Construct ⟨**repeat**⟩ enables the creation of browser-based user interfaces for editing and manipulating XML structures.

The children of element ⟨**repeat**⟩ define a user interface template that is instantiated for the members of the collection over which the ⟨**repeat**⟩ iterates. The *repeat index* determines the *current* member of this collection and is key to the functioning of the repeating construct. Access to this *repeat index* is carefully controlled, and XForms action ⟨**setindex**⟩ is the only means of changing the value of the *repeat index*.

Special XForms actions ⟨**insert**⟩, ⟨**delete**⟩, and ⟨**setindex**⟩ can be used to manipulate the underlying collection. XForms user interface controls can be used to view and update individual members of the collection. All such changes to the underlying collection are reflected in the user interface, and this creates dynamic user interfaces.

This design enables the nesting of repeating structures to create complex user interfaces. We detail one such use in Section 4.4 where we use nested, repeating structures to maintain a hierarchical task list. The preferred means of encoding repeating structures is via element ⟨**repeat**⟩. In addition, XForms 1.0 defines a set of *repeat attributes* that provide the same functionality as element ⟨**repeat**⟩ for use in container languages where the content model does not permit new elements.

4.4 Complete Example of an XForms User Interface

We conclude this chapter with a complete XForms example that uses nested repeating structures to create a dynamic task list. The resulting visual interface is shown in Figure 4.18.

The task list tracks a set of open tasks. Tasks are organized into sections such as `work` or `personal`; a user can add or remove sections as desired. A section consists of one or more tasks, and a *task* in turn holds information about a particular

Figure 4.18. Task list interface rendered by X-Smiles.

task, such as the date the task is due, a description of the task, and its current status. The task list interface we create allows the user to edit, maintain, and view the task list within a Web browser or other conforming XForms user agents.

In creating this example, we cover many of the concepts introduced so far in this book including:

- Declaring the data model by defining the structure of the task list via an XML Schema: Section 4.4.1

- Declaring the initial instance: Section 4.4.2

- Combining the schema and instance declarations into the XForms model and including this data model within an element (**head**) in an XHTML page: Section 4.4.3

- Creating the user interface via (**repeat**) and embedding the repeating structure within an XHTML table: Section 4.4.4

- Binding XForms user interface controls to the underlying data model: Section 4.4.5

- Creating the needed navigation controls: Section 4.4.6
- Encapsulating these into an XHTML document: Section 4.4.7

The example will be introduced in stages to cover each of these items.

4.4.1 Defining the Structure of the Task List

The structure of the task list is defined by an XML Schema as shown in Figure 4.19. A task list has element ⟨**todo**⟩ as its root element which consists of one or more ⟨**section**⟩ elements. The schema declares that element ⟨**todo**⟩ *must* have at least one ⟨**section**⟩ child by specifying a value of 1 for facet *minOccurs*.

Element ⟨**section**⟩ holds the name of the section in attribute *name*. A ⟨**section**⟩ can hold one or more ⟨**task**⟩ elements. A ⟨**task**⟩ element consists of four *required* child elements as follow:

⟨**date**⟩   Holds the due date for this task. The value is of type `xsd:date`.

⟨**description**⟩   Holds a human-readable description of the task. The value is of type `xsd:string`.

⟨**status**⟩   Holds a human-readable status of the task. The value is of type `xsd:string`.

⟨**done**⟩   An `xsd:boolean` that holds a `true` or `false` value indicating if the task has been completed. The schema declares a default value of `false` for this field.

We declare attribute *id* with value `todo-schema` for the schema definition, and this identifier will be used when connecting the instance declaration with the schema definition in the XForms model. The schema for the task list declares the target namespace for this schema in the statement

```
targetNamespace="http://example.com/todo"
```

to specify that elements defined by this schema are in the namespace identified by `http://example.com/todo`.

The local namespace prefix `t` is used within the schema in referring to types defined in this schema, for example, `t:task`.

Note that defining the instance data in an application-specific namespace is a powerful but fairly advanced feature. For the various elements being defined by this schema to be placed in the application-specific namespace, we add the attribute declaration

```
elementFormDefault="qualified"
```

```
<x:schema targetNamespace="http://example.com/todo"
  xmlns:t="http://example.com/todo"
  xmlns:x="http://www.w3.org/2001/XMLSchema"
  elementFormDefault="qualified" id="todo-schema">
  <x:element name="task">
    <x:complexType>
      <x:sequence>
        <x:element name="date" type="x:date"/>
        <x:element name="description"
        type="x:string"/>
        <x:element name="status" type="x:string"/>
        <x:element name="done" type="x:boolean"/>
      </x:sequence>
    </x:complexType>
  </x:element>
  <x:element name="section">
    <x:complexType>
      <x:sequence maxOccurs="unbounded">
        <x:element ref="t:task"/>
      </x:sequence>
      <x:attribute name="name" type="x:string"/>
    </x:complexType>
  </x:element>
  <x:element name="todo">
    <x:complexType>
      <x:sequence maxOccurs="unbounded">
        <x:element ref="t:section"/>
      </x:sequence>
    </x:complexType>
  </x:element>
</x:schema>
```

Figure 4.19. XML Schema that defines the data model for the task list.

to the root of the schema element. Because of the way XML namespaces interact with XPath, XForms binding expressions need to *namespace qualify* individual components of the XPath locator.

As an example, note the namespace prefix t: in each step of the XPath locators used when binding user interface controls. If we omitted the namespace prefix in this case, the binding expression would fail. Writing

```
/todo/section/task
```

would use the default namespace when looking for these nodes; as a consequence, todo would use the default namespace, which in the case of the user interface markup is different from the namespace that contains the task list.

4.4.2 Declaring the Task List Instance

Next, we create a skeleton XML instance for holding the task list. This skeleton serves as the initial data for the task list; it also serves as a declaration that is used when creating new sections and tasks in the task list. The instance declaration is shown in Figure 4.20.

The namespace for the task list is declared as the default namespace using the statement

```
xmlns="http://example.com/todo"
```

```xml
<todo xmlns="http://example.com/todo">
  <section name="business">
    <task>
      <date>2003-01-07</date>
      <description>XForms Call</description>
      <status/><done/>
    </task></section>
  <section name="personal">
    <task>
      <date>2003-04-15</date>
      <description>Tax Deadline</description>
      <status/><done/>
    </task></section>
  <section name="writing">
    <task>
      <date>2003-04-01</date>
      <description>Complete book</description>
      <status/><done/>
    </task></section>
</todo>
```

Figure 4.20. Instance declaration for the task list.

to avoid having to namespace qualify the various elements in the task list. The task list starts with three sections named work, personal, and writing. Each section contains one partially filled-in ⟨**task**⟩ element.

4.4.3 Declaring the Data Model within XHTML ⟨head⟩

Next, we create the XForms data model within element ⟨**head**⟩ of an XHTML document in Figure 4.21. We assume that the XHTML namespace has been declared as the default namespace. Element ⟨**model**⟩ contains the XForms model, and we temporarily make the XForms namespace the default namespace with an appropriate *xmlns* attribute. Element ⟨**model**⟩ carries two attributes in this example:

schema   Identifies the schema that defines the type and structure of instance data to be used in this model. Here, we use #todo-schema to identify the schema for the task list via its unique identifier shown in Figure 4.19.

The instance data is specified by reference in the line

```
<xf:instance src="todo-instance.xml"/>
```

where the location todo-instance.xml contains the skeleton instance shown in Figure 4.20. For brevity, we have replaced the schema definition for the task list shown in Figure 4.19 with a one-line comment.

```
<head><title>Editing Task List</title>
  <model xmlns="http://www.w3.org/2002/xforms"
    id="todo" schema="todo-schema.xsd">
    <!-- instance declared by reference-->
    <instance src="todo-instance.xml"/>
    <submission id="s01" method="post"
    action="http://examples.com/"/>
  </model>
  <style type="text/css">
    @namespace xf url(http://www.w3.org/2002/xforms);
    xf|input.edit {font-weight:bold; ...}
    xf|label.sectionLabel {font-weight:bold; ...}
    xf|submit {font-family: Arial;...}
  </style>
</head>
```

Figure 4.21. XHTML ⟨head⟩ for the task list.

In addition to the schema and instance declarations, the XForms model also declares a ⟨**submission**⟩ element that specifies the *what*, *where*, and *how* of submit processing. The result of *submitting* will be to update the user's saved task list.

Finally, element ⟨**head**⟩ contains a CSS style section in element ⟨**style**⟩ that contains CSS style rules for rendering specific aspects of the user interface. The CSS rules declared here will be used in Section 4.4.4 to style the various user interface controls.

4.4.4 Creating the User Interface Via Nested Repeats

The XForms user interface for editing and viewing the task list within an XHTML page can be thought of as a Web browser window onto the XML document shown in Figure 4.20. Thus, the actual document that the user is viewing and editing is the XML task list; the XForms user interface hosted in an XHTML page enables the user to maintain the task list without having to edit the raw XML source. In this section, we enable such browser-based editing by binding a user interface consisting of XForms constructs and controls to the task list data model; see Figure 4.22.

A key feature of the task list is its hierarchical nature and the ability to grow and shrink dynamically. The task list has been organized into a set of logical sections comprising the various tasks. On the user interface side, we mirror this structure by creating XHTML sections that correspond to the sections in the task list. In doing so, we can use the section name as encapsulated by attribute *name* of element ⟨**section**⟩ in constructing the section title that is displayed to the user. Since the number of sections can grow or shrink at run-time, XForms aggregation construct ⟨**repeat**⟩ is a natural choice for creating a *scrolling* view-port that allows the user to view a portion of the task list. We will create the necessary controls for adding, removing, and scrolling these sections and aggregate these controls to create navigation toolbars.

The tasks appearing in each section have additional substructure, and aligning the fields making up each task is an appropriate visual representation. We use XHTML tables to achieve this visual display. The user can add, remove, and scroll tasks appearing in a given section, and we use a repeating construct to achieve this end result. However, since we are using XHTML tables to render the list of tasks in a given section, we use *repeat attributes* rather than element ⟨**repeat**⟩ to create XHTML tables that grow or shrink dynamically during user interaction.

The consequence of this design is that we create nested repeat structures, with the outer ⟨**repeat**⟩ iterating the sections appearing in the task list and the inner repeat iterating tasks in a given section. Finally, notice that this form of nesting requires

```
<xf:repeat xmlns="http://www.w3.org/1999/xhtml"
  xmlns:t="http://example.com/todo"
  xmlns:ev="http://www.w3.org/2001/xml-events"
  xmlns:xf="http://www.w3.org/2002/xforms"
  id="rs" nodeset="/t:todo/t:section">
<h2><xf:input ref="@name">...</xf:input></h2>
<table>
  <tr xf:repeat-nodeset="t:task" xf:repeat-id="rt">
    <td><xf:input ref="t:date">
    <xf:label>Date</xf:label></xf:input></td>
    <td><xf:input ref="t:description">
    <xf:label>Task</xf:label></xf:input></td>
    <td><xf:input ref="t:status">
    <xf:label>...</xf:label></xf:input></td>
    <td><xf:input ref="t:done">
  <xf:label>Done</xf:label></xf:input></td></tr>
  <tr><td><xf:trigger ev:event="DOMActivate">
      <xf:label>New Task</xf:label>
      <xf:insert at="index('rt')"
        position="after"
      nodeset="/t:section[index('rs')]/t:task"/>
  </xf:trigger></td>
  <td><xf:trigger ev:event="DOMActivate">
      <xf:label>Delete Task</xf:label>
      <xf:delete at="index('rt')"
      nodeset="/t:section[index('rs')]/t:task"/>
  </xf:trigger></td>
  <td><xf:trigger ev:event="DOMActivate">
      <xf:label>Scroll Forward</xf:label>
      <xf:setindex repeat="rt"
  index="index('rt')+1"/></xf:trigger></td>
  <td><xf:trigger ev:event="DOMActivate">
      <xf:label>Scroll Back</xf:label>
      <xf:setindex repeat="rt"
      index="index('rt')-1"/>
</xf:trigger></td></tr></table></xf:repeat>
```

Figure 4.22. User interface for editing a hierarchical task list.

no special attention on the author's part; the design of the XForms repeat construct ensures that nested repeats work as the author would expect.

Note that for this example, we assume the XHTML namespace as the default; see relevant declaration in Figure 4.25. Hence, we prefix all elements from the XForms namespace via the local namespace prefix xf.

Outer ⟨repeat⟩.   The outer ⟨repeat⟩ iterates over the ⟨section⟩ children of the task list and is identified by setting attribute *id* to rs. This unique identifier will be used when manipulating the state of this repeating structure via XForms actions ⟨insert⟩, ⟨delete⟩, and ⟨setindex⟩.

We identify the node-set to iterate via the binding expression

```
nodeset="/todo/section"
```

which selects all ⟨section⟩ children of element ⟨todo⟩. Given the instance declared in Figure 4.20, this would select a set consisting of 3 ⟨section⟩ nodes. Notice that since there is only one ⟨model⟩ in this complete example, we do not need to specify attribute *model* in the binding expression; by default XForms uses the first model in the document. The binding expression appearing on element ⟨repeat⟩ also establishes the XPath evaluation context when evaluating relative XPath locators within the body of element ⟨repeat⟩.

For brevity, we have not set optional attributes of element ⟨repeat⟩ such as *startindex*. In this case, the browser can display as many sections as appropriate for the connecting device.

The markup appearing within element ⟨repeat⟩ declares the template user interface to be applied to each member of the node-set being iterated. We first create a section header via XHTML element ⟨h2⟩ that displays an editable field bound to attribute *name* of element ⟨section⟩. Notice that XForms user interface control ⟨input⟩ is used as the contents of the XHTML section header created by element ⟨h2⟩. The result is to create a Web page where the section headings are editable by the user. Within this ⟨input⟩ control, we use a relative XPath locator @name to address attribute *name* of the *current* ⟨section⟩. In the current example, the instance shown in Figure 4.20 results in the creation of 3 XHTML ⟨h2⟩ elements, with each displaying attribute *name* from the corresponding ⟨section⟩ element. Editing the displayed value results in the underlying XML instance being updated, and the display is refreshed to show the new value.

The key thing to notice is that relative XPath locators appearing within the body of element ⟨repeat⟩ are evaluated in the evaluation context established by the binding expression on the containing ⟨**repeat**⟩ and with the *current* member of the node-set being iterated as the *context* node. Thus, the binding expression on control ⟨**input**⟩

```
ref="@name"
```

is interpreted as `./@name`, where `.` refers to the *current* node, that is, the current ⟨**section**⟩. This is key to understanding the functioning of nested repeat structures as we will see when we examine the inner repeat next.

Inner repeat. The outer ⟨**repeat**⟩ creates an XHTML ⟨**table**⟩ for displaying the tasks in a given section. The context node for the outer ⟨**repeat**⟩, that is, `.` refers to the *current* ⟨**section**⟩ from the task list, and this *current* ⟨**section**⟩ sets up the evaluation context as explained earlier. We want the XHTML table that displays the individual tasks to grow or shrink with the tasks in a section. We achieve this by turning XHTML element ⟨**tr**⟩ into a repeating structure via *repeat attributes* described in Section 4.3.6. In this case, the template user interface for this repeating construct is an XHTML table row that displays the fields making up an individual task.

The inner repeat is created via *repeat attributes* on XHTML element ⟨**tr**⟩ with the line

```
<tr repeat-nodeset="task" repeat-id="rt">
```

which declares that the repeating structure being created will be identified via the unique identifier `rt`. The binding expression that locates the set of nodes to iterate uses the current evaluation context as set up by the outer ⟨**repeat**⟩. Thus, the XPath locator in the statement

```
repeat-nodeset="task"
```

is interpreted as `./task` and selects all ⟨**task**⟩ children of the current ⟨**section**⟩. Thus, the outer ⟨**repeat**⟩ determines the specific ⟨**section**⟩ to operate on; the inner repeat structure selects the ⟨**task**⟩ of a specific ⟨**section**⟩. The result is that, as the user changes the ⟨**section**⟩ that is *current* via add, delete, or scroll operations, the inner repeat structure is correctly updated to display the tasks from the right ⟨**section**⟩.

The contents of the table row as given by the children of element ⟨**tr**⟩ declare the template user interface that is applied to each task appearing in the collection being iterated. We have created individual table cells via XHTML element ⟨**td**⟩ for each of these fields. Each table cell contains an XForms user interface control that binds to the corresponding field in element ⟨**task**⟩.

Adding, removing, and scrolling tasks   Before closing off element ⟨**table**⟩ created by the outer ⟨**repeat**⟩, we create a table row that holds user interface controls for adding, removing, and scrolling tasks in the current section. These controls use XForms action handlers ⟨**insert**⟩, ⟨**delete**⟩, and ⟨**setindex**⟩ in a manner similar to that explained in Figure 4.13. Within these controls, we address the inner repeat via its unique identifier rt and the outer ⟨**repeat**⟩ via its unique identifier rs. Since the ⟨**section**⟩ on which the inner repeat operates is completely determined by the state of the outer ⟨**repeat**⟩, the add, delete, and scroll controls in this example are identical in operation to what we saw when creating the shopping cart in Section 4.3.4.

Following, we examine one of these controls in detail to explain the functioning of the nested repeats. Consider the control that adds a new task. The new task is added by invoking XForms handler ⟨**insert**⟩. This invocation needs to specify the node-set to which the new ⟨**task**⟩ node should be added and the position at which it should be inserted. The node-set in question is the set of all ⟨**task**⟩ children of the *current* ⟨**section**⟩.

The position of the current ⟨**section**⟩ within the node-set of all ⟨**section**⟩ children of the task list can be accessed by invoking XPath extension function *index*, as in

```
index(rs)
```

which returns the value of the repeat index for the outer ⟨**repeat**⟩. This expression can in turn be used to locate the desired set of ⟨**task**⟩ children of the current ⟨**section**⟩ as in

```
nodeset="section[index('rs')]/task"
```

which selects the set of all ⟨**section**⟩ nodes, filters it by the predicate index(rs), and finally selects all ⟨**task**⟩ children of the result. Next, we specify where in this set of ⟨**task**⟩ elements the insertion should happen. This is expressed via the following:

```
xf:insert at="index('rt)" position="after"
```

where XPath extension function *index* is used to access the current value of the repeat index for the inner repeat identified by rt.

Finally, notice that the add, delete, and scroll controls described earlier appear *within* the outer ⟨**repeat**⟩. The effect is to create a toolbar consisting of these controls for *each* ⟨**section**⟩ of the task list.

4.4.5 Binding User Interface Controls to the Task List

Next, we examine the binding expressions used in the user interface controls in Figure 4.22. As before, the evaluation context and *context node* for evaluating these XPath locators are determined by the containing ⟨**repeat**⟩. The user interface in Figure 4.22 creates four input controls that each binds to one of the four child elements of ⟨**task**⟩. The binding expressions in each of these controls are relative XPath expressions that are all evaluated with the *current* ⟨**task**⟩ as the context node. Thus, the binding expression on the first ⟨**input**⟩ control

```
<input ref="date">...</input>
```

binds that input control to the ⟨**date**⟩ of the ⟨**task**⟩ node that is *current*, that is, the node at the position given by index('rt').

Notice also that we have bound XForms control ⟨**input**⟩ to each of the four child elements of ⟨**task**⟩. Recall from the schema shown in Figure 4.19 that the children of ⟨**task**⟩ are *typed*. This type information can be used to create user interface controls appropriate to a given interaction modality and device. Thus, the ⟨**input**⟩ control bound to field ⟨**date**⟩ of type xsd:date might be rendered as a date picker control on a given device. The date picker on a desktop client might take the form of a simple calendar widget; the date picker on a cell phone with a small display might be rendered as a text field with smart completion. Child element ⟨**done**⟩ is of type xsd:boolean; this information can be used to render the associated ⟨**input**⟩ control as a checkbox where appropriate.

4.4.6 Adding a Toolbar for Navigation

Controls for adding, removing, and scrolling tasks are described in Section 4.4.4. The controls for adding, removing, and scrolling the sections in the task list are similar in structure and functionality. Placing these controls in element ⟨**group**⟩ as shown in Figure 4.23 turns these controls into a conceptual toolbar that can be placed at the appropriate point in the containing user interface.

Notice that creating a new section in the task list effectively clones the prototypical ⟨**section**⟩ element declared in Figure 4.20. Binding the user interface shown in Figure 4.22 to the new collection results in an additional section appearing in the user interface.

This newly created section has an empty ⟨**task**⟩ node, and this ⟨**task**⟩ node in turns gets bound by the inner repeat structure that is part of the newly created table row. Notice also that depending on the available display real estate, a fixed number

```
<group xmlns="http://www.w3.org/2002/xforms"
 xmlns:ev="http://www.w3.org/2001/xml-events"
 xmlns:t="http://example.com/todo">
<trigger ev:event="DOMActivate">
  <label>New section</label>
  <insert nodeset="t:section" at="index('rs')"
position="after"/></trigger>
<trigger ev:event="DOMActivate">
  <label>Delete section</label>
  <delete nodeset="t:section" at="index('rs')"/>
</trigger>
<trigger ev:event="DOMActivate">
  <label>Scroll Forward</label>
  <setindex repeat="rs" index="index('rs')+1"/>
</trigger>
<trigger ev:event="DOMActivate">
  <label>Scroll Back</label>
  <setindex repeat="rs" index="index('rs')-1"/>
</trigger>
</group>
```

Figure 4.23. Toolbar for manipulating sections in the task list.

of sections will be shown to the user at any given time. Since the toolbar consisting of the controls for operating on sections is placed outside the outer ⟨**repeat**⟩ structure, that toolbar will never scroll off the display while the user is working with the task list.

The end result is to divide the displayed page effectively into a fixed toolbar and a scrolling region that displays the sections of the task list. Each displayed section is in turn subdivided into a toolbar for manipulating the tasks in that section and a scrolling view-port that displays the tasks in that section. We show a conceptual overview of this visual display in Figure 4.24.

4.4.7 Putting It Together inside an XHTML Page

In Figure 4.25, we bring together the various pieces of the task list example in an XHTML page that creates the complete task list application. Element ⟨**html**⟩ is the root of this document, and it declares the XHTML namespace to be the

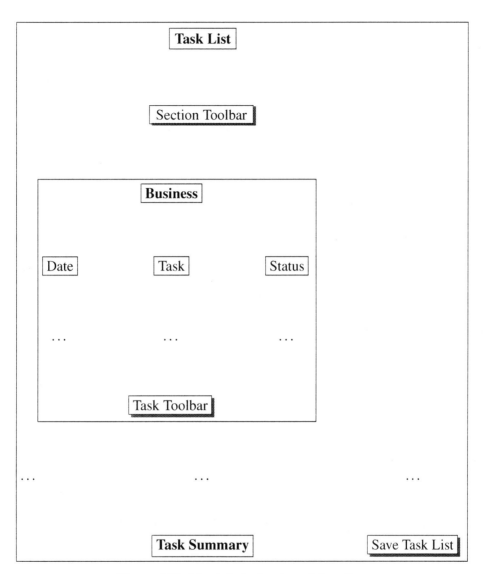

Figure 4.24. Visual display for the task list editor.

default namespace. We declare local namespace prefixes for the various namespaces used by the task list application as follows:

xf   The XForms 1.0 namespace.

xsd The XML Schema namespace corresponding to XML Schema 1.0. XML Schema became a W3C Recommendation in 2002.

```
<html xmlns="http://www.w3.org/1999/xhtml"
  xmlns:xf="http://www.w3.org/2002/xforms"
  xmlns:xsd="http://www.w3.org/2001/XMLSchema"
  xmlns:todo="http://example.com/todo"
  xmlns:ev="http://www.w3.org/2001/xml-events">
  <!-- insert head element here -->
  <body>
    <h1>Task List</h1>
    <!-- insert section toolbar here. -->
    <!-- insert nested repeating here-->
    <!-- Insert task list summarizer here. -->
    <!--Insert submit control here-->
</body></html>
```

Figure 4.25. Dynamic XHTML user interface for editing a hierarchical task list.

ev   The XML Events namespace. XML Events is currently a W3C Candidate Recommendation, but the namespace URI is not expected to change when XML Events becomes a W3C Recommendation.

t   The namespace containing elements in the task list instance. This namespace is private to the task list application.

Next, we insert XHTML element ⟨**head**⟩ as shown in Figure 4.21. This contains the XForms ⟨**model**⟩ and the CSS style rules used to style various aspects of the presentation.

The user interface described in Section 4.4.4 and Section 4.4.6 appears within XHTML element ⟨**body**⟩. Notice that in the resulting interface, the level one heading produced by XHTML element ⟨**h1**⟩ is fixed with respect to the scrolling view-port created by the ⟨**repeat**⟩ structure that binds to the hierarchical task list.

We follow the ⟨**repeat**⟩ that holds the task list user interface with other XForms controls that display a summary of the task list; see Figure 4.26. Like the title produced via element ⟨**h1**⟩, this summary section is also fixed with respect to the scrolling task list.

The summary section displays the number of sections in the task list and a count of the tasks that remain to be completed. Since this computed information is not stored in a specific node in the task list instance, we cannot use a binding expression

```
<group xmlns="http://www.w3.org/2002/xforms"
  xmlns:t="http://example.com/todo">
  You have <output value="count(/t:todo/t:section)"/>
  sections in your task list with a total of
  <output value=
    "count(//t:task[
  not(boolean-from-string(t:done))])"/>
unfinished tasks.</group>
```

Figure 4.26. Displaying a summary of the task list.

in control ⟨**output**⟩ to look up this information. We therefore use attribute *value*[2] on control ⟨**output**⟩ to specify the expression to compute. This information is computed dynamically at run-time and updates as the user interacts with the task list.

We conclude the example by adding a ⟨**submit**⟩ control that enables the user to save the task list.

4.4.8 Submitting the Task List

We began this section by introducing the XML document that holds the task list in Figure 4.20. The primary purpose of the user interface we have created so far is to edit, maintain; and view this XML document within a standard browser interface without having to worry about the details of the XML markup. The interface we have created provides the user the necessary interface controls to view and manipulate the task list XML document. The key advantage with the interface we have created is that the underlying task list remains valid XML at all times. We can complete the circle by *submitting* the task list in order to save the current state.

Creating such *save task list* functionality requires the addition of a ⟨**submit**⟩ control (see Figure 4.27) that *binds* to the ⟨**submission**⟩ element we created in the XForms ⟨**model**⟩ in Figure 4.21. Activating control ⟨**submit**⟩ results in the current state of the task list being serialized as an XML document and the result of this serialization being transmitted to the URI specified in the ⟨**submission**⟩ element.

---

[2] This was an oft-requested feature that was added following public feedback during the Last Call period.

```
<submit xmlns="http://www.w3.org/2002/xforms"
  submission="s01">
  <label>Save Task List</label><help>...</help>
</submit>
```

Figure 4.27. Submitting the task list saves the current state.

4.5 XForms User Interface at a Glance

This has been a long chapter, and we close it with Table 4.2 that gives a summary of the various XForms user interface constructs we have covered. For each user interface construct, we give a succinct reminder of the usage patterns addressed by that construct.

Table 4.2. XForms User Interface at a Glance

Construct	Purpose
⟨**group**⟩	• Group related controls to ease refactoring
	• Enable structured navigation
	• Factor common parts of binding expressions
⟨**switch**⟩	• Enable conditional user interfaces
	• Enable interaction-based switching
	• Create user interface wizards and multipage tab dialogs
	• Progressively reveal complex user interfaces
⟨**repeat**⟩	• Iterate collections
	• Create user interfaces that grow or shrink as needed
	• Enable creation and maintenance of hierarchical content

CHAPTER 5

XForms Model Properties

5.1 Introduction

XForms element ⟨**model**⟩ holds the instance data along with its associated type constraints. Constraints on XML instance data can be static type constraints as expressed via XML Schema; static constraints are suitable for capturing aspects of the data that are not likely to change during user interaction. Typical examples of such constraints include data type and structural constraints. In addition to holding the instance data, the schema for that instance data, and the submission details, the XForms model can encapsulate additional properties that refine the static schema constraints.

XForms defines a small number of such *model properties* that can be used to express dynamic constraints. These properties, in contrast to constraints expressed via XML Schema, are *dynamic* and are recomputed during user interaction; their updated value is immediately reflected in the user interface. The dynamic nature of model properties is key to creating online forms that exhibit a high degree of interactivity.

Model properties are authored via element ⟨**bind**⟩ described in Section 5.2. We described interaction-based switching in Section 4.2; model-based switching for creating conditional interaction is enabled via boolean property *relevant* described in Section 5.3. Property *relevant* can be used to advantage in dynamically revealing or hiding portions of a complex user interface.

During user interaction, it may be useful to indicate that a certain piece of data is *required* in order to ensure successful completion of a task; this is enabled via boolean property *required*, described in Section 5.4. Properties *relevant* and *required* can be used in combination in creating sophisticated electronic work-flow applications.

As an example, the user's response to an initial set of questions can be used to determine the value of *relevant* on portions of the model; this automatically *enables* portions of the user interface that *bind* to the fields that are *relevant*. Setting property *required* to `true` on these *relevant* fields can in turn ensure that the user gets appropriate feedback when interacting with the associated controls.

Finally, boolean property *readonly*, described in Section 5.5, enables certain fields to be made temporarily *read-only* during user interaction. This feature can prove extremely useful in work-flow applications where users with different *roles* work on the same form.

Complex forms can express dynamic validity constraints that are computed from the state of the current data instance; for example, a shopping application might declare that to obtain a discount, the user *must* buy a specific number of items. Dynamic constraints are expressed via property *constraint* described in Section 5.6. In addition, XForms authors can constrain the cardinality of a given set of nodes (*e.g.,* the number of items in a shopping cart) by creating model properties that constrain the number of nodes in a set via property *constraint*.

XForms enables the automatic computation of nodes in the data instance; we saw an example of this in the shopping cart application in Figure 4.10. Model property *calculate* is used to achieve this functionality and is described in Section 5.8.

Finally, model property *type* enables XForms authors to extend schemas that cannot be modified; such *external schema augmentation* is enabled by property *type*, described in Section 5.9.

5.1.1 Model Properties and CSS Style

The purpose of the XForms user interface is to convey the state of the XForms model to the user at all times. Toward this end, the current value of model properties *required*, *relevant*, *readonly*, and *constraint* for a given node in the instance tree need to be reflected in the user interface. Thus, if a field is presently *read-only*, it is useful to convey this information, perhaps by styling controls bound to that field using a particular presentation style.

There are also boundary conditions where the XForms model and user interface might be out of sync, for example, when a ⟨**range**⟩ control specifies *start* and *end* values subset the allowable values for the underlying instance; notice that in such a case, it is possible for the instance to hold a value *outside* this subset. As an example, consider a specialized volume control authored using ⟨**range**⟩ that allows the user to adjust the volume within the interval [25, 75], where the permissible values for volume lie in the interval [0, 100]. Assume further that the user interface provides a specialized *mute* control authored via element ⟨**trigger**⟩ that sets the volume to 0. When the user activates this *mute* control, the volume gets set to 0; consequently, the value is now *outside* the interval displayed by our specialized volume control, even though it is still *valid* with respect to the overall application; see Figure 5.1.

XForms uses a relatively advanced CSS feature called *pseudoclasses* to enable the styling of form controls to reflect the state of the underlying data. We have seen the use of attribute *class* in many of the user interface examples in this book when creating CSS style rules to apply to a set of controls. CSS pseudoclasses can be thought of as creating an imaginary *class* attribute on elements, based on the state of the underlying document tree.

Consider the creation of a CSS style rule that specifies how *required* fields should be presented to the user. Property *required* can have one of two possible boolean values. We use *pseudo classes :required* and *:optional* that correspond to these two values. We then specify the CSS style to be used for *:required* and *:optional* using the syntax defined in CSS3 for associating style rules with pseudo classes.

When property *readonly* on an instance node becomes `true`, the XForms processor sets controls bound to this node to have pseudoclass *:required*; similarly, when property *required* becomes `false`, controls bound to that node get pseudoclass *:optional*. The CSS-aware browser can then use this information to update the presentation. For the case of the specialized volume control described in Figure 5.1, we use CSS pseudoclass *:out-of-range* to attach a special style to be used when control ⟨**range**⟩ is out-of-sync with the underlying data. Notice that this out-of-sync condition can also arise with control ⟨**select1**⟩ when the displayed choices are a subset of the permissible values and the underlying instance holds a permissible value outside this subset.

We list the proposed CSS3 pseudoclasses with their corresponding XForms model properties in Table 5.1 and show an example of their use in Figure 5.2. Note that these pseudoclasses are being defined jointly by the CSS and XForms working groups and might be updated in the future.

Table 5.1. CSS3 Pseudoclasses and the Associated XForms Model Properties

Property	CSS3	CSS3
readonly	*:readonly*	*:readwrite*
required	*:required*	*:optional*
relevant	*:enabled*	*:disabled*
constraint	*:valid*	*:invalid*
	:out-of-range	

```
<html xmlns="http://www.w3.org/1999/xhtml">
  <head>
    <model xmlns="http://www.w3.org/2002/xforms"
      id="sound" schema="units.xsd">
    <instance>
      <settings xmlns="">
        <volume xsi:type="percentage"/>
      </settings></instance>
    </model>
    <style type="text/css">
      @namespace xf
      url(http://www.w3.org/2002/xforms);
      /* blue background
      for out of range form controls */
      *:out-of-range {background-color:blue; }
  </style></head>
  <body>
    <group xmlns="http://www.w3.org/2002/xforms">
      <range ref="/settings/volume"
        start="25" end="75" step="5">
      <label>Adjust Volume</label></range>
      <trigger ev:event="DOMActivate">
        <label>Mute</label>
        <action>
          <setvalue ref="/settings/volume">
          0</setvalue>
      <message>Muted</message></action></trigger>
</group></body></html>
```

Figure 5.1. Conveying that model and user interface are *out of sync* via styling.

```
<style xmlns:xf="http://www.w3.org/2002/xforms">
  @namespace xf url(http://www.w3.org/2002/xforms);
  /* Red background on all invalid form controls */
  *:invalid {background-color:red; }
  /* Red asterisk after all required form controls */
  *:required::after {content: "*"; color:red; }
  /* Do not render non-relevant form controls */
  *:disabled {visibility: hidden; }

  /* Display non-relevant repeat items
  in the system GrayText color */
  *::repeat-item:disabled {
  visibility: visible; color: GrayText;}
</style>
```

Figure 5.2. CSS style rules using pseudoclasses.

5.2 Attaching Constraints Via Element ⟨bind⟩

Model properties are created via element ⟨**bind**⟩. We encountered this element when creating *binding sites* in Section 3.2.2.[1] The ⟨**bind**⟩ element is also used for attaching model properties to a set of nodes in the instance. When used in this manner, element ⟨**bind**⟩ specifies the set of nodes to which the property is being applied via XForms binding attributes. All allowed model properties are legal attributes on element ⟨**bind**⟩; model properties are applied by specifying an appropriate attribute-value pair. Thus, element ⟨**bind**⟩ has the following general form:

nodeset   Locates set of nodes to which a model property is to be applied. The specified property will be applied to *each* node in the node-set.

property   The name of the property to be applied.

Model property bindings created via ⟨**bind**⟩ can be collected inside a container ⟨**bind**⟩ element for authoring convenience. When collected inside a ⟨**bind**⟩ container, this container can use XForms binding expressions to define the evaluation context for the binding expressions that appear within contained ⟨**bind**⟩ elements. We show a template ⟨**bind**⟩ in Figure 5.3.

---

[1]With the benefit of hindsight, we should probably have named this ⟨**assert**⟩, that is, it was probably a mistake to overload element ⟨**bind**⟩ to play both roles, and this may well be revisited in a future version of XForms.

```
<model xmlns="http://www.w3.org/2002/xforms">
  <instance>
    <root xmlns="">
      <c1><c11/><c12/></c1>
      <c2><c21/><c22/></c2>
  </root></instance>
  <bind nodeset="/root">
    <bind nodeset="c1/c11" required="value"/>
    <bind nodeset="*" type="xsd:string"/>
</bind></model>
```

Figure 5.3. Element ⟨**bind**⟩ is used to attach model properties.

5.3 Property *relevant* for Model-based Switching

Property *relevant* takes an XPath expression that is evaluated during user interaction to return a boolean value. By default, all nodes in the instance tree have this property set to `true`. When a node gets its *relevant* property set to `false`, user interface controls that bind to that node become *unavailable* to the user; that is, the user is not presented with these values. Property *relevant* enables the creation of dynamic applications that use model-based switching to create conditional user interfaces. Compare this to the interaction-based switching enabled by construct ⟨**switch**⟩ described in Section 4.2.

When property *relevant* is applied to a node, it applies to that node and all its descendant children. Thus, property *relevant* makes it possible to make entire subtrees in the instance become *relevant*. This can be used to advantage in making large portions of a complex user interface conditional upon the current state of the instance being populated by the user.

5.3.1 Insurance Form Using Model-based Switching

We illustrate the use of property *relevant* with an example of an insurance application form. This form collects personal information in order to prepare an appropriate insurance policy and is divided into different sections. Not all sections of the form are *relevant* to every individual; the user's answer to specific questions is used to determine the *relevance* of each section.

As an example, if the user responds yes to the question

Do you smoke?

```
<model xmlns="http://www.w3.org/2002/xforms"
  id="i1" schema="insurance.xsd">
  <instance>
    <person xmlns="">
      <diet>...</diet>
      <habits>
        <smoker>false</smoker>...
      </habits>
      <health><chest/><lungs/><heart/></health>
    </person>
  </instance>
  <bind nodeset="/person/health">
    <bind nodeset="chest"
      relevant=
      "boolean-from-string(../habits/smoker)"/>
    <bind nodeset="lungs"
      relevant=
      "boolean-from-string(../habits/smoker)"/>
  </bind>
</model>
```

Figure 5.4. Property *relevant* makes portions of the data instance irrelevant.

```
<group xmlns="http://www.w3.org/2002/xforms"
  ref="/person">
  <input ref="habits/smoker">
  <label>Do you smoke?</label></input>
  <group ref="health/chest">
  <label>Chest Conditions</label>...</group>
  <group ref="health/lungs">
  <label>Lung Conditions</label>...</group>
</group>
```

Figure 5.5. Property *relevant* enables model-based conditional user interfaces.

the user might be asked a series of questions pertaining to prior smoking-related health conditions. We first define a partial data model for this insurance application in Figure 5.4.

Next, we bind a user interface to this model in Figure 5.5. In this example, the user interface pertaining to the user's smoking-related health conditions are initially hidden because of the default value provided in the instance for field ⟨**smoker**⟩. A value of `false` is used in the expression

```
relevant= "boolean-from-string(../habits/smoker)"
```

to set model property *relevant* on fields ⟨**chest**⟩ and ⟨**lungs**⟩ to `false`.

If the user changes this initial state by answering `yes` to the question

Do you smoke?

the *relevant* property applied to the nodes corresponding to ⟨**chest**⟩ and ⟨**lungs**⟩ becomes `true`. As a consequence, user interface controls that bind to the subtree that collects details about smoking-related health conditions are displayed to the user.

5.4 Property *required* for Mandatory Fields

Property *required* can be used to ensure that the user supplies values for a given field or set of fields. Such mandatory fields may be declared via the schema; in that case, the values are *always* required. Model property *required* is for use in those cases where certain fields become mandatory, depending on the input provided by the user when interacting with the XForms application.

The value of property *required* is an XPath expression that is evaluated to return a boolean value. Like property *relevant*, it is computed at run-time. When a node in the instance gets *required* set to `true`, the user interface is updated appropriately to convey this state. As an example, a visual user agent might use appropriate visual styling to indicate to the user that a certain field is *required*. Such styling is achieved via the use of CSS3 pseudoclasses *:required* and *:optional*, described in Section 5.1.1.

5.4.1 Extending Insurance Form with Property *required*

Continuing the example of the insurance application form shown in Figure 5.4 and Figure 5.5, we can add ⟨**bind**⟩ declarations to the data model to state the following effect. If the user has answered `yes` to the question

Do you smoke?

then the user *must* answer *relevant* questions about existing health conditions; see Figure 5.6. Thus, property *relevant* causes the needed user interface controls for answering these questions to be presented to the user; property *required* ensures that

```
<model xmlns="http://www.w3.org/2002/xforms"
  id="i1" schema="insurance.xsd">
<instance>
  <person xmlns="">
    <diet>...</diet>
    <habits>
    <smoker>false</smoker>...</habits>
    <health>
    <chest/><heart/><lungs/></health>
</person></instance>
<bind nodeset="/person/health">
  <bind nodeset="chest"
    relevant=
    "boolean-from-string(/person/habits/smoker)"
    required=
    "boolean-from-string(/person/habits/smoker)"/>
  <bind nodeset="lungs"
    relevant=
    "boolean-from-string(/person/habits/smoker)"
    required=
    "boolean-from-string(/person/habits/smoker)"/>
</bind></model>
```

Figure 5.6. Property *required* makes fields *mandatory*.

the user answers these questions. CSS3 pseudoclasses *required* and *optional* style controls to reflect model property *required*; for example, fields that are *required* might be displayed using a different font and color in a visual interface.

5.5 Property *readonly* for Controlling Changes

XForms controls bound to the instance data make it possible to modify the values stored in the instance. Property *readonly* makes it possible to create dynamic applications where the user is allowed to change certain values only if some other condition holds true. Property *readonly* takes an XPath expression that evaluates to a boolean value. All nodes in the instance start off with property *readonly* set to true. The expression for the value of property *readonly* for a given node is recomputed whenever the nodes that the property depends on are modified.

```
<model xmlns="http://www.w3.org/2002/xforms">
  <instance>
    <root xmlns="">
      <c1><c11/><c12/></c1>
      <c2><c21/><c22/></c2>
    </root></instance>
  <bind nodeset="/root">
    <bind nodeset="c1/c12"
    readonly="c1/c11&gt;10 and c1/c11&lt;100"/>
</bind></model>
```

Figure 5.7. Property *readonly* can temporarily prevent editing of certain fields.

5.5.1 Conditional Editing Using *readonly*

We illustrate the use of property *readonly* with an XForms interface that enables *conditional* editing of portions of an XML document. Consider the model shown in Figure 5.7.

Property *readonly* is attached to node c1/c12. The value is computed by evaluating an XPath expression

```
c1/c11 &gt; 10
```

which evaluates to true if and only if value of c1/c11 is greater than 10. Notice that when writing the comparison operator within an XPath expression, we need to use XML character entity >.

XForms user interface controls that bind to field c1/c12 will reflect the state of property *readonly*; for example, a visual browser might style the controls to indicate that the value may not be edited. Attempting to edit c12 when *readonly* is true would result in the XForms user agent signaling an error to the user with an appropriate message.

5.6 Property *constraint* for Dynamic Validation

Model property *constraint* can be used to declare validity constraints to be evaluated during user interaction. These serve to refine the static constraints defined via XML Schema. Property *constraint* takes an XPath expression that is evaluated to return a boolean value. XForms user interface controls can be styled to reflect the state of this model property via CSS3 pseudoclasses *:valid* and *:invalid*. See Section 5.1.1.

```
<model id="t" xmlns="http://www.w3.org/2002/xforms"
  xmlns:xsd="http://www.w3.org/2001/XMLSchema"
  xmlns:xsi=
  "http://www.w3.org/2001/XMLSchema-instance">
  <instance>
    <trip xmlns="">
      <depart xsi:type="xsd:date"/>
      <return xsi:type="xsd:date"/>
  </trip></instance>
  <bind nodeset="/travel">
    <bind nodeset="return"
      constraint="days-from-date(return)
      - days-from-date(depart) &gt; 0"/>
  </bind>
</model>
```

Figure 5.8. Constraining return date via property *constraint*.

Property *constraint* is especially useful in constraining the cardinality of node-sets used with ⟨**repeat**⟩; this usage will be described separately in Section 5.7. Additionally, property *constraint* is useful in creating XForms user interfaces where values provided by the user can be used in computing additional constraints on the remaining fields in a form.

5.6.1 Constraining Travel Dates Using *constraint*

Consider a travel application that needs to collect departure and return dates. The XForms author can use property *constraint* to declare that the return date must come *after* the departure date and that the departure and return dates *may not* be the same. XForms extends XPath with the functions needed to perform such date comparisons; see Figure 5.8. Function *days-from-date* takes a string representing a value of type xsd:date and returns the number of days since January 1, 1970. We use this function to compute the number of days between the departure and return dates in property *constraint*.

5.7 Constraining the Number of Permitted Entries

XForms uses XML Schema for defining the structure of the instance data. However, XML Schema may not always be implementable on all clients, for example, mobile clients requiring a small footprint. In recognition of this fact, XForms defines two conformance profiles for XForms implementations:

Basic   Basic profile for running on small devices
Full   Full profile for running on platforms that do not have footprint constraints

The only difference between these conformance profiles is the extent of XML Schema support that is needed. XForms Basic does not require XML Schema structures. In addition, it eliminates some of XML Schema's built-in types that rarely if ever occur in XForms applications.

The lack of XML Schema structures in XForms Basic means that an XForms Basic client does not have access to cardinality constraints expressed via attributes *minOccurs* and *maxOccurs*; these are defined by XML Schema structures; See Section 2.5.3. The absence of these attributes is felt in XForms Basic when working with ⟨**repeat**⟩ structures; XForms Basic clients need to be able to ensure that a collection of nodes being operated on by ⟨**repeat**⟩ remains valid with respect to cardinality constraints such as

The shopping cart *must* contain at least 3 items.

Such cardinality constraints can be expressed via model property *constraint* described in Section 5.6. Here, we illustrate the use of property *constraint* in expressing such cardinality constraints with an example in Figure 5.9.

The key thing to notice is that the cardinality constraint is expressed by applying model property *constraint* to the container—in this case, the shopping cart. In this

```
<model xmlns="http://www.w3.org/2002/xforms"
  xmlns:xsd="http://www.w3.org/2001/XMLSchema"
  id="cart" schema="cs.xsd">
  <instance id="c1">
    <line-item xmlns="">
      <item><product>...</product></item>
      <quantity>1</quantity><cost/>
  </line-item></instance>
  <bind nodeset="/cart"
  constraint="count(line-item) &gt; 3"/>
</model>
```

Figure 5.9. Expressing cardinality constraints via property *constraint*.

sense, ⟨**cart**⟩ can be thought of as an *array* of ⟨**item**⟩ elements, and property *constraint* defines the bounds on the dimensions of this array.

5.8 Property *calculate* for Dynamic Computation

We saw an example of model property *calculate* in the shopping cart example in Section 4.3.3. The value of property *calculate* is an XPath expression that computes the value to be stored in the node to which the *calculate* property applies. Thus, when an instance node has model property *calculate* applied to it, it does not make sense to bind an XForms input control to that node. The XForms processor will automatically update the value of nodes having property *calculate* by evaluating the XPath expression provided after first updating the value of dependent nodes.

5.8.1 Examples of Property *calculate*

XPath expressions for property *calculate* can be cumbersome to write for a first-time XPath user. The advantage with using XPath as the expression language for this purpose is that XPath is side-effect free. Thus, even though XPath may appear cumbersome at first flush when compared to full-blown programming languages like Javascript, the decision to use XPath within XForms is a conscious one. A consequence of XPath expressions being side-effect free is that complex XForms become easier to debug since the *calculate* property on a node can affect only the value of that particular node.

Contrast this with using a full-blown programming language, where the programmer would be free to create data models where calculating the value of a particular node might affect other unrelated parts of the form. By design, the dependency relationship set up among nodes in the XForms model by property *calculate* can be statically analyzed. The result of this analysis is a dependency graph that is used by the XForms processor in determining the order of automatic updates to the instance as the user interacts with the XForms application.

Note that property *calculate* sets up one-way dependencies among nodes in the instance; it is not meant to define a general constraint-solver. To see this, consider the temperature converter shown in Figure 5.10. Model property *calculate* on ⟨**Fahrenheit**⟩ relates this value to ⟨**Centigrade**⟩. We bind control ⟨**input**⟩ to field ⟨**Centigrade**⟩ and control ⟨**output**⟩ to field ⟨**Fahrenheit**⟩. Providing a value for ⟨**Centigrade**⟩ automatically updates field ⟨**Fahrenheit**⟩, and the updated value is displayed by the ⟨**output**⟩ control that is bound to this field.

In XForms 1.0, binding an input control to field ⟨**Fahrenheit**⟩ and providing a new value for that field would not automatically update field ⟨**Centigrade**⟩; that is,

```
<html xmlns="http://www.w3.org/1999/xhtml"
  xmlns:xf="http://www.w3.org/2002/xforms">
  <head><title>Temperature Converter</title>
    <xf:model id="temp">
      <xf:instance xmlns="">
        <temperature>
          <Centigrade>100</Centigrade><Fahrenheit/>
      </temperature></xf:instance>
      <bind nodeset="/temperature/Fahrenheit"
      calculate="../Centigrade *9  div 5 +32"/>
  </xf:model></head>
  <body>
    <xf:group ref="/temperature"
      xmlns="http://www.w3.org/2002/xforms">
      <input ref="Centigrade">
      <label>Celsius</label></input>
      <output ref="Fahrenheit">
      <label>Fahrenheit</label></output>
  </xf:group></body></html>
```

Figure 5.10. Property *calculate* to convert temperature.

the processor does not build the inverse relation between fields (**Fahrenheit**) and (**Centigrade**). This is also why it does not make sense to bind XForms input controls to fields that have an associated *calculate* property.

5.9 Augmenting Schemas with Type Constraints

Type declarations are mostly achieved via XML Schema. However, there may be situations where the XForms' author wishes to refine the type constraints provided by an existing schema. If the author has write access to the schema, such refinements might be implemented by modifying the schema. Model property *type* is for use in those cases where this is not possible.

Model property *type* provides functionality similar to XML Schema attribute *xsi:type*. However, notice that being an attribute itself, *xsi:type* cannot be used to specify type information for attributes. Using model property *type* via element (**bind**) does not suffer from this restriction. We show an example of this in Figure 5.11.

```
<model xmlns="http://www.w3.org/2002/xforms"
  xmlns:xsd="http://www.w3.org/2001/XMLSchema">
  <instance>
    <person xmlns="" serial="1">
    <name/><age/></person>
  </instance>
  <bind nodeset="/person">
    <bind nodeset="@serial" type="xsd:integer"/>
    <bind nodeset="age" type="xsd:integer"/>
  </bind>
</model>
```

Figure 5.11. Declaring type information via property *type*.

Property *type* can also be used to advantage to provide basic type information on XForms environments where XML Schema is not available.

5.10 Declaring Privacy Level Via P3P

Protection of individual privacy and ensuring the safety of personal information are becoming increasingly important on the Internet. XForms—as the next generation of Web forms—enables Web authors to declare the policies used to protect the information they collect via a standardized mechanism. This is enabled via model property *p3ptype*, based on Platform For Privacy Preferences (P3P[2]), a W3c recommendation that enables Web sites to express their privacy practices in a standard format that can be retrieved automatically and interpreted easily by user agents. P3P user agents will allow users to be informed of site practices (in both machine and human-readable formats) and to automate decision making based on these practices when appropriate. Thus, users need not read the privacy policies at every site they visit.

Property *p3ptype* holds a value of type xsd:string that describes the kind of data collected by the associated instance data node, based on the P3P data type system. The P3P data type system helps reconcile among different names that might be used for the same piece of data. XForms' authors, deploying large scale Web applications, are encouraged to use this feature so that users are made aware of the policies used to protect their personal data. This will in turn encourage users to provide such information when appropriate.

---

[2]http://www.w3.org/tr/p3p

5.11 XForms Model Properties at a Glance

We conclude this chapter with a summary of the various model properties and their role in the overall XForms application in Table 5.2. For each property, we give a brief review of the motivating use cases.

Table 5.2. XForms Model Properties at a Glance

Property	Description
relevant	• Model-based switching for conditional interfaces • Dynamically reveals appropriate portions of an interface • Enables controls based on state-of-instance data
required	• Conditionally makes fields *required*
readonly	• Conditionally edit data • Dynamic user interaction based on instance values
constraint	• Refines static schema constraints • Constrains values based on previous user interaction • Expresses cardinality constraints on node-sets
calculate	• Creates computational dependency among instance nodes • Automatically computes fields based on user input • Enables spreadsheet-like functionality within XForms
type	• Extends schema type definitions • Useful when the schema cannot be modified
p3ptype	• Holds P3P type information

CHAPTER 6

XForms Functions

6.1 Introduction

The previous chapter showed how XPath expressions can be used in calculating the values of certain form fields. When writing such expressions, it is useful to have a standard set of utility functions for performing common computations. As explained in Section 2.2, XPath expressions can use functions that are defined in the XPath specification. In addition, XPath makes it possible to define extension functions for use in languages that adopt XPath as the base expression language. XForms 1.0 defines a handful of such extension functions, and these will be described in the rest of this chapter along with motivating examples for each. We refer to this collection of functions as the XForms core function library. XForms authors can depend on the availability of all core XForms functions in addition to the predefined XPath functions.

XForms 1.0 uses XPath 1.0, which has a comparatively restrictive set of data types compared with XML Schema. XPath 1.0 defines only four basic types:

1. `boolean`
2. `number`
3. `string`
4. *nodeset*

XPath 2.0, currently under development, has support for the full set of XML Schema data types, and future versions of XForms will use the richer function libraries provided by XPath 2.0. When working with XForms 1.0, the restricted access to types in XPath 1.0 needs careful attention when working with XML Schema types such as xsd:date. Many of the extension functions provided by the XForms core function library are designed to hide some of these difficulties from the XForms author.

Functions in the XForms core can be classified according to the data types they operate on, and we will use this classification to organize the rest of this chapter into sections. In addition to the XForms core function library, XForms like XSLT 1.0[1] encourages experimentation by allowing authors and implementations to provide additional extension functions. Such extension functions, if used, must be declared via attribute *functions* on element ⟨**model**⟩. This enables XForms processors to check for the availability of all needed functions when loading a document, rather than encountering a fatal error during user interaction.

6.2 Boolean Functions

This section defines the various boolean functions provided by the XForms core function library.

6.2.1 Function *boolean-from-string*

Function *boolean-from-string* was added to the XForms core to ease the use of XML Schema's xsd:boolean type and to assist in correctly mapping the string representation of xsd:boolean to the appropriate logical value. XML Schema defines the string representations for the logical values true and false as shown in Table 6.1. XPath in turn represents *logical true* as true() and *logical false* as false().

Table 6.1. String Representation of Legal xsd:boolean Values

Logical Value	xsd:boolean	XPath
true	1 true	*true()*
false	0 false	*false()*

---

[1]http://www.w3.org/tr/xslt

Function *boolean-from-string* converts an `xsd:boolean` value to the correct XPath boolean value. This function is case-insensitive with respect to its argument and throws an error if called with an illegal `xsd:boolean` value. We used function *boolean-from-string* in Figure 4.26 when counting the number of open tasks with the expression

```
"count(//task[not(boolean-from-string(done))])"
```

The XPath boolean value returned by function *boolean-from-string* is negated via a call to XPath core function *not*. This predicate is in turn used to filter the set of nodes returned by XPath locator `//task`, and the resulting node-set is passed to XPath core function *count*.

6.2.2 Function *if*

XForms model property *calculate* enables the creation of instance data that is automatically computed as the user interacts with portions of a form. This functionality is often used to implement simple spreadsheet-like interfaces. In creating such interfaces, a common use case is to test for a specific condition and return one of two values depending on the value returned by the test condition.

XForms defines function *if* to enable this use case. Function *if* takes three `string` arguments; it evaluates the first argument as an XPath expression to compute a boolean value. If this evaluates to `true()`, the result of evaluating the second argument is returned; if it evaluates to `false()`, the function returns the result of evaluating its third argument.

Note that *if* is a function and not an *if statement* as found in programming languages like C or Java. This distinction is important to ensure that the expression language used in XForms does not turn into a programming language of its own. We use function *if* to compute the cost of shipping, as shown in Figure 6.1. For orders of $100 or more, shipping is free. For orders of less than $100, the user is charged a fixed percentage of the total cost for shipping and handling.

6.3 Number Functions

This section defines the various number functions provided by the XForms core function library. These functions were added to the XForms core because they were missing in the XPath core but deemed necessary for typical form-based applications. Some of these functions are being adopted by the XPath working group for inclusion in XPath 2.0.

```
<model id="iv" xmlns="http://www.w3.org/2002/xforms">
  <instance>
    <invoice xmlns="">
      <items><item/>...</items>
      <cost/><shipping/><total/>
  </invoice></instance>
  <bind  nodeset="/invoice">
    <bind nodeset="total" calculate="cost+shipping"/>
    <bind nodeset="shipping"
     calculate=
     'if(cost &gt; 100.00, "0.0", "cost * 0.05")'/>
  </bind>
</model>
```

Figure 6.1. Using function *if* to compute shipping cost.

6.3.1 Computing Minimum, Maximum, and Average

The XPath core function library defines a number of functions like *sum* that *reduce* a node-set by applying a given mathematical operation. XForms extends these with the following functions:

avg   Function *avg* computes the *average value* from a node-set. This average is computed by

1. Converting the string representation of each node in the node-set to a number,

2. Reducing the resulting set of numbers by applying function *sum* to *sum* these values, and

3. Dividing this sum by the number of elements in the node-set as computed by function *count*.

min   Function *min* computes the minimum value given a node-set. This minimum is computed by

1. Converting the string representation of each node in the node-set to a number and

2. Reducing this set by computing the *minimum* value.

```
<html xmlns="http://www.w3.org/1999/xhtml"
  xmlns:xf="http://www.w3.org/2002/xforms">
  <head><title>Census Report</title>
    <xf:model id="data">
      <xf:instance xmlns="">
        <census>
          <state><population/></state>
        </census></xf:instance>
    </xf:model></head>
    <body>
      <xf:group xmlns="http://www.w3.org/2002/xforms">
        <output value="min(/census/state/population)">
        <label>Smallest population</label></output>
        <output value="max(/census/state/population)">
        <label>Largest population</label></output>
        <output value="avg(/census/state/population)">
        <label>Avg state population</label></output>
      </xf:group></body>
  </html>
```

Figure 6.2. Functions *min*, *max*, and *avg* used in a census report.

max   Function *max* computes the maximum value given a node-set. This maximum is computed by

1. Converting the string representation of each node in the node-set to a number and
2. Reducing this set by computing the *maximum* value.

In Figure 6.2, we illustrate the use of these functions with a fragment from a census report.

6.3.2 Function *index* for Addressing ⟨repeat⟩ Structures

Function *index* takes a string argument that is the id of a ⟨**repeat**⟩ structure. It returns the current value of the *repeat index* for that ⟨**repeat**⟩ structure. We used function *index* in creating add, remove, and scroll controls in Figure 4.13 and Figure 4.23.

6.3.3 Function *count-non-empty*

The XPath core contains function *count* that returns the number of nodes in a node-set. XForms adds a *count-non-empty* function, which first reduces the input node-set by removing all *empty* nodes before applying function *count*. Here, a node is said to be *empty* if and only if the string representation of the contents of that node has length 0.

6.4 String Functions

XPath provides a standard set of functions for string manipulation, and these are felt to be adequate for forms-based applications. This section defines string function *property* provided by the XForms core function library.

Function *property* takes a single `string` argument that names a feature of an XForms implementation and returns a `string` value describing that feature. Possible values for the argument to function *property* along with the defined return values are shown in Table 6.2.

We illustrate the use of function *property* in Figure 6.3 with a sample that displays information about the XForms client that is processing the page.

When loaded into a browser that implements all features of XForms 1.0, this might display the output shown in Figure 6.4.

Table 6.2. Function *Property*—Arguments and Return Values

Argument	Return	Description
version	*1.0*	Specification Version
conformance-level	*full*	XForms Full
	basic	XForms Basic

```
<group xmlns="http://www.w3.org/2002/xforms">
   This XML powered web form uses XForms
   <output value="property('version')"/>
   and conforms to
   <output value="property('conformance-level')"/>
</group>
```

Figure 6.3. Displaying information about the XForms processor using function *property*.

```
<model id="tc" xmlns="http://www.w3.org/2002/xforms"
  xmlns:xsd="http://www.w3.org/2001/XMLSchema">
  <instance>
    <tc xmlns="">...<stamp xsi:type="xsd:date"/></tc>
  </instance>
  <submission id="submit-tc">
    <action>
      <setvalue ref="/tc/stamp" value="now()"/>
      <message>Submitted your time-card  with
        time-stamp <output ref="/tc/stamp"/>
    </message></action>
</submission></model>
```

Figure 6.4. Time-stamping a time card using function *now*.

This XML powered Web form uses XForms 1.0 and is being displayed by an XForms user agent that conforms to profile XForms *full*.

6.5 Date-time Functions

This section defines the various date-time functions provided by the XForms core function library. The mismatch between the data types available in XML Schema and XPath is most noticeable when working with values of type xsd:date and xsd:duration or any of their derived data types. This discrepancy is being addressed in XPath 2.0. XForms 1.0 provides an interim solution by defining date-time functions in the XForms core to meet the most common use cases encountered when creating electronic forms.

The date-time functions in the XForms core accept string representation of the appropriate schema types and return a numeric XPath result. They have been designed for use within XPath expressions that appear within property *calculate* or *constraint*. Note that all of these functions take legal string representations of the underlying XML Schema type such as xsd:date or xsd:dateTime.

days-from-date   This function takes a string representing a value of type date or dateTime (see XML Schema data types in Table 2.3) and returns the number of days since January 1, 1970.

The minute, hour, and seconds components are ignored if called with a dateTime value; it returns a negative number if the value represents a date before January 1, 1970. As an example,

```
days-from-date('1971-01-01')
```

returns 365.

seconds-from-dateTime This function is similar, except that it accepts a string representing a `dateTime` and returns the number of seconds since January 1, 1970. The value returned is numeric (possibly including a fractional part). As an example,

```
seconds-from-dateTime(
'1970-01-02T00:00:00Z')
```

returns 86400.0, the number of seconds in one day.

seconds This function takes a string representing a subtype of `duration`, for example, the duration of a meeting. See type `duration` in Table 2.3. It returns the number of seconds in the specified duration. As an example,

```
seconds('P1DT0H0M0.0S')
```

returns 86400.0, the number of seconds in a 24-hour day.

months This function is similar, except that it returns a number of months in the specified time period. As an example,

```
months('P1Y0M')
```

returns 12.

We used function *days-from-date* in model property *constraint* in Figure 5.8. Date and time functions are most useful when creating XForms applications that manipulate XML documents dealing with time values, for example, travel bookings or task lists.

6.5.1 Function *now*

Online transactions may need to capture the time at which a transaction was completed. This can be done by including the current time in the submitted instance. The XForms core library defines a *now* function that returns the string representation of the current time as represented by type `xsd:dateTime`.

The value returned by this function can be used in a variety of use cases, for example, to time-stamp data that is being submitted (see Figure 6.4). This is achieved by creating an action handler[2] within element ⟨**model**⟩ that stores the value returned by *now* in the instance to be submitted.

6.6 Node-set Functions

The XForms core function library provides function *instance* for use when the XForms model contains more than one ⟨**instance**⟩ element. Multiple instances in a model are useful in forms that wish to store temporary values that are not submitted. Function *instance* can be used within binding expressions to address instance nodes from an ⟨**instance**⟩ different from the one that contains the *current context node* but belonging to the *same* model as the ⟨**instance**⟩ containing the current context node.

Function *instance* takes a string that identifies the instance to address. If it succeeds in locating an ⟨**instance**⟩ with attribute *id* equal to the specified string argument, it returns a node-set containing the root node of that ⟨**instance**⟩. In all other cases, it returns an empty node-set. The effect of returning the root node has a subtle but significant effect on the use of this function within binding expressions, and we illustrate this using the example shown in Figure 6.5 after first detailing the process by which binding expressions are evaluated. In addition, refer to the examples shown in Figure 4.12 where we used function *instance* to address nodes in the catalog while iterating items in the shopping cart instance.

6.6.1 Binding Expressions: The Full Story

Throughout this book, we have used relative and absolute XPath locators in binding expressions. To keep the explanation simple, we have glossed over some minor details, but now it's time to reveal the full story.

As explained in Section 2.2, the *current* context node is key to determining the result of evaluating an XPath expression. When working with an XForms document that contains one or more models, binding expressions use attribute *model* in determining the ⟨**model**⟩ to address; if attribute *model* is absent, we default to the *first* ⟨**model**⟩ in document order.

Next, the binding expression needs to determine the ⟨**instance**⟩ to address. Again, we default to the first ⟨**instance**⟩ in the model, as seen in this section. This can be overridden by explicitly naming the ⟨**instance**⟩ via a call to function *instance*.

---

[2]The full complement of action handlers provided by XForms will be described in Chapter 7.

```
<html xmlns="http://www.w3.org/1999/xhtml">
  <head>
    <model xmlns="http://www.w3.org/2002/xforms">
      <instance id="i1">
        <root xmlns="">
          <child>As easy as   3.14159265359</child>
      </root></instance>
  </model></head>
  <body>
    <group xmlns="http://www.w3.org/2002/xforms">
      <label>The three controls shown below all
        address node /root/child of instance i1
        and display the same message, As easy as
        3.14159265359.</label>
      <!--absolute locator:  first instance-->
      <output ref="/root/child"/>
      <!--relative locator default context is root-->
      <output ref="child"/>
      <!-- Use instance function -->
    <output ref="instance('i1')/child"/></group>
  </body></html>
```

Figure 6.5. Using *instance* to address multiple instances in an XForms model.

Finally, we need to determine the *context node* for XPath locators addressing nodes in this instance; XForms sets the *root* node of the selected 〈**instance**〉 as the default context.

Applying these rules to the model shown in Figure 6.5, we see that the three binding expressions shown in that example all address the *same* node.

/root/child	This uses the first 〈**model**〉 in document order and the first 〈**instance**〉 in that 〈**model**〉. Since we have an absolute locator, we do not need to locate the *context node* any further in determining the result of evaluating this expression.
child	The 〈**model**〉 and 〈**instance**〉 are determined as before. This is a *relative* XPath locator, so to evaluate it we need first to establish the *current* context node. XForms uses the *root* node of the 〈**instance**〉

in use, in this case ⟨**root**⟩. Expression `child` is evaluated with `/root` as the current context and returns the same node as the absolute XPath locator detailed earlier.

`instance('i1')/child`   The model is chosen as before. This time the locator uses function *instance*; it is called to locate the instance to use. This function call locates element ⟨**instance**⟩ having attribute *id* with value `i1`. It returns a node-set containing the *root* node of this instance, `/root`. This ⟨**root**⟩ node is now used as the context node for evaluating the remainder of the expression. The result is element ⟨**child**⟩.

6.7 XForms Functions at a Glance

We conclude this chapter with a summary of the various XForms functions defined in this chapter; see Table 6.3. For each function, we give its argument type, return type, and a brief description.

Table 6.3. XForms Functions at a Glance

Function	Argument	Return	Description
avg	node-set	number	Average
boolean-from-string	string	boolean	Type coercion
count-non-empty	node-set	number	Count nodes
days-from-date	string	number	Days in epoch
if	boolean, string, string	string	Conditional
index	string	number	Repeat index
instance	string	node-set	Locate instance
max	node-set	number	Maximum
min	node-set	number	Minimum
months	string	number	Months
now		string	Current time
property	string	string	Feature value
seconds	string	number	Seconds
seconds-from-dateTime	string	number	Seconds

CHAPTER 7

XForms Actions

7.1 Introduction

A key goal when designing XForms 1.0 was to enable common online forms' functionality without resorting to extensive scripting via languages like Javascript. HTML forms that make extensive use of Javascript have been a very good vehicle for deploying highly interactive user experiences on the Web. The ability to access the Document Object Model (DOM) from within scripts has also made it easy to experiment and innovate on the Web.

However, all this comes at a price; user interaction that depends heavily on scripting becomes difficult to deploy on a variety of different devices and environments. In addition, HTML pages that rely heavily on scripting are hard to maintain. XForms 1.0 attempts to minimize the need for scripting by creating declarative XML event handlers that cover common use cases. The realization is that scripting will always be a convenient means for innovating on the Web; XForms codifies those scripting innovations that have survived the test of time on the Web to prove truly useful into a set of declarative handlers that can be implemented reliably on a variety of platforms.

We have encountered some XForms actions in earlier examples, for example, when creating add, delete, and scroll controls within the shopping cart and task list examples in Figure 4.13 and Figure 4.23. The rest of this chapter defines the various XForms actions along with examples as appropriate.

XForms action handlers are designed to be used in conjunction with XML Events described in Section 2.3. The XForms processing model is defined declaratively in terms of events and actions. Toward this end, XForms 1.0 defines a standard set of events described in Chapter 8. These events, together with the actions defined in this chapter, give the XForms author complete access to the XForms processing model from within XML markup. A key consequence of this design is that authors can *hook* into the XForms processing model at a number of predetermined points to attach *custom behavior* via specified actions. Such custom behaviors extend the look and feel provided by XForms user interface controls in a consistent and predictable manner.

Like the user interface controls, XForms action handlers have been designed to capture high-level semantics of a given action and to leave the actual implementation to the run-time environment. The resulting design is significantly more accessible than earlier Web technologies that relied exclusively on scripting.

7.2 Declarative Event Handlers

Declarative action handlers capture the high-level meaning of the action to perform. The details of how the action is implemented in a given client or device is left to the underlying implementation. This allows XForms authors to focus on the higher-level aspects of the interaction they create; it also ensures that such interaction is easily deployed to a variety of devices and environments.

XForms action handlers encode the following pieces of information:

Eventing   Event wiring using the facilities provided by XML Events described in Section 2.3.2

Binding   XForms binding expression that connects the handler to the underlying model where appropriate

Arguments   Arguments that need to be passed to the handler

XForms action handlers are used within control ⟨**trigger**⟩ as seen in numerous examples in this book. The type of information that needs to be passed to a handler is different for each action based on the functionality it provides. The description that follows will focus on these differences; the eventing attributes common to all XForms actions will not be mentioned explicitly in the description for each action handler.

The mechanism provided by XML Events is used to connect events to the handlers they invoke. The actions performed by these declarative handlers can in turn be described in terms of the events they dispatch. The description of the actions in this chapter will mention this correspondence between actions and the events they dispatch where appropriate. The complete mapping between XForms actions and XForms events will be presented in Chapter 8 after we have covered the events defined in XForms 1.0.

7.2.1 Action ⟨setfocus⟩

Action ⟨**setfocus**⟩ is used to move focus to a specified XForms control. Element ⟨**setfocus**⟩ uses attribute *control* to identify the control that will receive focus. The value of this attribute is an `idref` of an XForms user interface control.

Action ⟨**setfocus**⟩ can be used to implement custom navigation within an on-line form. It can also be used to enable accessibility related functions such as quick navigation to a specified control.

7.2.2 Action ⟨setvalue⟩

Action ⟨**setvalue**⟩ can be used to set a specific value in the ⟨**instance**⟩. Attributes of element ⟨**setvalue**⟩ specify what value to set and where that value should be assigned. Thus, action ⟨**setvalue**⟩ can be thought of as an assignment statement, and its attributes can be classified as specifying the two sides of this assignment:

LHS The left side of the assignment is specified using XForms binding attributes. This is consistent with the mechanism used when binding controls to the ⟨**instance**⟩; in fact, the various user interface controls can be viewed as performing an implicit ⟨**setvalue**⟩ action when the user enters a value.

RHS The value to assign can be specified in one of two ways:

1. Specified via an XPath expression using attribute *value*. The expression will be evaluated, and the result becomes the right side of the assignment. Notice that using an XPath locator to address portions of the instance data can be used to advantage in copying values from one portion of the data model to another. Action ⟨**setvalue**⟩ assigns the `string` result of evaluating attribute *value*. Contrast this with element ⟨**copy**⟩ that can be used to copy entire subtrees.

2. The right side of the assignment can be specified as text content of element ⟨**setvalue**⟩.

If neither attribute *value* nor text content is present, the effect is to set the value of the selected node to the empty string. If both are present, attribute *value* is used.

7.2.3 Action ⟨load⟩

Action ⟨**load**⟩ is used to load a specified resource, for example, an external document specified by its URL. The *resource* to load is specified in one of two mutually exclusive ways:

Instance The URI to load can be located in the instance data by specifying an XForms binding expression.

XLink XLink[1] is a W3C Recommendation for specifying extensible linking behavior. This mechanism can be used to specify the resource to load and the behavior that is exhibited in loading that resource via attributes *resource* and *show*.

7.2.4 Action ⟨send⟩

We described user interface control ⟨**submit**⟩ and the associated submit processing in Section 3.8. Control ⟨**submit**⟩ achieves the functionality described by implicitly invoking action ⟨**send**⟩. The submission to invoke is specified via attribute *submission* of action ⟨**send**⟩, and its meaning is the same as the attribute of the same name on control ⟨**submit**⟩.

Having access to submit processing via an explicit action handler has a number of advantages when creating rich user experiences. As an example, XForms authors can create an *implicit* submit control by invoking action ⟨**send**⟩ when the user finishes interacting with a given control.

We illustrate such *implicit* submission in Figure 7.1 where we attach action ⟨**send**⟩ to control ⟨**input**⟩ used to collect the user's id. When the user completes this field, the resulting **DOMActivate** event invokes the attached ⟨**send**⟩ action. The submission performs a lookup of the user's subscription information, and the results are reflected in the user interface. This is achieved by specifying a value of instance for attribute *replace* in element ⟨**submission**⟩.

Following we enumerate the sequence of events and actions for the example shown in Figure 7.1:

1. _____

[1] http://www.w3.org/tr/xlink

```
<html xmlns="http://www.w3.org/1999/xhtml"
  xmlns:ev="http://www.w3.org/2001/xml-events"
  xmlns:xf="http://www.w3.org/2002/xforms">
<head>
  <xf:model id="profile" schema="person.xsd">
    <xf:instance xmlns="" id="p1">
    <person><id/>...</person></xf:instance>
    <submission id="lookup" replace="instance"
    action="http://examples.com/person/lookup"/>
</xf:model></head>
<body>
  <group xmlns="http://www.w3.org/2002/xforms">
    <input ref="/person/id"><label>User ID</label>
      <help>...</help>
      <hint>If subscribed, providing your ID will
      display  your current profile.</hint>
      <send ev:event="DOMActivate"
      submission="lookup"/></input>
      <!-- UI bound to <person>...</person>-->
  </group>
</body></html>
```

Figure 7.1. Reflecting the result of an automatic lookup.

User enters value for ⟨**id**⟩.

2. Completing the entry; for example, pressing enter raises event
   DOMActivate.

3. The event is dispatched according to the rules defined by DOM2 Events and
   outlined in Figure 2.1.

4. The event is handled by action ⟨**send**⟩. Action ⟨**send**⟩ causes submit
   processing as declared in element ⟨**submission**⟩. This is initiated by
   dispatching event **xforms-submit** to the specified ⟨**submission**⟩ element.

5. The current ⟨**instance**⟩ is serialized and transmitted as specified by element
   ⟨**submission**⟩.

6. This performs a lookup, and the result is an XML instance that holds the
   user's current profile.

7. This XML instance is returned as the server response. The value of attribute *replace* is *instance*; consequently, the server response is interpreted as an update to the instance data.

8. The updated instance is *loaded* into the form; as a result, user interface controls bound to the instance data are updated to display the newly received values.

Notice that action ⟨**send**⟩ performs its action by dispatching event **xforms-submit** to the desired ⟨**submission**⟩ element. An immediate consequence of this design is that the XForms author can *hook* custom behavior that is invoked before the submission takes place. We saw an example of this in Figure 6.5 where we attached action ⟨**message**⟩ to element ⟨**submission**⟩.

7.2.5 Action ⟨reset⟩

Action ⟨**reset**⟩ can be used to clear all values entered by the user and to restore the instance data to its initial state. This action affects only the specified model and can therefore be used in an XForms application with multiple models. The id of the ⟨**model**⟩ to reset is specified via attribute *model*. Action ⟨**reset**⟩ dispatches an **xforms-reset** event to the specified model. Thus, like the rest of the XForms processing model, authors can *hook* custom behavior to reset processing by attaching an event listener that responds to event **xforms-reset**. An accessibility application might use this feature to advantage in alerting the user that the form is about to be cleared.

7.2.6 Action ⟨message⟩

Action ⟨**message**⟩ *displays* (or otherwise conveys) the specified message to the user. The message to convey can be specified in multiple ways as with action ⟨**setvalue**⟩.

Inline   The message can be provided inline as text content within body of element ⟨**message**⟩.

Instance   The message can be placed in the instance data and addressed via an XForms binding expression.

External   The message can be located in an external resource that is specified via XLink.

Required attribute *level* specifies the behavior to use when displaying the message. XForms specifies the following predefined values for attribute *level*:

ephemeral   The message is displayed for a short duration.
modal   Explicit user action is needed to clear the message.
modeless   This is used in visual environments for displaying pop-up help.

As with attributes like *appearance*, implementors can experiment with other values for attribute *level* as long as these values are in a specific namespace.

Notice that the ⟨**help**⟩ and ⟨**hint**⟩ facilities provided by all XForms user interface controls is syntactic sugar for attaching action ⟨**message**⟩ to the corresponding events as follows:

Element	Event
⟨help⟩	xforms-help
⟨hint⟩	xforms-hint

We demonstrate this equivalence in Figure 7.2 by creating two instances of the same input control. The first uses elements ⟨**help**⟩ and ⟨**hint**⟩; the second encodes the same information via action ⟨**message**⟩.

```
<group xmlns="http://www.w3.org/2002/xforms"
  xmlns:ev="http://www.w3.org/2001/xml-events">
  <!--Using elements help and hint -->
  <input ref="age"><label>Age</label>
    <help>Specify your age as a number.</help>
  <hint>How old are you?</hint></input>
  <!-- Using  action message -->
  <input ref="age"><label>Age</label>
    <message ev:event="xforms-help" level="modal">
    Specify your age as a number.</message>
    <message ev:event="xforms-hint" level="modeless">
    How old are you? </message>
</input></group>
```

Figure 7.2. Action ⟨**message**⟩ used to implement ⟨**help**⟩ and ⟨**hint**⟩.

7.2.7 Action ⟨action⟩

Action ⟨**action**⟩ can be used to group handlers when more than one action is to be attached for a specified event. Thus, its role is similar to that played by braces in languages like C and Java when creating compound statements. Actions enclosed in ⟨**action**⟩ have one additional special behavior: Steps performed by the XForms processing model such as rebuilding dependency relations is deferred while the actions inside an ⟨**action**⟩ grouping are invoked. See Section 7.2.9 for a list of such actions. This deferred processing is relevant in advanced applications where it can be advantageous to recompute interdependencies after a group of changes has been propagated to the model.

The role of action ⟨**action**⟩ is to attach a group of handlers to a single event. The event to *listen for* must be specified on element ⟨**action**⟩, *not* via event attributes on any of the contained actions. The reason for this is the default rules used by module XML Events in determining the *observer* (see Section 2.3). We illustrate this with an example in Figure 7.3.

The example contains a ⟨**trigger**⟩ control that implements a specialized *insert* control. A new node is inserted into a ⟨**repeat**⟩ collection, and the value of the newly inserted node is set to 9. Notice that, in this example, XML Events attribute *ev:event must* be placed on element ⟨**action**⟩. Placing this attribute on either of the contained actions would have no effect. This is because the example relies on the defaulting of XML Events attributes *observer* and *handler*. As defined in the XML Events specification, if both *observer* and *handler* are omitted, then the parent is the observer. Thus, placing attribute *ev:event* on the children of element ⟨**action**⟩ would cause element ⟨**action**⟩ to become the *observer* for the individual events.

```
<group xmlns="http://www.w3.org/2002/xforms"
  xmlns:ev="http://www.w3.org/2001/xml-events">
  <trigger>
    <label>Add Special Item</label>
    <action ev:event="DOMActivate">
      <insert nodeset="cart" at="index('cart')"
      position="after"/>
      <setvalue ref="cart[index('cart')]" value="9"/>
  </action></trigger>
</group>
```

Figure 7.3. Insert control that sets the value of the inserted node.

Consequently, these actions will never be triggered, since events arrive at element ⟨**trigger**⟩, not at element ⟨**action**⟩.

7.2.8 Action ⟨dispatch⟩

Action ⟨**dispatch**⟩ enables the XForms author to *dispatch* explicit events during the course of user interaction. As mentioned earlier, the operation of the various declarative actions can be described in terms of the events they dispatch; in fact, many of these actions can be thought of as syntactic sugar for action ⟨**dispatch**⟩ with the appropriate arguments. Action ⟨**dispatch**⟩ takes the following items of information:

name   Names the event to dispatch
target   Identifies the *target node* to which the event should be dispatched

Events that are defined as part of the XForms processing model—see Chapter 8—start with the prefix **xforms-**. These events have special *bubble* and *cancel* semantics as defined in the XForms 1.0 specification. For all other event types, the XForms author can specify *bubble* and *cancel* behavior via the XML Events attributes of the same name.

7.2.9 Invoking XForms Processing

The XForms processing model is responsible for keeping the rendered user interface in sync with the underlying data model. As the user interacts with the XForms application, values in the instance get updated, and this triggers default XForms processing which involves the following steps:

Rebuild   Rebuild dependency relations among the nodes in the instance data.
Recalculate   Using the updated dependency relationships, recalculate the value of instance data nodes that need updating.
Revalidate   Ensure that the updated instance satisfies all static and dynamic validity constraints specified in the model.
Refresh   Refresh the user interface by reflecting all updates to the instance data in the presentation layer. This includes refreshing all controls whose underlying data has changed, as well as displaying the necessary *alert* messages for invalid instance data.

Table 7.1. Events and Corresponding
Actions That Invoke XForms Processing

Action	Event
⟨rebuild⟩	xforms-rebuild
⟨recalculate⟩	xforms-recalculate
⟨revalidate⟩	xforms-revalidate
⟨refresh⟩	xforms-refresh

By default, the XForms processor invokes the above steps as the user interacts with the various user interface controls. However, authors can explicitly invoke these steps via declarative action handlers. These actions, enumerated as follows, have the same names as the processing step they invoke. In addition to the standard eventing attributes, each of these actions takes the id of the (**model**) to process via attribute *model*. When these actions are enclosed within action ⟨**action**⟩, their processing is *deferred*.

⟨**rebuild**⟩   Rebuilds the dependency relations for the specified model
⟨**recalculate**⟩   Recalculates all instance nodes having property *calculate* in the specified model
⟨**revalidate**⟩   Revalidates instance data in the specified model
⟨**refresh**⟩   Redisplays all user interface controls that bind to updated instance data in the specified model

Each of these actions invokes the specified processing step by *dispatching* the appropriate event to the specified model; the correspondence between these declarative actions and events is shown in Table 7.1.

7.2.10 Actions ⟨insert⟩, ⟨delete⟩, and ⟨setindex⟩

XForms defines three special declarative handlers for use with ⟨**repeat**⟩. These action handlers are described in Section 4.3.4 and are summarized following for completeness.

⟨**insert**⟩   Enables insertion of a node when using ⟨**repeat**⟩, for example, adding a new item to a shopping cart
⟨**delete**⟩   Enables deletion of a node when using ⟨**repeat**⟩, for example, removing an item from a shopping cart
⟨**setindex**⟩   Used to scroll through the underlying nodes when using ⟨**repeat**⟩

7.3 XForms Actions at a Glance

We conclude this chapter with a table summarizing the declarative action handlers defined by XForms. Note that host languages like XHTML typically add their own action handlers, for example, element ⟨**script**⟩ in XHTML for holding action handlers written in a scripting language.

Table 7.2. XForms Actions at a Glance

Action	Description
⟨**setfocus**⟩	Move focus
⟨**setvalue**⟩	Assign value
⟨**load**⟩	Load URI
⟨**send**⟩	Initiate submission
⟨**reset**⟩	Clear form
⟨**message**⟩	Display message
⟨**action**⟩	Group handlers
⟨**dispatch**⟩	Send event
⟨**rebuild**⟩	Rebuild dependencies
⟨**recalculate**⟩	Recompute values
⟨**revalidate**⟩	Revalidate all values
⟨**refresh**⟩	Update user interface
⟨**insert**⟩	Insert node
⟨**delete**⟩	Delete node
⟨**setindex**⟩	Scroll ⟨**repeat**⟩

CHAPTER 8

XForms Events

8.1 Introduction

We conclude our description of the XForms architecture and its inner workings with a description of the events and event flow that define the XForms processing model. The normative definition of this processing model is given in the XForms Processing Model (XPM[1]); that description has been written explicitly with implementors in mind to ensure interoperability.

The purpose of this chapter is to give a gentle introduction to the XForms processing model with a view to helping authors understand how they can leverage the XForms functionality in their own Web applications. To this end, we will cover only those aspects of the processing model that are most likely to be accessed by Web authors and point the XForms implementor and other interested readers to the XForms specification for the precise details.

XForms markup and the processing that is applied to that markup have both been designed to be *hosted* within a variety of *Web containers*. We have used XHTML as the host markup language for many of the examples in this book. This aspect of hosting XForms markup describes only the syntax of XForms contained within XHTML documents. The *behavior* of such XHTML documents that host XForms constructs is defined by the model given in the standard DOM Level 2 Events specification and exposed to the XML author by module XML Events

---

[1] http://www.w3.org/tr/xforms/slice4.html

(see Section 2.3). Thus, to complete the picture regarding the behavior of XForms constructs hosted in a DOM2-compliant XHTML container, all that remains is a description of how these various XForms constructs interact with the DOM2 events flow implemented by standard XHTML-aware Web browsers.

Thus, the description of the XForms Processing Model reduces to enumerating the following aspects of eventing in the context of XForms constructs:

What Define the various XForms-specific events that can be raised
When Specify at what points in the XForms processing model these events are raised
Where Specify where these events are targeted
Who Define the various actors responsible for handling these events
How Specify how these actors handle these events

We will organize the rest of this chapter by grouping XForms events based on *when* and *how* they are raised. Using this classification, XForms events can be grouped into the following classes:

Initialization Events raised as the various XForms components are initialized as an XForms document is being loaded (see Section 8.2). These initialization events are of interest mostly to XForms implementors. Some advanced XForms applications might find it useful to *hook* special behavior by attaching custom handlers to these events.
Interaction Events raised by user interaction (see Section 8.3). These events are raised by user interaction *gestures*, for example, a request for help, and will be of interest to XForms authors when creating rich user interaction.
Notification Events raised by the XForms processing model to trigger different steps in XForms processing (see Section 8.4). Events in this class are of interest to XForms authors when attaching custom behavior at specific points in the XForms processing model.
Errors Notifications raised when specific types of error conditions are encountered. Events in this class are of interest mostly to implementors and are enumerated following for completeness.

xforms-binding-exception Fatal error in evaluating a binding expression
xforms-link-exception Fatal error traversing a link

xforms-link-error	Recoverable error while traversing a link
xforms-compute-exception	Fatal error in a computation

8.2 Initialization Events

XForms initialization events are raised as the XForms document is being loaded by the host processor. Just as XForms markup is contained within a host language, for example, XHTML, the XForms processor can be *contained* within a processor for the host language. In this framework, XForms initialization events define the mechanism by which the host, an XHTML browser, interfaces with the XForms processor to initialize the XForms model and user interface.

The initialization process consists of setting up the XForms model, followed by initializing all XForms user interface controls that bind to the model. Initialization in turn consists of two phases: a construct phase where things are created in memory and an initialization phase where these newly created objects are initialized.

Following, we give a short description of these events. The details of the processing steps that occur for each of these events are not covered since that is of interest mostly to XForms implementors and are already described in the XForms specification. Notice that all initialization events are targeted at the corresponding ⟨**model**⟩ and that they *must* be handled at the model; that is, these events cannot be *canceled* at the model.

xforms-model-construct

This event is raised for each ⟨**model**⟩ in the document. The event is targeted at element ⟨**model**⟩ and *must* be handled there; it cannot be *canceled*. The event is handled by loading all specified resources, such as schema definitions and instance declarations. If no error results, processing continues to the next stage.

Element ⟨**instance**⟩ is processed to construct an in-memory representation of the XML instance that holds values collected during user interaction. Model properties declared by element ⟨**bind**⟩ are applied to this instance.

Processing concludes by applying standard XForms processing steps of

Rebuild	Rebuild dependency relations
Recalculate	Recalculate fields that need updating
Revalidate	Validate the instance

When these processing steps are completed, the XForms model is initialized and ready to be populated during user interaction.

xforms-model-construct-done This event is raised when all models are initialized and ready for user interaction. In response to this event, processing continues by initializing the user interface that binds to the model. Initializing the user interface results in all user interface controls being bound to the instance data. This initialization consists of

1. *Wiring* the control to the instance using the specified binding expression.

2. *Refreshing* the presentation of the control to reflect the state of the underlying instance data. Controls are refreshed by dispatching event **xforms-refresh**.

xforms-ready This notification event is sent to each model to indicate that the user interface has been initialized.

xforms-model-destruct This event is raised when an XForms processor is about to be shut down and is available for clean-up processing. It is targeted at the ⟨**model**⟩ and *must* be handled there.

Once all of these initialization steps have completed without an error condition, the XForms application is ready to process user interaction events.

8.3 Interaction Events

Once the XForms model and user interface have been initialized, the stage is set for user interaction. As the user interacts with the various controls and user interface constructs described in Chapter 3 and Chapter 4, the data model and user interface are kept synchronized by the XForms processor.

8.3.1 XForms Processing Events

This model-view synchronization is achieved by implementing the *rebuild, recalculate, revalidate*, and *refresh* loop in response to user interaction events that change values in the data model. We encountered these operations as XForms actions in Section 7.2.9; these raise the corresponding XForms events shown in Table 7.1. All of these events are targeted at ⟨**model**⟩ to be affected. Following, we briefly outline the processing that takes place as these steps are performed.

The goal of the XForms processing model is to maintain consistency between the user interface (the view) and the underlying data model. Providing new values via controls bound to the instance data results in these new values being stored in the instance. This triggers the XForms processing loop to actuate the following steps:

Rebuild   User interaction may have added or deleted nodes in the instance, and the result of this change may have affected the dependency relations that were computed earlier. This step rebuilds the dependency graph that records interdependencies among nodes in the instance data that are the result of model properties, such as *relevant* and *calculate* (see Chapter 5).

Recalculate Using the updated dependency graph, the XForms processor recomputes the values and state of instance nodes affected by model properties. This results in recomputing the various dynamic model properties described in Chapter 5.

Revalidate   The updated instance is revalidated against the static and dynamic validity constraints defined by the model.

Refresh   The newly computed state information is communicated to the user interface that is *bound* to instances in the model. This update includes

1. Reflecting new data values in the presentation of the user interface controls that *bind* to these values, and

2. Reflecting the updated setting of model properties.

Event **xforms-refresh** communicates this updated state to the user interface by dispatching notification events detailed in Section 8.4.

8.3.2 Navigation Events

Navigation events are dispatched in response to user actions that direct the browser displaying the XForms document to *navigate* among the various user interface controls. XForms navigation events are the mechanism by which the browser keeps the presentation synchronized with the XForms processing model. This synchronization is essential to ensure that user interface controls and aggregation constructs such as ⟨**repeat**⟩ and ⟨**switch**⟩ exhibit their expected behavior.

Event **xforms-focus** corresponds to XForms action ⟨**setfocus**⟩ covered in Section 7.2.1; that action achieves its effect by dispatching event **xforms-setfocus** to the specified user interface control. The result is to give input focus to the specified control. This event is targeted at the control that should receive focus; it *must* be handled at the control; that is, this event cannot *bubble*. In addition, standard DOM2 notification events **DOMFocusIn** and **DOMFocusOut** can be used to advantage in attaching special behavior to XForms controls, for example, an accessibility aid might use these to track focus changes.

Event **xforms-focus** and the associated ⟨**setfocus**⟩ action enable moving the focus to any user interface control. Events **xforms-next** and **xforms-previous** enable sequential navigation through the various controls in an XForms application. The navigation sequence defaults to document order and can be influenced by attribute *navindex* (see Section 3.2.4). XForms user agents can implement sequential navigation by dispatching event **xforms-previous** and **xforms-next** in response to the appropriate navigation keys, for example, `tab` and `shift-tab`.

8.3.3 Help Events

The user can request help explicitly, for example, by pressing a *help* key or implicitly, for example, by hovering over a control in a visual interface or by not responding within a specified timeout when using a voice interface. Such user actions raise events **xforms-help** and **xforms-hint** respectively. These events are targeted at the *current* user interface control, that is, the control that has input focus.

As described in Section 3.2.1, user interface controls capture the metadata needed to display help and tooltips via elements ⟨**help**⟩ and ⟨**hint**⟩. As shown in Figure 7.2, these elements handle events **xforms-help** and **xforms-hint**. These events can *bubble*; that is, a form control can delegate the handling of these events to one of its parents. Alternatively, a control may choose to handle these events by displaying the available help and to allow the event to *bubble* to the parent that might be able to provide additional contextual feedback.

8.3.4 Submit and Reset

XForms events **xforms-submit** and **xforms-reset** correspond to actions ⟨**send**⟩ and ⟨**reset**⟩, respectively. The former is targeted at element ⟨**submission**⟩ that is specified by action ⟨**send**⟩; the latter is targeted at the ⟨**model**⟩ being reset as specified by action ⟨**reset**⟩. Both of these events may be *canceled* and are allowed to *bubble*.

Event **xforms-submit** is handled by initiating submit processing as described in Section 3.8. Event **xforms-reset** results in the instance data within the specified ⟨**model**⟩ being reset to its initial state.

8.4 Notification Events

Interaction events are raised as a result of explicit user action, for example, changing a value or navigating to a user interface control. In contrast, notification events are raised by the XForms processor to signal changes of state that require other processing steps to be initiated. Notification events provide a useful *hook* for XForms authors to attach custom behaviors. Below, we group these various notification events based on their function.

8.4.1 Setting Values

User input provided via XForms controls is *finalized*, that is, propagated to the bound instance when the user *activates* the control. The specific user action that activates a control varies, based on the user interface control as well as on the device in use. As an example, a desktop browser might use the pressing of the `enter` key to activate an input control. All such *activation* raises event **DOMActivate**, and this event provides a platform-neutral means for attaching custom behavior to be triggered when a control is activated. We used this event in attaching action ⟨**send**⟩ in Figure 7.1 to trigger an automatic lookup. This event is targeted at the user interface control to activate; the event can be *canceled* or allowed to *bubble*.

Event **xforms-value-changed** is raised when the value is finalized and can be used to create custom controls that alert the user to such state changes, for example, by triggering an action that speaks a confirmatory message.

8.4.2 Select and Deselect Notifications

XForms defines events **xforms-select** and **xforms-deselect** that are raised in response to user actions that result in selection and deselection. XForms selection controls ⟨**select1**⟩ and ⟨**select**⟩ allow the user to *select* from a set of values (see Section 3.4). Both of these controls use common element ⟨**item**⟩ to specify the alternatives in the case of static selections and element ⟨**itemset**⟩ when creating dynamic selections. User interaction with static and dynamic selections raises events **xforms-select** and **xforms-deselect**. The events are targeted at the *item* that is being selected or deselected.

Advanced XForms applications can attach actions to these events to update other portions of the interface automatically as the user changes the state of controls ⟨select⟩ or ⟨select1⟩. As an example, consider an online bookstore that displays a list of authors and the list of books by a selected author. The XForms author can create a dynamic end-user experience by attaching an implicit ⟨send⟩ action to event xforms-select for the author list control. This results in the displayed list of books being automatically updated whenever the user selects a different author (see Figure 8.1).

```
<html xmlns="http://www.w3.org/1999/xhtml"
  xmlns:ev="http://www.w3.org/2001/xml-events"
  xmlns:xf="http://www.w3.org/2002/xforms">
  <head><title>Book Catalog</title>
    <model id="books" schema="bookstore.xsd">
      <instance id="authors" src="authors.xml"/>
      <instance id="s" xmlns="">
        <shelf>
          <author/>
          <books><book>...</book></books>
      </shelf></instance>
      <submission id="update" replace="instance"
        ref="instance('s')"
      action="http://example.com/bookstore/lookup"/>
  </model></head>
  <body xmlns="http://www.w3.org/2002/xforms">
    <select1 ref="instance('s')/author">
      <label>Select Author</label>
      <itemset ref="instance('authors')/author">
        <label ref="."/><value ref="@author-id"/>
        <send ev:event="xforms-select"
        submission="update"/>
    </itemset></select1>
    <table>
      <tr repeat-nodeset="instance('s')/books/book">
      ...</tr>
</table></body></html>
```

Figure 8.1. Dynamically updating a book list as authors are selected.

Notice that this usage is similar to the automated profile lookup demonstrated in Figure 7.1.

These events are also raised when the user changes the *selected* ⟨**case**⟩ in interacting with a conditional interface created via construct ⟨**switch**⟩ (see Section 4.2). In this situation, the selected ⟨**case**⟩ receives event **xforms-select**; the previously selected ⟨**case**⟩ receives event **xforms-deselect**. XForms authors can use this to attach additional custom behavior to such dynamic interfaces; as an example, a speech-enabling extension might trigger a spoken message that speaks the ⟨**label**⟩ of the ⟨**case**⟩ that got selected.

8.4.3 Interacting with Repeat Collections

User interaction with repeating structures can directly affect the underlying collection by the addition or deletion of nodes. Nodes are added and deleted by actions ⟨**insert**⟩ and ⟨**delete**⟩; events **xforms-insert** and **xforms-delete** are notification events raised by these actions. These events are targeted at the ⟨**instance**⟩ affected by the insert or delete operation. They carry the XPath locator of the node to operate on as part of the context information. These events are allowed to *bubble* to enable centralized handling of these notifications; this means that the XForms author can attach a single custom action handler at the ⟨**model**⟩ that notifies the user about all insertions and deletions that affect any contained ⟨**instance**⟩ in the ⟨**model**⟩.

User interaction with ⟨**repeat**⟩ structures can also change the portion of the underlying collection that is presented; notification events **xforms-scroll-first** and **xforms-scroll-last** are raised when the user attempts to *scroll* off either end of the collection. These events are targeted at the ⟨**repeat**⟩ and can be *canceled* or allowed to *bubble*. As an example, an accessibility aid might use these events to attach an action that produces an audible cue when the user hits either end of the collection.

8.4.4 Listening for Changes in State

Notification events enumerated in this section are raised in response to changes of state in the instance data. Such changes of state reflect updated values of the various model properties introduced in Chapter 5. We detailed the CSS pseudoclasses that can be used explicitly to style user interface controls based on the state of these properties in Table 5.1. There is a one-to-one correspondence between these pseudoclasses and the notification events that are raised in response to changes in state. All of these events are targeted at the affected user interface control and can be either *canceled* or allowed to *bubble*. XForms authors can use these notification

Table 8.1. Notification Events that Signal
State Changes

Notification	CSS Pseudoclass
xforms-out-of-range	`:out-of-range`
xforms-in-range	`default`
xforms-valid	`:valid`
xforms-invalid	`:invalid`
xforms-readonly	`:readonly`
xforms-readwrite	`:readwrite`
xforms-required	`:required`
xforms-optional	`:optional`
xforms-enabled	`:enabled`
xforms-disabled	`:disabled`

events to attach custom behavior that extends beyond merely styling user interface controls.

8.4.5 Submit Notifications

We conclude our roundup of notification events with **xforms-submit-done** and **xforms-submit-error**. As their names imply, these are raised to indicate the result of submit processing. Successful completion, including interpretation of the server response as specified by the corresponding ⟨**submission**⟩ element raises event **xforms-submit-done**. It is targeted at element ⟨**submission**⟩, and it can be either *canceled* or allowed to *bubble*. Error during submit processing raises event **xforms-submit-error**; the event is targeted at the ⟨**model**⟩ containing the submission that failed, with the context information supplying details on the method that failed.

We conclude this section with a summary of how XForms events relate to the various XForms actions defined in Chapter 7 by giving the complete mapping between the declarative XForms actions and the XForms events they dispatch in Table 8.2.

8.5 XForms Events at a Glance

The previous sections have described the various events in detail; we give a succinct summary of the behavior of these events in Table 8.3. Note that ⟨**control**⟩ refers to XForms user interface controls in this summary.

Table 8.2. Correspondence between XForms Actions and XForms Events

Action	Event
⟨**delete**⟩	xforms-delete
⟨**insert**⟩	xforms-insert
⟨**rebuild**⟩	xforms-rebuild
⟨**recalculate**⟩	xforms-recalculate
⟨**refresh**⟩	xforms-refresh
⟨**reset**⟩	xforms-reset
⟨**revalidate**⟩	xforms-revalidate
⟨**send**⟩	xforms-submit
⟨**setfocus**⟩	xforms-setfocus

Table 8.3. XForms Events at a Glance

Event	Cancel	Bubbles	Target
Initialization Events (Section 8.2)			
xforms-model-construct	N	Y	⟨**model**⟩
xforms-model-construct-done	N	Y	⟨**model**⟩
xforms-ready	N	Y	⟨**model**⟩
xforms-model-destruct	N	N	⟨**model**⟩
Processing Events (Section 8.3.1)			
xforms-rebuild	Y	Y	⟨**model**⟩
xforms-recalculate	Y	Y	⟨**model**⟩
xforms-revalidate	Y	Y	⟨**model**⟩
xforms-refresh	Y	Y	⟨**model**⟩
Interaction Events (Section 8.3)			
xforms-previous	Y	N	⟨**control**⟩
xforms-next	Y	N	⟨**control**⟩
xforms-focus	Y	N	⟨**control**⟩
xforms-help	Y	Y	⟨**control**⟩
xforms-hint	Y	Y	⟨**control**⟩
xforms-reset	Y	Y	⟨**model**⟩
xforms-submit	Y	Y	⟨**submission**⟩
DOMActivate	Y	Y	⟨**control**⟩
Notification Events (Section 8.4)			
DOMFocusIn	N	Y	⟨**control**⟩
DOMFocusOut	N	Y	⟨**control**⟩
xforms-value-changing	N	Y	⟨**control**⟩

continued

Table 8.3. *Continued*

Event	Cancel	Bubbles	Target
xforms-value-changed	N	Y	⟨**control**⟩
xforms-select	N	Y	⟨**item**⟩ or ⟨**case**⟩
xforms-deselect	N	Y	⟨**item**⟩ or ⟨**case**⟩
xforms-scroll-first	N	Y	⟨**repeat**⟩
xforms-scroll-last	N	Y	⟨**repeat**⟩
xforms-insert	N	Y	⟨**instance**⟩
xforms-delete	N	Y	⟨**instance**⟩
xforms-valid	N	Y	⟨**control**⟩
xforms-invalid	N	Y	⟨**control**⟩
xforms-in-range	N	Y	⟨**control**⟩
xforms-out-of-range	N	Y	⟨**control**⟩
xforms-readonly	N	Y	⟨**control**⟩
xforms-readwrite	N	Y	⟨**control**⟩
xforms-required	N	Y	⟨**control**⟩
xforms-optional	N	Y	⟨**control**⟩
xforms-enabled	N	Y	⟨**control**⟩
xforms-disabled	N	Y	⟨**control**⟩
xforms-submit-done	N	Y	⟨**submission**⟩
xforms-submit-error	N	Y	⟨**model**⟩
Error Notifications			
xforms-binding-exception	N	Y	⟨**bind**⟩
xforms-link-exception	N	Y	⟨**model**⟩
xforms-link-error	N	Y	⟨**model**⟩
xforms-compute-exception	N	Y	⟨**model**⟩

PART III

XForms and the Next Generation Web

CHAPTER 9

Connecting the User to
Web Services

9.1 A Human-centric View of Web Services

The widespread adoption of XML as the common means of exchanging structured information on the Internet has made XML an ideal choice for connecting disparate information technologies. This in turn lays the groundwork for finally achieving the vision of distributed computing where information processing is seamless in a world of heterogeneous computing systems. Where previous distributed systems relied on specialized protocols and programming conventions, using XML as the common interchange format enables the creation of loosely coupled distributed systems that can be combined to deliver end-to-end customer solutions.

This is the underlying vision that drives Web services. It enables computing solutions that run on different platforms and originate from a variety of vendors (and possibly implemented using a variety of implementation approaches) to collaborate seamlessly. In this context, the evolving stack of Web service standards is primarily focused on ensuring the following:

Discovery	To enable the *discovery* of Web services that have been published
Invocation	To enable the invocation of Web services once they have been discovered
Communication	To ensure that Web services can communicate with one another

The focus in all of these is the need to seamlessly connect distributed systems to automate business processes and related information processing needs.

Notice that as the Web services vision comes to be realized, structured XML documents become the means by which one invokes a desired information service and that the response from such a service in turn is an appropriately structured XML document. This is well suited for machine-to-machine interaction; in fact, it's the lack of structure in documents created for human consumption that has traditionally made the vision of completely automated business workflows difficult to achieve.

However, information that is well structured, rigorously validated, and ready for machine processing is often not well suited for human consumption. Although machines may communicate with one another to achieve a high degree of automation, at the end of the day these services, to be useful, need to be invoked by end users. The final response that such services deliver also needs to be presented in a form that is suitable for human consumption.

XForms plays a key role in providing this *last mile* in connecting humans to information technologies deployed as Web services. XForms enables the creation and editing of structured XML content within a familiar Web browser environment. The XForms processing model ensures that the content being manipulated by the end user is structurally valid and that the data being provided meets the various application constraints at all times. But the end user remains insulated from the syntactic details of ensuring that the XML being manipulated is structurally valid. The XForms components described in the previous part of this book work behind the scenes in presenting the user with an intuitive user interface that aids in the creation and management of the XML structure.

When the user is done manipulating the XML structure in question, XForms submit processing can take over to create a syntactically valid XML document that is ready for being passed on to the Web service that implements the desired processing. The final result of processing is returned by the Web service as an XML structure; binding an XForms user interface to this structure once again hides syntactic details, leaving the user free to focus on the information that is returned.

Thus, where the emerging stack of Web services standards focuses on ensuring a well-engineered machine-to-machine distributed system, XForms provides the icing on the cake by enabling end users to interact with the exciting possibilities presented by the promise of Web services (see Figure 9.1).

9.1.1 XForms Access to Weather Service

As an example, consider a Web service that provides weather forecasts by area code. The availability of such a service is published as a WSDL document; WSDL

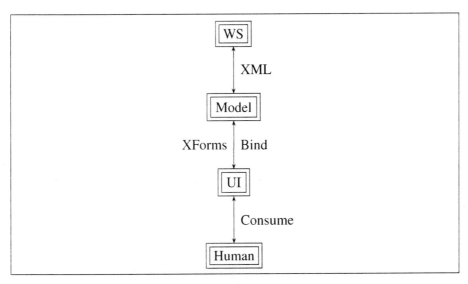

Figure 9.1. XForms puts a human face on Web services.

(Web Services Description Language) is a declarative means of specifying the calling convention for a Web service and the type of results that the service returns. To invoke this weather service, one sends an XML document that specifies the area code of interest; such XML *messages* are serialized using SOAP (Simple Object Access Protocol) and transmitted over HTTP. The SOAP message consists of a header and body; the message body carries information needed by the service being invoked, in this case, an XML document that specifies the area code.

To create a friendly browser-based interface to this weather service, we can create an XForms model that declares the type and structure of the XML document to be transmitted within the body of the SOAP message. Binding an XForms user interface allows the end user to specify the area code without having to work with the raw XML message. This user interface might be deployed to a variety of end-user devices; as an example, when deployed to a GPS-enabled mobile phone, the user interface might be initialized with the area code for the user's current location.[1] The mobile phone user can either accept the initial default or edit the area code; completing the area code might invoke an XForms submission that results in the specified area code being packaged into the appropriate SOAP message.

Notice that in this process, the end user never deals with raw XML. Ensuring that the area code being supplied is valid as specified by the weather service happens

---

[1] The conversion of the GPS location coordinates to an area code might itself happen by invoking an appropriate Web service.

through the XForms model. As an example, if the user specifies an invalid area code in the process of editing the initially supplied default, the XForms user interface would provide appropriate feedback and allow the submission to proceed only after the error has been corrected.

Invoking the weather service results in a SOAP response whose body gives the weather forecast for the specified area. Updating the instance in the XForms model with the newly obtained data automatically refreshes the user interface. Once again, the end user works with the information in a form that is ready for human consumption, rather than the raw XML that was returned as a response. Notice, however, that the XML data that made up the weather forecast is not lost; it is present as structured XML in the model and is therefore available for further use. As a further example, the user might be able to pass portions of the weather forecast just received to a different service that locates areas that are experiencing better weather.

9.2 Connecting Users to Their Data

Information technologies deployed on the Internet owe their success to connecting people together effectively in performing complex tasks. Web services are about connecting distributed systems to enable complex information workflows. To be useful, such information systems need to interface effectively with the end user as seen in the previous section. Thus, at the end of the day, effective deployment of these information services is a function of how well they succeed in connecting users to their data (see Figure 9.2). In this context, enabling seamless access to XML content is key to creating end-user applications.

9.2.1 Leveraging XML for Collecting Information

Business work flows are about collecting and categorizing information that starts off in semistructured documents, for example, a travel expense report, and eventually moving the fully structured information into the relevant back-end information processing system. Until now, structured data has been the purview of database applications, while semistructured documents have been managed with a variety of tools including word processors and spreadsheet programs. With the advent of the Web, such data gathering has also come to include user interfaces that are typically deployed to a universal Web client.

Though this move to online interaction has brought significant productivity gains, businesses and end users still fail to reap the full benefits of electronic

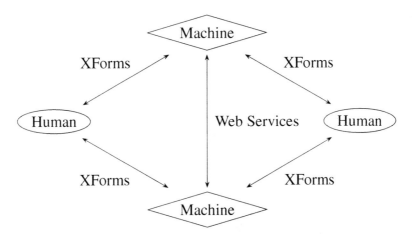

Figure 9.2. XForms: Connecting humans to XML powered Web Services.

documents because of the need to move data across disparate information processing systems. Traditionally, business critical information has been entered in largely semistructured documents, for example, word-processor files, because the user interface provided by well-structured forms packages, for example, the front-end to a database, has been too inconvenient to use for the end user. At the same time, the tools used to create business critical information, such as sales reports and market analysis, have tended to lock this critical information within proprietary file formats that make it hard to export and import structured data.

Thus, while it is convenient for users to work with information in a semi-structured format that is designed for easy human consumption, this factor becomes a strong negative when it comes to extracting and further processing the data contained in these business documents.

XML promises to bridge this gap by enabling the interchange of structured and semistructured information. The Web services architecture has already picked XML as its means for exchanging structured information. In this context, XForms enables the creation of browser-based interfaces for editing and submitting XML documents.

By enabling the collection and validation of data from within a Web browser, XForms makes the original promise of *the document is the interface* a reality; users can now interact with Web pages that present a document-centric view of the underlying structured data.

A key consequence of this evolution is that data collected via such interfaces will no longer need to be re-entered into the relevant back-end information system; instead, the collected XML data can be directly submitted to a Web Service to connect the user with the underlying information technology effectively (see Figure 9.1).

Thus, XForms looks and feels to the end user like today's online Web forms enhanced with all of the data-capture functionality one expects from a traditional forms package. In addition, it has been designed to be suitable for delivery to the merging plethora of pervasive devices ranging from PDAs to smart phones. Built from the ground up to work with XML, XForms can gather information that has been structured to conform to the customer's document schema, where the structure and type of content that each data element can contain have been designed to suit the needs of a specific business application. The XML instance that results from a user interacting with such a form can then be integrated with existing databases and servers, making it easier to reuse data across the enterprise via XML Web services.

9.2.2 XForms Collect Structured Data

One of the key innovations introduced by XForms is the separation of the *data* being collected from the *interaction* that is presented to the user. This separation of the *model* from the *view* is a key enabler with respect to creating document-based user interfaces that collect and validate structured data.

In this context, XForms is designed to be embedded within other XML document formats, such as XHTML. When embedded in XHTML, the XForms model defines regions of *structured data* within the overall XHTML document which continues to provide a traditional *semistructured* document view. XForms user interface controls embedded within the XHTML markup connect to the underlying XForms model, thereby enabling the display and update of the values stored in the XForms instance.

Finally, the data collected by the XForms application can be cleanly extracted and serialized as a structured XML document for submission to a Web Service. XForms can thus address the entire continuum, ranging from fully structured documents such as database queries to semistructured documents like expense reports, project reviews, and travel itineraries.

Thus, XForms documents, when deployed inside a Web browser, provide the best of both worlds; they provide the ease of use and platform independence provided by Web forms, along with the rigorous data-capture capabilities of traditional forms packages. The end result is that users end up creating structured information where they would have earlier created completely unstructured content within a myriad of desktop applications, all having their own proprietary data formats; the collected data need no longer be reentered to get it ready for processing by the underlying information technology.

A key consequence of this evolution is that information technologists can continue to model business data using abstract structures that are amenable to machine processing. XForms binds a user-friendly Web browser interface to such abstract XML models, thereby empowering the average user to edit and update these abstract structures. In this sense, XForms enables a standard Web browser to associate *editable views* to the underlying abstract XML models. This ability to view and edit XML documents from within a standard Web browser is likely to prove a key empowering technology.

In addition, industry-standard XML Schema validation and business logic validation through the XForms model enable error checking at each stage, thereby avoiding costly data errors.

Finally, the XForms design enables the creation of off-line forms, *i.e.,* users can save forms to their computers and work on them when not connected. Such off-line use is an automatic consequence of the separation of the model from the view and the resulting design that stores the instance data in an XML document that is separable from the XForms document. Enabling offline use of forms, as well as advanced features, such as suspend and resume, follow cleanly in this architecture the XForms browser can enable the user to save the currently provided instance data to an XML file and resume the interaction by reloading this XML file as the initial instance data.[2]

9.3 Creating Personalized Information Views

Just as Web services derive their power from the ability to mix and match different services in creating complete solutions, there is enormous value in bringing end-user access to such diverse services from within a single well-integrated user interface. This idea has gained significant momentum on the Web with the move toward *portals*, Web sites that aggregate content from a variety of sources to provide an *online dashboard*.

9.3.1 What Is a Portal?

A Web *portal* typically aggregates a number of useful end-user information services for access from within a *single page*. Portals are not new; they have been around since the early days of the Web, and most users are familiar with using portals such as Yahoo[3] since the mid-1990s. Over time, such portals have increased in sophistication

---

[2]This was a key motivator for allowing attribute *src* on element (**instance**).
[3]http://www.yahoo.com

and today offer additional features such as personalization, for example, my.yahoo[4] allows registered users to *configure* a personalized portal that aggregates information services that are of interest to a given user.

Such personalized portals are extremely convenient to use from an end-user perspective; however, until now they have been complex to create. The next evolution in this fast evolving area of Web applications is the advent of the *portal server*, a server component that aids in the rapid creation and deployment of a myriad of information services on a portal site. Such component applications are called *portlets*, a name chosen as a follow up to calling Web applications that run on a server *servlets*.[5]

The previous section describes how the XForms model and user interface can be used for putting a human face on Web services. Such Web services can be aggregated by portals to enable a single point of access to all of the Web services of interest to a given user. XForms plays a significant role in the human side of this equation when enabling a consistent user interface to the aggregation of services exposed by a portal.

Web services based portals are presently an area of intense activity. Following, we summarize some of the relevant open standards that are expected to make a significant contribution in this area.

9.3.2 Content Syndication Using RSS

Rich Site Syndication (RSS) is an RDF-based means for content-rich sites to publish a conceptual *table of contents*. These conceptual RSS *feeds* can then be aggregated to create *news portals*. As an example, see Meerkat[6] from the O'Reilly network.

XForms proves extremely useful in creating personalized newspapers built using a collection of RSS feeds. Such a personalized newspaper consists of the following conceptual components:

Feeds   The set of feeds to which the user is *subscribed*

Sources   The set of feeds that are *available* to the user

View   The *presentation* to be used in displaying the content from the various feeds

---

[4]http://my.yahoo.com

[5]The name *servlets* was chosen to contrast it with *applets*, which referred to small pieces of code that ran inside the Web browser application.

[6]http://meerkat.oreillynet.com

These components map cleanly to the model-view separation that is at the heart of the XForms design. An XForms-based content portal that uses RSS feeds can be constructed by

Model Creating an XForms model with two (**instance**) elements, one to hold the subscribed feeds and the second to point to the available feeds

UI Bind XForms user interface controls that allow the user to

- Browse the available feeds
- Preview a given feed
- Subscribe to a selected feed
- Update the view by adding content from the newly subscribed feed
- Persist the instance that holds subscription details for later access

Notice that a personalized newspaper like the one created earlier has all the immediate benefits of using XForms.

- The newspaper will be accessible from a variety of different end-user devices and modalities.
- The newspaper is *designed for accessibility* because of the accessibility inherent in the XForms design.
- By having the instance that holds the available feeds refer to a master list of sources via a URI, the personalized newspaper can automatically update its user interface as new feeds become available.

We show such a personalized newspaper in Figure 9.3.

9.3.3 UI Syndication Using WSRP

The personalized newspaper described in Section 9.3.2 relies on aggregating content feeds into a personalized newspaper. In the case of such content syndication, the raw XML content is ideally suited for being styled and presented in a consistent manner by the portal. However, information services that require a higher degree of user interaction may find this form of content aggregation unsatisfactory; this is because styling and adding behavior to the raw XML content can require significant effort.

```
<html xmlns="http://www.w3.org/1999/xhtml"
  xmlns:ev="http://www.w3.org/2001/xml-events"
  xmlns:xf="http://www.w3.org/2002/xforms">
  <head><title>Personalized News Portal</title>
    <model xmlns="http://www.w3.org/2002/xforms">
      <instance id="s"
      src="http://example.com/subscr?u=aster"/>
      <instance id="f"
      src="http://example.com/feeds?u=aster"/>
      <instance id="n"
      src="http://example.com/news?u=aster"/>
      <submission id="update" ref="instance('s')"
      action="http://example.com/subscr?u=aster"/>
      <submission  ref="instance('n')"
        replace="instance" id="news"
      action="http://example.com/news?u=aster"/>
  </model></head>
  <body>
    <group xmlns="http://www.w3.org/2002/xforms">
      <label>News Portal</label>
      <select ref="instance('s')">
        <label>Add/Remove Feeds</label>
        <itemset ref="instance('f')">
          <label ref="title"/><value ref="@rss"/>
        </itemset>
        <send ev:event="DOMActivate"
      submission="update"/></select>
      <submit submission="news">
        <label>Get News</label>
      </submit>
      <table>
        <tr repeat-nodeset="instance('n')">...</tr>
    </table></group>
</body></html>
```

Figure 9.3. XForms news portal using RSS feeds.

This aspect of aggregation is being addressed by Web Services For Remote Portals (WSRP),[7] an emerging Web services standard from OASIS. Just as the XForms architecture enables the *binding* of multiple views to the XForms model, approaches like WSRP have the potential to extend this approach one step further by enabling the creation of reusable Web user interfaces. Such user interfaces can themselves be syndicated to create complex end-user applications that have been put together from a collection of *LEGO blocks* comprising Web services that provide either content or user interfaces that *bind* to different content services.

9.4 XForms Web Services at a Glance

We conclude this chapter with a summary of the relationship between XForms components and their application to Web services in Table 9.1.

Table 9.1. Web Services at a Glance

XForms	Web Services
model	• Collect data as XML
	• Serialize request as XML
	• Receive response as structured XML
Bind	• Connect distributed services
	• Connect user interfaces to actual data
	• Enable aggregation of information services
UI	• Connect users to their information
	• Enable ubiquitous information access
	• Enable delivery to multiple devices
	• Enable multimodal, mobile Web services
submit	• Serialize data as valid SOAP messages
	• Smart forms enable automatic data import and export

---

[7] http://www.oasis-open.org/committees/wsrp/

CHAPTER 10

Multimodal Access

10.1 Multimodal Interaction for Ubiquitous Access

XForms' separation of the *model* from the *view* makes it ideally suited to become a key building block for enabling ubiquitous access to Web applications and Web services. We focused on putting a human face to such Web services using XForms in Chapter 9; this chapter focuses on ensuring that the human facing interfaces we create are accessible from a variety of interaction modalities and access devices.

The focus in this chapter will be on accessing such information services with devices that vary in their capability; we will turn this around in the chapter on accessibility (see Chapter 11) where we will focus on ensuring that these same applications can be delivered to users with a wide range of capabilities. Notice that multimodal access to information services and ensuring the accessibility of such services to all users are, in fact, two sides of the same coin. The XForms design leverages this fact in solving the issues of multimodal interaction and accessibility by depending on the same set of features inherent in the XForms design.

10.1.1 Multimodal Access

With the coming of age of speech technology, spoken interaction can be integrated as a first-class modality for creating multimodal user interaction. Such multimodal interaction is especially relevant in the context of mobile devices where traditional user interface peripherals may not be available or appropriate. Rich multimodal interfaces that integrate new user interaction modalities will need to be based on a set of user interface metaphors and design principles that leverage the presence of these new forms of interaction. These metaphors will manifest themselves within application and user interface frameworks where they play the role of integrating user input arriving from different modalities and in synthesizing output to multiple media.

The next section will enumerate a set of user interface principles that are essential for good multimodal interaction. The remaining sections of this chapter will demonstrate how the various components in the XForms architecture aid in realizing multimodal interfaces that satisfy these principles.

10.2 Multimodal User Interface Principles

10.2.1 Multiple Modalities Need to Be Synchronized

Spoken interaction is highly *temporal*, whereas visual interaction is *spatial*. When combining these modes of interaction in a multimodal interface, synchronization is a key feature that determines overall usability of the interface. Synchronization is key to the following *multimodal acts*:

Point and Talk User points at a location on the map while speaking a question.

Redundant Confirmation The user interface *supplements* visual output with a spoken confirmation; for example, a travel reservation system might highlight the user's selection while speaking an utterance of the form

> Leaving from *San Francisco*

If not synchronized, this can increase the cognitive load on the user significantly and prove a source of confusion.

Parallel Communication The user interaction leverages the availability of multiple streams of output to increase the band width of communication. For example, a travel reservation system might visually present a list of available flights and speak a prompt of the form

> There are *seven* flights that match your request, and the flight at *8:30*A.M. appears to be the most convenient.

To be effective, such *complementary* use of multiple modalities needs to be well synchronized with respect to the underlying interaction state.

10.2.2 Multimodal Interaction Should Degrade Gracefully

Human interaction degrades gracefully; for example, a face-to-face conversation degrades gracefully in that the communication still remains effective when one of the participants in the conversation is functionally blind, for example, when talking over a telephone. This form of *graceful degradation* is due to the high level of redundancy in human communication. As man-machine interfaces come to include multimodal interaction, we need to ensure that these interfaces degrade gracefully in a manner akin to human conversation. Such graceful degradation is important since the user's needs and abilities can change over time, for example, a user with a multimodal device moving between a noisy environment where spoken interaction fails and an eyes-free environment where visual interaction is unavailable.

Supplementary Modalities	The use of multiple modalities to *supplement* one another leads to user interfaces that degrade gracefully.
Complementary Modalities	Portions of the interface that use multiple modalities to *complement* one another are natural points where the interface will fail to degrade gracefully. When complementary modalities are used, the underlying system needs to be aware of the modalities that are currently available and ensure that *all* essential items of information are conveyed to the user. This is a key accessibility requirement when ensuring that the user interface is usable by individuals with different needs and abilities.
Changing Capabilities	Capabilities can change rapidly in the case of mobile users. These include available bandwidth between the mobile device and the network, as well as changes in the bandwidth of communication between device and user. To be useful, multimodal interaction that is deployed to mobile devices needs to adapt gracefully to such changes.

10.2.3 Multiple Modalities Should Share a Common Interaction State

Consider the user task of setting up a travel itinerary using a multimodal interface, for example, one that allows the simultaneous use of spoken and visual interaction. Successful task completion during such a conversation requires that the participants share a common mental model, and this is true in the case of man-machine interaction as well. When using multiple modalities in a user interface, it is important that the various modes of interaction share a common interaction state that is used to update the presentation in the various available output media. Such a common interaction state is also essential for rapid completion of the conversation, since the various *multimodal interactors* can examine this shared interaction state in determining the next step in the dialog. A shared interaction state is important for the following *multimodal acts*:

Switching Modalities	User switches between interaction modalities owing to a number of external factors such as the available bandwidth among the user, the device, and the network. As an example, the user might answer the first few questions using spoken input and then use the visual interface to complete the conversation. For such transitions to be seamless, the data collected by each interaction modality, as well as the information conveyed via the available output media, needs to be driven by a shared interaction state.
History	The shared interaction state can track the *history* of user interaction, and this history can be useful in determining the most appropriate path through the dialog to achieve rapid task completion. For example, if the user had requested nonstop flights earlier in the conversation, this knowledge can be used in customizing the visual presentation by filtering out flights that do not meet this requirement.
Multidevice Interaction	A user with a mobile device might use a large visual display upon entering a conference room. To achieve a synchronized multimodal experience, the user's mobile device and the conference room display will need to share some interaction state.

Distributed Multimodality   It is advantageous to offload complex speech processing to network servers when using thin clients such
as cell phones. As an example, a cell phone might be
capable of local speech processing sufficient to enable
the user to dial a small number of frequently used entries by speaking a name. If the name is not found in
this list, it may be looked up in a larger phone book,
for example, a company directory, and the speech processing required might be best offloaded to a network
server. Sharing a common interaction state between
the visual and spoken components of the cell phone
is essential for synchronized multimodal interaction
in such distributed deployments.

10.2.4 Multimodal Interfaces Should Be Predictable

Multimodal interaction provides the user with a multiplicity of choices and often
enables a given task to be performed in a number of different ways. But to be effective, the interface needs to empower the user to arrive intuitively at these different
means of completing a given task. Symmetric use of modalities where appropriate
can significantly enhance the usability of applications along this dimension; for example, an interface that can accept input via speech or pen might visually highlight
an input area while speaking an appropriately designed prompt. Where a specific
modality is unavailable for a given task, for example,

> signatures may only be entered via pen input

appropriate prompt design can help make the user implicitly aware of this restriction. Predictable multimodal user interfaces are important for the following:

Eliciting Correct Input   Appropriately designed prompts are important for get-
ting the desired user input. This in turn can lead to rapid
task completion and avoid user frustration when using
noisy input channels such as speech.

What Can I Do?   Rich user interfaces can often leave the user impressed
with the available features but baffled as to what can be
done next. Spoken interaction, combined with good
visual user interface design, can be leveraged to overcome

this *lost in space* problem. Rich multimodal interfaces can use the shared interaction state and dialog history to create user interface wizards that guide the user through complex tasks.

10.2.5 Multimodal Interfaces Should Adapt to Users Environment

Finally, multimodal interfaces need to adapt to the user's environment to ensure that the most optimal means of completing a given task are made available to the user at any given time. In this context, *optimality* is determined by

- The user's needs and abilities
- The abilities of the connecting device
- Available bandwidth between device and network
- Available bandwidth between device and user
- Constraints placed by the user's environment, for example, the need for hands-free, eyes-free operation

10.3 Creating Multimodal Interfaces Using XForms

This section details the effectiveness of the XForms components in realizing effective multimodal interaction conforming to the user interaction principles described in Section 10.2. The XForms model is ideally suited to hold the interaction state that is to be shared among the different interaction modalities (see Section 10.3.1). Abstract XForms user interface controls are well suited to creating user interfaces that are later mapped to different devices (see Section 10.3.2). The XForms user interface constructs encourage intent-based authoring, and the resulting interfaces can be easily refactored for delivery to clients with a variety of different display form factors (see Section 10.3.3). Finally, XForms' use of XML Events makes it ideally suited for attaching event handlers that respond to user input received from different modalities such as speech (see Section 10.3.4).

10.3.1 One Model to Bind Them All

The XForms model holds instance data and associated constraints. The XForms binding mechanism enables multiple *views* to bind to this model. A key consequence of this architecture is that multiple views that bind to the single model are automatically synchronized. Thus, in a multimodal interface that integrates visual and spoken interaction, user input that arrives via either interaction modality is placed in the model and becomes immediately available to all available modalities.

The ability to hold more than one (**instance**) in the model allows XForms applications to store both application state as well as *interaction* state within the model. The application state holds user input that is to be transmitted to the application; the interaction state can hold intermediate results that reflect user interaction. We demonstrated this form of interaction state in Figure 4.7 and Figure 8.1. This use of an instance within the model to hold interaction state can be used to create smart user interfaces that take the history of user interaction into account. Thus, a multimodal interface might use this XForms feature to track the progress of the man-machine conversation via an appropriately designed interaction state and use this in guiding the user toward rapid task completion. Thus, the XForms model is ideally suited to be used as a building block in implementing various *dialog managers*.

Since the effect of user interaction in the different modalities is ultimately reflected in the XForms model, higher level software components such as *interaction managers* that work on *integrating* across user input received from various modalities to infer *user intent* can use the XForms model as the central repository that tracks the needed information. As an example, the (x, y) coordinates specified via a pointing device and the spoken utterance

How do I get here?

by themselves do not fully express the user's intent. However, when the result of both of these interaction *gestures* is stored in a common model along with the necessary time-stamping information, these utterances can be *integrated* to derive the expressed user intent.

10.3.2 Abstract Controls Enable Flexible Access

Abstract XForms user interface controls when combined with the type information available from the XForms model can be turned into rich user interface controls that are appropriate for the connecting device and interaction modality. We demonstrated this with an example of control (**input**) bound to a field of type date that gets rendered as a *date picker*. This form of *late binding* of user interface widgets is extremely useful when authoring Web applications that are to be accessed from a variety of interaction modalities and end-user devices. Notice that the user interface we created by binding control (**input**) to a field of type date degrades gracefully;

that is, it uses a date picker widget when delivered to an environment that supports such a widget but can be presented as a simple text field on environments where no such widget is available.

XForms user interface controls encapsulate all relevant metadata needed for interaction with a control. A key consequence is that these controls can be turned into appropriate spoken dialogs. As an example, the design of XForms control ⟨**select1**⟩ enables the generation of smart spoken prompts; for instance, consider the example shown in Figure 3.9. The markup contains sufficient information to be able to generate a spoken prompt of the form

Please specify your gender; default is *male*.

10.3.3 XForms UI Creates Synchronized Views

XForms user interface constructs are designed to capture the underlying intent of the interaction, rather than a specific manifestation of that interface. Aggregation constructs like ⟨**group**⟩ enable the XForms author to provide information that is sufficient to refactor the resulting interface as needed. Dynamic user interface constructs like ⟨**switch**⟩ and ⟨**repeat**⟩, in conjunction with model-based switching that is enabled via model property *relevant*, enable the creation of user interfaces that adjust to the current interaction state. These features can be used to advantage when creating rich multimodal interaction.

We demonstrated an insurance application form in Figure 5.4 and Figure 5.5 that used model-based switching to enable portions of the interface conditionally. This application can be extended to support rich multimodal interaction by allowing the user to answer a set of "yes" or "no" questions that populate fields corresponding to the user's habits. As the user answers these questions using speech input, the XForms model gets updated, and this automatically updates the visual interface to hide portions of the insurance form that are not *relevant*. Finally, user commands that are available as ⟨**trigger**⟩ controls and use one of the XForms declarative action handlers are ideal candidates when speech enabling the interface. Since the effect of these declarative action handlers is predictable, they can be activated via speech input to create simple *command and control* speech interaction.

Finally, notice that just as the XForms user interface can adapt itself based on previous user input, it can also adapt itself based on changes in the user environment. This flexibility comes from the use of XML Events and the ability to *dispatch* such events into the XForms model or user interface as appropriate. As an example, a smart multimodal device might represent the current user environment in an XForms model and update it accordingly as it detects changes in the environment, for example, increased noise level that makes speech interaction impossible. The device can arrange for appropriate event handlers that dispatch information about the updated device state to various XForms applications running on the device. These applications can, in turn, handle these events by appropriately updating the user interface, for example, by displaying a visual prompt indicating that spoken interaction is unavailable or by turning off the microphone to avoid spurious speech recognition results.

10.3.4 XML Events Enable Rich Behavior

The use of XML Events enables XForms constructs to be extended with rich behavior. One such example is given by the ability to attach voice dialogs as event handlers at various points in the XForms user interface. Voice dialogs are typically authored in Voice Extensible Markup Language (VoiceXML[1]). Such dialogs can be attached to the various XForms user interface controls and aggregation constructs to create Web interfaces that *speak* and *listen*. This form of multimodal interaction is presently an area of intense activity in the W3C, and these standards are still evolving. For one example of how declarative voice handlers can be integrated using XML Events to produce multimodal interfaces, see XHTML+Voice (X+V[2]).

The use of XML Events enables the creation of consistent, predictable user interfaces. XForms applications can attach default event handlers for most common cases; the XForms processing model exposes a set of standard events that can be *hooked* to attach specific behaviors at various points during XForms processing as described in Section 8.3 and Section 8.4.

This design encourages the authoring of consistent user interaction when creating XForms applications. The definition of a set of abstract XForms event types also enables a given platform or device to map platform-specific events to these generic XForms events. As an example, a desktop interface might map the `enter` key to event **DOMActivate**; a mobile phone might map the * key to this same event. XForms applications that use this event consistently for attaching specific behaviors will exhibit a *predictable* interface when deployed to both a desktop client as well as a mobile phone. This architecture enables the creation of Web applications that react as users expect on a given device and can be a key determining factor in the overall usability of an application.

---

[1]http://www.w3.org/TR/voicexml20
[2]http://www.w3.org/tr/xhtml+voice/

10.4 Multimodal Interaction at a Glance

We conclude this chapter with a summary of the role played by the XForms architecture in multimodal interaction in Table 10.1. XForms has been designed as a reusable forms module for use within the W3C's Web architecture. It can be used today within XHTML 1.1 and is slated to become the default forms module in XHTML 2.0. With the intense level of standards activity at the W3C and other standards organizations like the Open Mobile Alliance (OMA) around multimodal interaction and mobile access, XForms can be expected to play a pivotal role in the evolving next generation Web.

Table 10.1. XForms Architecture in Multimodal Interaction

XForms	Multimodal Interaction
model	• Hold interaction state • Support multidevice access • Enable synchronized views
Bind	• Connect multiple interaction modalities • Connect user interfaces to data
UI	• Enable late binding of user interaction • Enable ubiquitous information access • Enable delivery to multiple devices • Enable multimodal, mobile user experience

CHAPTER 11

XForms and Accessibility

11.1 XForms Enables Universal Access

We conclude this book with an overview of XForms features that ensure that Web applications are accessible to users with different needs and abilities. This chapter has been held back until the end because accessibility is a key design feature that is built in to all aspects of the XForms architecture. This means that XForms applications are *designed for accessibility*. Where previous Web standards required a large set of authoring guidelines that enumerated HTML design idioms that would either help or hinder accessibility, the XForms author is assured of meeting a large set of accessibility needs by creating Web applications the *XForms way*.

This chapter will start by enumerating a set of user interface principles that ensure universal access (see Section 11.2) and conclude by describing aspects of the XForms architecture that help fulfill these design principles in Section 11.3. We hope the material here is sufficient to convince Web developers to give up bad authoring habits that date back to early days of HTML and to switch to using XForms constructs that ensure the widest reach for the next generation of Web interaction.

In this context, XForms does not stand by itself in ensuring overall accessibility of Web content. Increasing adoption of CSS (Cascading Style Sheets) means that Web authors need no longer mix visual style markup within the content of XHTML Web pages. This separation of content from presentation is a major accessibility win, and XForms with its use of some of CSS3's more advanced features goes even further in ensuring that Web content is access ready.

As an example, we demonstrated the use of CSS pseudoclasses in styling XForms controls based on the state of the underlying instance in Section 5.1.1. The use of nested HTML tables for achieving visual layout has become a serious stumbling block for accessibility over the last few years. The XForms specification contains examples of an advanced CSS feature called *pseudoelements* that can be used to achieve the same layout effect as when using HTML tables but without polluting the content with extraneous table markup. We describe this aspect of Web authoring in Section 11.3.2.

XForms' use of XML Events is another big win for accessibility. The somewhat adhoc nature of HTML eventing in HTML 4 can present serious accessibility challenges. This is because Dynamic HTML (DHTML) content that is created using the HTML 4 framework depends almost exclusively on imperative scripts to create user interaction behavior. Such scripts are hard to analyze with respect to their final behavior, and adaptive technologies suffer a serious breakdown when accessing such content. We describe how XML Events can be used to speech-enable content as an example of how this new technology enables first-class access (as opposed to retrofitting adaptive technology) in Section 11.3.3.

At the end of the day, accessibility is determined by three factors that work in conjunction:

Content   The quality of the content. Content that has been created with accessibility issues in mind is the first—and perhaps most critical—element in ensuring accessibility. Throughout this book, we have focused on the content aspects of XForms; we summarize some of the salient accessibility features in Section 11.3.1.

User Agent   Content alone is not very useful unless there are end-user clients that can enable the user to interact with it. As XForms clients gain wider adoption, these will have to focus on leveraging the accessibility features inherent in the XForms content and to turn these into real end-user benefits. We cover user agent issues in Section 11.3.4.

Access Aid   In an ideal world, all users would interact with well-designed content with user agents that best match the user's needs and abilities. However, we live in an imperfect world, and it is often necessary to enhance the final user experience by resorting to adaptive technologies that extend standard user interaction with the features needed by users with special needs. We describe how adaptive technologies can leverage the XForms processing model in Section 11.3.5.

Finally, all of the accessibility features covered here apply equally well to the need for accessing Web applications from a variety of different devices. As pointed out earlier, device independence and multidevice access focuses on the varying capabilities of the device, whereas accessibility focuses on the varying abilities of the end user.

11.2 Design Principles for Accessible Interfaces

This section enumerates a set of design principles that ensure accessible user interface design. These design principles are phrased in the context of user interaction authored via markup languages and deployed to a Web browser; however, many of them are applicable to general user interface design as well.

11.2.1 Content Should Encapsulate Relevant Metadata

When creating user interfaces via markup languages such as XHTML, the content designer should ensure that all relevant metadata for each user interface element is *contained within* the declarative markup for that element. As an example, if the user interface contains a widget that is created via markup element (**gadget**), then all metadata pertaining to this user interface *gadget*, for example, the label to display, the tooltip that is popped up, or the help information that is displayed upon request, should all be encapsulated by the markup for element (**gadget**).

Legacy HTML fails to meet this design principle but instead relies on visual layout to help the reader associate various user interface controls with their labels.

Meeting this guideline requires that the markup language being used contain the necessary constructs for such encapsulation. It also requires that the markup language enable designers to achieve the various layouts they need when using the structured markup provided by the language.

11.2.2 Separate Content from Layout and Presentation

Separating details of layout and presentation from the content markup is a key requirement for ensuring the accessibility and device independence of the resulting user interface. HTML started as a simple markup language but over time degraded into a confused mix of structure and presentation markup. The increased adoption of CSS for styling has finally enabled sites to factor out presentational rules into style sheets.

This still leaves the problem of HTML authors using multiple levels of tables for achieving a desired visual layout. More advanced CSS features, such as CSS pseudoelements and CSS absolute positioning, are beginning to provide a solution to this problem. The advantage of these modern approaches to customizing the style and layout of Web content is that the resulting XHTML documents are easily rendered on a variety of display devices. In addition, using CSS to design visually pleasing pages has the advantage that the resulting Web pages display significantly faster than the earlier HTML tables solution. The success of this approach can be judged by the fact that recently, Wired[1] magazine (a site that was notoriously inaccessible due to its attempt to create a magazine-like appearance using HTML tables) switched to XHTML 1.1 and CSS 2. The resulting site downloads and renders significantly faster while being fully accessible.

11.2.3 Ensure That Content Can Be Refactored

Well-structured XML content has the advantage of being suitable for generating *multiple* views; in fact, this is one of the original motivations behind structured markup languages. As an example, when a book is authored as a well-structured XML document, it is extremely easy to generate a table of contents, or to display only the figures in the book. This form of content refactoring and filtering is extremely useful when building alternative modes of information access. For example, such content refactoring and filtering enables efficient eyes-free access to information.

The advantages enumerated in the case of structured documents apply equally well to the domain of user interfaces created via markup languages, where the document *is* the interface. Markup languages that provide structural elements that can be used to group related elements of the user interface are well suited for this form of accessibility. Examples of these include the ability to group related choices in a menu or to group related user interface controls to appear within a common container. The ability to refactor the user interface, rearrange elements of the user interface, and progressively reveal relevant portions of an interface is significant both to users of small devices and to users with special needs.

11.2.4 Ensure That Rich Content Degrades Gracefully

To ensure that Web interfaces remain accessible and device independent, the underlying user interface framework should ensure that rich content degrades gracefully. As an example, stock market performance may be displayed as a bar graph when using a rich visual display, as a table of numbers on a textual display, and as a succinct spoken summary when using an eyes-free interface. In a well-designed system, all three of these representations should be derivable from the same underlying representation. In a system that fails to degrade gracefully, the information might get hard coded as a table or a graphic and prove impossible to access via a cell phone with a small display or with a speech-only interface.

---

[1]http://www.wired.com

11.2.5 Avoid Device-specific Events

The *behavior* of a user interface is often a function of the interaction events to which it responds. When creating accessible Web interfaces designed to be used from a variety of end-user devices, it is important to ensure that the events the Web application responds to are not device specific.

As an example, a Web page that is explicitly authored to respond to mouse movement events is impossible to use in the absence of a pointing device; such pages are unusable by a functionally blind user. Authoring the same Web application to respond to a more generic event, for example, **DOMFocusIn** can make the same application usable from a variety of devices and ensure accessibility. This is because the specific device in use can map the available device-specific events to platform-independent events such as **DOMFocusIn**. The result is that a blind user might generate the **DOMFocusIn** event by moving focus with a press of the tab key, while the cell phone user might generate the same event with a special navigation key. In either case, the application continues to function correctly.

A corollary to this principle is the consistent use of accelerator keys to ensure that an application is keyboard accessible. Keyboard accessibility is often cited as an essential requirement to ensure that an application is accessible to blind users. However, lack of keyboard access is usually symptomatic of the bigger problem of relying on platform- or device-specific events.

11.2.6 User Interfaces Should Exhibit Predictable Behavior

Predictability is a key factor in determining the overall usability of a user interface. Web interfaces often attempt to grab the user's attention by using fancy gimmicks in the user interface. Although these do succeed in drawing the user's attention, they do not necessarily aid in rapid task completion.[2] Where predictability in the user interface speeds task completion for the average user, it can often be the difference in being able to complete a task at all in the case of users with special needs.

Consistent use of keyboard shortcuts and, more generally, consistent binding of device-specific events to standard actions can significantly enhance overall accessibility.

11.2.7 Allow for Late Binding of Interaction Behavior

A follow-up to the previous principle of graceful degradation is the late binding of presentation and interaction behavior to structured content. We emphasized

---

[2] A point that was probably in their favor during the eye-ball counting dot-com boom.

the importance of separating content from presentation and interaction earlier; ensuring the late binding of presentation and interaction semantics ensure that a user interface can be best customized to match the user's needs and abilities.

11.2.8 Enable Centralized Event Handling

Adaptive technologies often need to attach additional handlers that alert the user to changes in application state. Such *behaviors* are best attached at a centralized location in the interface hierarchy rather than at each widget making up the user interaction.

As an example, an adaptive technology might wish to attach a special alert message whenever the user is about to send out personal information. A complex Web interface may provide many points in the user interface where the user is likely to trigger such a submission. Attaching the specialized alert message to each such point in the application can be tedious and can result in errors. Centralized event handling, that is, the ability to attach the custom behavior at a single point in the user interface hierarchy, provides a reliable means of ensuring that the user *always* receives the alert message.

Notice that this design pattern is not specific to adaptive technology alone; it is a key requirement for enabling any kind of augmentative behavior in the user interface.

11.2.9 Raise Notification Events for Key State Changes

Adaptive technologies and augmentative user interfaces that cater to a user's special needs often perform their function by triggering specialized handlers that produce custom behaviors at appropriate points during user interaction. But to be effective, this design pattern requires that the underlying user interface framework raise a rich set of notification events that can be responded to by such handlers.

Notification events need to encapsulate sufficient contextual information about the state change that is being communicated. The eventing framework that is exposed by the underlying platform also needs to be sufficiently flexible to allow such behaviors to propagate these notification events to a central point in the interface hierarchy where they can be handled in a consistent manner.

11.2.10 Provide Hooks for Attaching Special Behavior

The right set of notification events and a flexible eventing framework are necessary conditions for *hooking* specialized behaviors. To be sufficient, the framework also needs to enable complete access to the current interaction context from within handlers that implement specialized behavior. In addition, handlers that implement augmentative behaviors may need to pass information about their actions to the rest of the interaction framework.

Thus, in a well-designed user interface framework, augmentative behaviors that have been created as specialized event handlers that respond to state changes and other notifications blend into the main application and become an integral part of the final user experience. In this sense, creating such accessible behaviors as an augmentation—rather than as a part of the original application—is mostly a programming convenience that enables the core interaction framework to carry functionality that is needed by all users while enabling specific augmentations to be added based on a given user's needs and abilities.

11.2.11 Use Declarative Handlers in Favor of Scripts

Event handlers written in scripting languages like Javascript can prove an effective means to experiment with new user interaction behaviors. Once a set of effective behaviors has been arrived at, it is often advantageous to recast these behaviors as declarative handlers that are authored via XML markup. In addition to being more maintainable and allowing the binding of different programming languages to the declarative handler at runtime, this approach also has a significant benefit when it comes to adding augmentative behaviors to match a user's special needs.

Once a commonly used handler has been codified using declarative markup, this establishes a clear contract as to the actions that that handler is expected to perform. As a result, XML documents that use such declarative handlers to attach interaction behavior can be statically analyzed and the results of such analysis used in automatically attaching specialized behavior.

As an example, consider a Web application that invokes an action handler to display a help message in a pop-up window. If this is achieved via a standard declarative handler, all instances of its use can be automatically augmented with an additional handler that also speaks the help message. However, if this same action is achieved via a fragment of imperative Javascript, such augmentation would require human intervention since it would be impossible to derive the result of invoking the script fragment automatically.

11.3 Leveraging XForms Accessibility Features

This section details how various aspects of the XForms architecture can be leveraged in meeting the accessibility design principles covered in Section 11.2.

11.3.1 XForms Creates Accessible Content

The separation of model from view that is inherent in the XForms architecture is a key enabler with respect to creating accessible content. In addition, all XForms controls and user interface constructs have been designed to encapsulate relevant metadata such as ⟨**label**⟩, ⟨**help**⟩, and ⟨**hint**⟩ (see Section 3.2.1). XForms user interface controls encourage platform-independent eventing and support consistent keyboard navigation (see Section 3.2.1) for a description of attributes *accesskey* and *navindex*.

The XForms vocabulary has been designed to encourage intent-based authoring and provides the constructs needed to express the logical grouping of user interface elements. Constructs ⟨**group**⟩ and ⟨**switch**⟩ create user interfaces that can be easily refactored (see Section 4.1 and Section 4.2). In conjunction with model property *relevant* and the resulting ability to create conditional interaction, this enables the creation of user interfaces that reveal themselves progressively during user interaction.

11.3.2 Accessibility in Style

CSS plays a key role in creating accessible XForms user interfaces. HTML 4 failed to encapsulate key items of metadata as part of its user interface markup because visual designers relied exclusively on tables to position user interface controls correctly with respect to their labels. For the XForms design of encapsulating such metadata within each user interface control to gain wide-spread adoption, Web designers need to be assured of being able to style user interfaces created using the XForms vocabulary to the same degree as when using explicit HTML tables. A new CSS feature—CSS pseudoelements—is a key enabler in styling XForms controls (see CSS3 UI[3] for the complete details). Using this feature, style sheet authors can specify that user interface controls and their labels should be displayed *as if* they were authored using an HTML table.

We demonstrate this use in Figure 11.3. This feature of CSS is named *pseudoelements* because the style sheet author is able to refer to *pseudo* nodes in the markup tree. As an example, the markup tree for control ⟨**input**⟩ that collects the user's e-mail address is shown in Figure 11.1, and the corresponding CSS fragments is shown in Figure 11.3. Conceptually, the presentation of this input control has two distinct visual components, the presentation of the edit field and the associated label.

---

[3] http://www.w3.org/tr/css3-ui

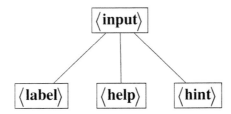

Figure 11.1. Markup tree corresponding to control ⟨**input**⟩.

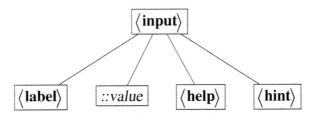

Figure 11.2. Pseudo markup tree corresponding to control ⟨**input**⟩.

However, examining the markup tree shown in Figure 11.1, we see that there is no explicit node that corresponds to the *value* in the edit field itself. In the absence of CSS pseudoelements, a style sheet author would not be able to attach a visual presentation to the value in the edit field that is distinct from the presentation style used for the rest of the input control.

CSS pseudoelements enable the style sheet author to refer to *pseudo* nodes in the markup tree. The set of predefined pseudoelements is shown in Table 11.1. Like the CSS pseudoclasses described in Section 5.1.1, CSS pseudoelements provide the necessary place holders in the markup tree needed by the style sheet to attach the appropriate presentation rules. The syntax used to refer to such pseudoelements in the style-sheet is : : and parallels that used for referring to pseudoclasses covered in Section 5.1.1.

We show the markup tree augmented with the pseudoelement for the edit field in Figure 11.2. The CSS style rules shown in Figure 11.3 use these pseudoelements to align the labels and their associated controls.

This is achieved by specifying that

⟨**group**⟩   Element ⟨**group**⟩ should be treated as a table for display purposes.
⟨**input**⟩   Element ⟨**input**⟩ should be treated as a conceptual row of this table.
::value   Pseudoelement *::value* for control ⟨**input**⟩ should be treated as a cell in this table row.
⟨**label**⟩   Element ⟨**label**⟩ should be treated as another cell in the table row.

```
<html xmlns="http://www.w3.org/1999/xhtml"
  xmlns:xf="http://www.w3.org/2002/xforms">
  <head><title>Email With Style</title>
    <style type="text/css">
      @namespace xf
      url(http://www.w3.org/2002/xforms);
      /*This causes form controls and their labels
      to align, as if a two-column table were used */
      xf|group { display: table; }
      xf|input { display: table-row; }
      xf|input>xf|label {
      display: table-cell; }
      xf|input::value {
      border: thin black solid;
      display: table-cell; }
      /* Display repeat-items with a dashed border */
      *::repeat-item { border: dashed; }
      /*Current item gets  a teal highlight*/
      *::repeat-index { background-color: teal;}
  </style>...</head>
  <body>
    <group xmlns="http://www.w3.org/2002/xforms">
      <input ref="email"><label>Email</label>
        <help>Enter your email address</help>
      <hint>...</hint></input>
</group></body></html>
```

Figure 11.3. Aligning user interface controls and their labels using CSS.

The result is to achieve the same visual effect as when using HTML tables; however, the content markup remains independent of layout constructs.

11.3.3 Accessibility through Eventing

The accessibility design principles outlined in the previous section can be classified as pertaining to content, presentation, or interaction. All of the interaction-related design principles are met by XForms' use of XML Events as summarized in Table 11.2.

Table 11.1. CSS3 Pseudoelements for Styling XForms User Interfaces

Element	Description
::value	Represents the active area of a user interface control excluding its label
::repeat-item	Represents a single item from a repeating sequence
::repeat-index	Represents the current item of a repeating sequence

Table 11.2. XForms Eventing Enhances Accessibility

Principle	XForms Solution
Events	• Defines a set of high-level interaction events.
	• Exposes processing model through eventing.
Predictable	• User interface controls define consistent behavior.
	• Centralized event handling through XML Events.
	• Navigation sequence is well defined.
Late Binding	• XML Events enables attaching of new handlers.
	• Declarative handlers enable augmentative behaviors.
Notifications	• Defines notification events for all key state changes.
Hooks	• Processing model exposed through events.
	• Custom hooks at key points in the interaction.
Declarative	• Defines declarative handlers for all common operations.

11.3.4 User Agent Guidelines for Leveraging XForms Accessibility

User agents that implement XForms play a key role in ensuring that the accessibility features present in the XForms design benefit the end user. XForms user agents can provide direct support for accessibility; as an example, XForms user agents can directly augment the end-user experience by providing spoken feedback during user interaction. Implementing such spoken feedback is relatively straightforward, given a fully compliant XForms client. Since the XForms processing model and the underlying eventing framework expose all the needed hooks, augmenting the interface with custom behaviors that match a user's special needs only requires authoring event handlers and attaching them at the right points within the XForms client.

XForms user agents that do not directly implement such augmented behavior should expose all aspects of the XForms processing model and eventing framework.

This is essential to enable the creation of add-ons that augment an XForms browser with the specific behaviors needed by a particular user community.

11.3.5 Accessing XForms Features from Adaptive Technologies

When an XForms client does not directly implement the desired specialized behavior, it may be necessary to extend the client with an appropriate piece of adaptive technology. Such adaptive technologies will need to implement the DOM2 eventing framework and be capable of hooking into Web browsers that are fully DOM2 events compliant.

XForms content can also be augmented with special behaviors before the content is delivered to the client. Such server-side augmentation is likely to be a rich area of future investigation as we try to develop accessibility solutions that are usable on a variety of nondesktop information appliances.

11.4 XForms Accessibility at a Glance

We conclude this chapter with a summary of using XForms for creating accessible Web applications, shown in Table 11.3.

Table 11.3. XForms Accessibility at a Glance

XForms	Accessibility
Model	• Factors nonpresentational aspects. • Central point for hooking custom behavior.
Controls	• Designed for accessibility. • Encapsulate all relevant metadata. • Exhibit predictable behavior. • Enable consistent navigation.
UI	• Aggregation constructs encourage intent-based authoring. • Create content that enables refactoring. • Can progressively reveal complex interfaces.
Events	• Defines a flexible eventing framework. • Can attach custom behaviors.

COLOPHON

This book was authored in LaTeX on the Emacspeak[1] audio desktop with Emacs package AucTeX[2] providing authoring support. At a time when most of the attention around Open Source Software is focused on the operating system, I would like to draw readers' attention to the wonderful array of high-quality open source authoring and document preparation tools created over the last 25 years by the LaTeX community.

All figures in this book were drawn using package **pstricks**; the declarative markup enabled me to draw these diagrams reliably without having to look at the final output. XML examples were created as stand-alone XML files and processed using packages xmlindent[3] and xmllint[4] before being converted to LaTeX. The high-level markup makes the content long-lived and reusable. An immediate advantage is that the content can be easily made available using a variety of access modes ranging from high-quality print and online hypertext to high-quality audio renderings.

As proof of this fact, I was able to create the HTML version on the accompanying CD using package tex4ht[5] by author Eitan Gurari from the same markup sources used to produce the typeset output. I would like to thank him for his unflagging help and support as I learned my way around his wonderful creation. The HTML version includes the necessary Aural CSS style rules to produce high-quality audio

---

[1] http://emacspeak.sf.net
[2] http://mirrors.sunsite.dk/auctex/www/auctex/
[3] http://www.cs.helsinki.fi/u/penberg/xmlindent/src/
[4] http://xmlsoft.org/
[5] http://www.cis.ohio-state.edu/ḡurari/TeX4ht/mn.html

renderings of this book using Emacspeak and the Emacs W3 Web browser by William Perry.

Screen images for this book were produced by my XForms coeditor, Leigh Klotz, and I would like to thank him both for his help in creating these images and for carefully checking the text and examples against the XForms 1.0 specification. Screen images were produced using the X-Smiles, Novell, and FormsPlayer implementations.

I would like to thank author Nelson Beebe for his excellent collection of open-source tools for preparing and maintaining bibliographies. The document preparation tools used to prepare this book are well described in the Bibliography (entries 11, 12, and 13). I would like to thank author Sabastian Rahtz and publisher Addison-Wesley for providing access to the LaTeX sources for this book. Finally, I would like to thank author Donald E. Knuth for the TeX typesetting system.

BIBLIOGRAPHY

[1] M. Altheim. Modularization of XHTML. Technical report, W3C, 2001. W3C Recommendation available at http://www.w3.org/TR/xhtml-modularization/.

[2] Jonny Axelsson, Chris Cross, Håkon W. Lie, Gerald McCobb, T. V. Raman, and Les Wilson. XHTML+voice 1.0. Technical report, W3C, 2001. W3C Note available at http://www.w3.org/tr/xhtml+voice/.

[3] Mark Birbeck. *Professional XML*. Programmer to programmer. Wrox Press, Chicago, IL, second edition, 2001.

[4] Tim Bray, Jean Paoli, C. M. Sperberg-McQueen, and Eve Maler. Extensible markup language (XML) 1.0 (second edition). Technical report, W3C, 2000. W3C Recommendation available at http://www.w3.org/TR/REC-xml.

[5] Kurt Cagle and David Hunter. *Beginning XML*. Wrox Press, Chicago, IL, 2000.

[6] Wendy Chisholm, Gregg Vanderheiden, and Ian Jacobs. Web content access guidelines. Technical report, W3C, 1999. W3C Recommendation available at http://www.w3.org/tr/WAI-WEBCONTENT.

[7] James Clark. XSL transformations (XSLT) version 1.0. Technical report, W3C, 1999. W3C Recommendation available at http://www.w3.org/TR/xslt.

[8] James Clark and Steve DeRose. XML path language XPath version 1.0. Technical report, W3C, 1999. W3C Recommendation available at http://www.w3.org/TR/xpath.

[9] David C. Fallside. xml schema part 0: Primer. Technical report, W3C, 2001. W3C Recommendation available at http://www.w3.org/TR/xmlschema-0/.

[10] Khun Yee Fung. *XSLT: Working with XML and HTML*. Addison-Wesley, Reading, MA, 2000.

[11] Michel Goossens, Frank Mittelbach, and Alexander Samarin. *The LATEX Companion*. Addison-Wesley, Reading, MA, 1994.

[12] Michel Goossens and Sebastian Rahtz. *The LATEX Web Companion—Integrating TEX, HTML, and XML*. Addison-Wesley, Reading, MA, 1999.

[13] Michel Goossens, Frank Mittelbach, and Sebastian Rahtz. *The LATEX Graphics Companion: Illustrating Documents with TEX and PostScript*. Addison-Wesley, Reading, MA, 1997.

[14] Eric Hansen, Ian Jacobs, and Jon Gunderson. User agent accessibility guidelines 1.0. Technical report, W3C, 2002. W3C Working Draft available at `http://www.w3.org/TR/UAAG10/`.

[15] Dave Hollander, Andrew Layman, and Tim Bray. Namespaces in XML. Technical report, W3C, 1999. W3C Recommendation available at `http://www.w3.org/tr/rec-xml-names`.

[16] Michael Kay. *XSLT programmer's reference*. Programmer to programmer. Wrox Press, Chicago, IL, second edition, 2001.

[17] Chris Lilley, Ian Jacobs, Bert Bos, and Håkon Wium Lie. Cascading style sheets, level 2 (CSS2) specification. Technical report, W3C, 1998. W3C Recommendation available at `http://www.w3.org/TR/REC-CSS2`.

[18] Ashok Malhotra and Paul V. Biron. XML schema part 2: Datatypes. Technical report, W3C, 2001. W3C Recommendation available at `http://www.w3.org/TR/xmlschema-2/`.

[19] Scott McGlashan. Voice extensible markup language (voiceXML) 2.0. Technical report, W3C, 2003. W3C Candidate Recommendation available at `http://www.w3.org/tr/voicexml20/`.

[20] Noah Mendelsohn, Henry S. Thompson, Murray Maloney, and David Beech. XML schema part 1: Structures. Technical report, W3C, 2001. W3C Recommendation available at `http://www.w3.org/TR/xmlschema-1/`.

[21] David Orchard, Steve DeRose, and Eve Maler. XML linking language (XLink) version 1.0. Technical report, W3C, 2001. W3C Recommendation available at `http://www.w3.org/TR/xlink`.

[22] O'Reilly & Associates, Inc. *XML CD Bookshelf*. O'Reilly & Associates, Inc., Sebastopol, CA, 2002.

[23] Steven Pemberton. XHTML 1.0: The Extensible HyperText Markup Language—A reformulation of HTML 4 in XML 1.0. Technical report, W3C, 2000. W3C Recommendation available at `http://www.w3.org/TR/xhtml1`.

[24] Steven Pemberton, T. V. Raman, and Shane P. McCarron. XML events—an events syntax for XML. Technical report, W3C, 2002. W3C Candidate Recommendation available at `http://www.w3.org/TR/xml-events/`.

[25] Tom Pixley. Document object model (DOM) level 2 events specification. Technical report, W3C, 2000. W3C Recommendation available at `http://www.w3.org/TR/DOM-Level-2-Events/`.

[26] T. V. Raman. *Auditory User Interfaces—Toward the Speaking Computer*. Kluwer Academic Publishers, Boston, MA, 1997.

[27] Joseph Reagle, Lorrie Cranor, Massimo Marchiori Marc Langheinrich, and Martin Presler-Marshall. The platform for privacy preferences 1.0 (P3P1.0) specification. Technical report, W3C, 2001. W3C Last Call Working Draft available at `http://www.w3.org/TR/P3P/`.

[28] Aaron Skonnard and Martin Gudgin. *Essential XML quick reference: a programmer's reference to XML, XPath, XSLT, XML Schema, SOAP, and more.* DevelopMentor series. Addison-Wesley, Reading, MA, 2002.

[29] Eric van der Vlist. *XML Schema.* O'Reilly & Associates, Inc., Sebastopol, CA USA, 2002.

INDEX

Also Available from Addison-Wesley

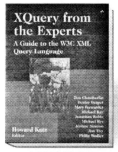

0-321-18060-7

0-201-84452-4

0-201-65796-1

0-321-15494-0

0-201-70046-8

0-201-61576-2

0-201-77004-0

0-201-77186-1

0-672-32374-5

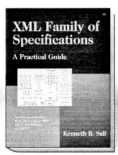

0-201-70359-9

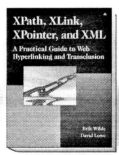

0-201-70344-0

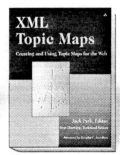

0-201-74960-2

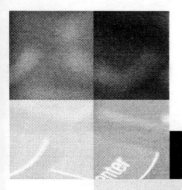

informIT

YOUR GUIDE TO IT REFERENCE

Articles

Keep your edge with thousands of free articles, in-depth features, interviews, and IT reference recommendations – all written by experts you know and trust.

Online Books

Answers in an instant from **InformIT Online Book's** 600+ fully searchable on line books. For a limited time, you can get your first 14 days **free**.

Catalog

Review online sample chapters, author biographies and customer rankings and choose exactly the right book from a selection of over 5,000 titles.

Register
Your Book

at www.awprofessional.com/register

You may be eligible to receive:

- Advance notice of forthcoming editions of the book
- Related book recommendations
- Chapter excerpts and supplements of forthcoming titles
- Information about special contests and promotions throughout the year
- Notices and reminders about author appearances, tradeshows, and online chats with special guests

Contact us

If you are interested in writing a book or reviewing manuscripts prior to publication, please write to us at:

Editorial Department
Addison-Wesley Professional
75 Arlington Street, Suite 300
Boston, MA 02116 USA
Email: AWPro@aw.com

Visit us on the Web: http://www.awprofessional.com

Addison-Wesley